D1327261

A TASTE FOR HOME

A TASTE FOR HOME

The Modern Middle Class in Ottoman Beirut

TOUFOUL ABOU-HODEIB

Stanford University Press
Stanford, California

Stanford University Press
Stanford, California

Printed in the United States of America on acid-free, archival-quality paper

Library of Congress Cataloging-in-Publication Data

Names: Abou-Hodeib, Toufoul, author.
Title: A taste for home : the modern middle class in Ottoman Beirut / Toufoul
   Abou-Hodeib.
Description: Stanford, California : Stanford University Press, 2017. |
   Includes bibliographical references and index.
Identifiers: LCCN 2016030501| ISBN 9780804799799 (cloth : alk. paper) |
   ISBN 9781503601475 (electronic)
Subjects: LCSH: Home—Lebanon—Beirut—History. | Middle
   class—Lebanon—Beirut—History. | Home
   economics—Lebanon—Beirut—History. | Consumer
   goods—Lebanon—Beirut—History. | Beirut (Lebanon)—Social life and
   customs. | Lebanon—Civilization—European influences.
Classification: LCC DS89.B4 A25 2017 | DDC 305.5/5095692509041—dc23
LC record available at https://lccn.loc.gov/2016030501

Typeset by Bruce Lundquist in 10.25/15 Adobe Caslon Pro

For Børre Ludvigsen

CONTENTS

ILLUSTRATIONS

Figures

Maps

ACKNOWLEDGMENTS

This research project has passed through several transformations over the past years, during which it benefited from the encouragement and feedback of many colleagues, friends, and family members.

The research was supported through generous grants from the Whiting Foundation and from the Andrew W. Mellon Foundation, the latter offered through the Council on Library and Information Resources. I wrote the bulk of this book during the academic year 2010–2011 in Berlin, as a postdoctoral fellow in Europe in the Middle East—The Middle East in Europe (EUME), a research program of the Berlin-Brandenburg Academy of Sciences and Humanities, the Fritz Thyssen Foundation, and the Wissenschaftskolleg zu Berlin. I am grateful to these institutions for providing me with the opportunity to work on my own project. The discussions during the EUME seminars and workshops and the exchanges with my co-fellows and colleagues from the Wissenschaftskolleg zu Berlin, the Zentrum Moderner Orient, and the Museum of Islamic Art have greatly enriched this project. In addition, my research was greatly facilitated by numerous archivists and librarians in Lebanon, Turkey, Great Britain, France, Norway, and the United States. I am particularly indebted to Abdel Hamid Shaito for helping me to navigate the Center for National Archives (Mu'assasat al-Mahfuzat al-Wataniyya) in Beirut and for graciously sharing his office space with me during the months I spent poring over microfilms from those archives.

Many colleagues, scholars, and friends have been a source of encouragement, inspiration, and intellectual development over the years. They include Abdul Rahim Abu-Husayn, Kamran Asdar Ali, Fadi Bardawil, Ralph Bodenstein, Nadia Maria El Cheikh, Paris Papamichos Chronakis, Gwyn Daniel, Kavita Datla, Ulrike Freitag, Rania Ghosn, Dyala Hamzah, Jens Hanssen, the late Vangelis Kechriotis, Georges Khalil, Elias Khoury, Ilham Khuri-Makdisi, Nora Lafi, Tamir el Leithy, Ussama Makdisi, Rania Maktabi, Adam Mestyan, Nada Moumtaz, Alidost Numan, Eugene Rogan, Nisreen Salti, Rosemary Sayigh, Roschanak Shaery, Malek Sharif, Holly Shissler, Avi Shlaim, Shayna Silverstein, Jihad Touma, Fawwaz Traboulsi, Eva Troelenberg, Jojada Verrips, Stefan Weber, and Michael Willis. I am especially grateful to Bill Brown, Martin Stokes, and Lisa Wedeen for their guidance and comments on previous drafts of this work, and to Orit Bashkin and Brigit Meyer for reading and commenting on chapters of this book. My thanks to Nada Moumtaz for providing a survey of the registers at the *shari'a* court in Tariq al-Jadida, Beirut. I am also indebted to Kate Wahl of Stanford University Press for her valuable feedback, her keen eye, and her encouragement to take this book further than the original manuscript.

Among my friends, I am grateful to Lama Bashour, Ameen Hannoun, Mustapha Jundi, and Stephanie and Sabah al-Wahid for providing a home away from home during the nomadic period of research. My parents, Diana Mahfouz and Khaled Ayed, have always supported me in their radically different ways and trusted the decisions I have made over the years, no matter how counterintuitive. For that I am eternally grateful. My father, also a historian, has been my intellectual interlocutor since before I knew what the word meant, and my academic trajectory is visibly marked by his influence. My heartfelt thanks to Alice Ludvigsen and Antonia, Morten, and Johanna Reime Aabø who continue to provide familial warmth in Norway. Finally, Børre Ludvigsen has accompanied this project from inception to completion and never complained of reading and commenting on seemingly endless drafts. He has been a tireless critic, a cheerful travel companion, and a wonderful father to our Miriam Amina. For this and so much more, I dedicate this book to him.

NOTE ON TRANSLITERATION, TRANSLATION, AND DATING

Transliteration and Translation

Transcription follows the language of the source: Arabic transcription for material from Arabic sources, modern Turkish for Ottoman Turkish sources. Arabic words are transliterated according to the simplified system employed by the *International Journal of Middle East Studies*. Although diacritical marks have been omitted, I use ' to represent the letter 'ayn and ' to represent the hamza. Arabic names are transliterated according to the same system, except where the person named has a preferred English spelling (e.g., Julia Tu'ma, not Julya Tu'ma). Place names with a common English spelling are given in that Anglicized version (e.g., Aleppo, not Halab). Arabic and Ottoman words in common English usage are also given in their Anglicized form (e.g., souk, not *suq*), the only exception being when the word forms part of a name (e.g., Suq al-Tawila).

All translations are mine unless otherwise noted.

Dating

Three calendar systems appear in this study: the Gregorian, the *hijri* (A.H.), and the *mali* (Ottoman financial) calendar (A.M.). The *mali* was a solar calendar, with a year that began on 13 March of the Gregorian calendar. Dates are given according to the dating system used in the source. Where a source gives more than one date, I give preference first to the Gregorian, then the *hijri*, and finally the *mali* date. In the two latter cases, the Gregorian equivalent is always indicated in parentheses. The spelling of the *hijri* months depends on the language of the source, Turkish or Arabic.

Most dates include the day, the month, and the year. Because the original documents are sometimes incomplete, a few dates include only the month and the year and a few supply only the year.

A TASTE FOR HOME

CHAPTER 1

BEIRUT, CITY OF THE LEVANT

The traveler who journeys to Beirut from the West is naturally
impressed by its scenes of Oriental life, but to one who has come
either from Lebanon or Damascus or even from Jerusalem, it seems
almost a European city.

Lewis Gaston Leary, *Syria, The Land of Lebanon*

We are in Beirut in 1910, a bustling port city on the Eastern Mediterranean
coast. 'Aysha al-'Aris, a resident of the Bab Idris neighborhood, walks out of
her home on a clear spring day in April. Fifteen years ago, 'Aysha had risked
losing the home that sheltered her, her husband, and children, after the municipal council demolished parts of their house and then demanded an urban
improvement tax she could not afford. After 'Aysha had made numerous petitions to the Sublime Porte and endured long years of conflict with the local
and provincial authorities, the municipal council had finally decided earlier
that month to reduce the tax she owed by half.

Not far away that same spring, in the government building housing the
Muslim Hanafi court, pregnant Hasiba brings a case against her husband,
Yusuf, a tramway company employee, for not having paid the remainder of
her dowry. When Yusuf puts forward his prized possessions, a phonograph
and sixteen records, as leverage in the bargaining process, the private life of
the young couple is suddenly pried open to the disapproving scrutiny of the
court. The case comes to an abrupt halt, with the judge rebuking Yusuf over
the worthlessness of the phonograph and ruling in Hasiba's favor.

On June 3rd of that same year, Julia Tu'ma is delivering a speech before the Greek Orthodox Benevolent Society in Tripoli while on a visit from
Beirut, where the twenty-eight-year-old Protestant educator will soon take
up the position of academic administrator of the Maqasid Islamic School for

girls. Referring to the home as *al-sama' al-ula*, the first heaven to be attained before actual heaven, Tuʿma describes the home as a kingdom and woman as its queen with a responsibility for the happiness and welfare of the family. Many in her audience were versed in at least two languages, and Tuʿma addresses her speech to the "Oriental woman," using the English word *home* to give her topic a more precise meaning.[1]

At the center of these three vignettes of daily life in Beirut stands the middle-class home. Beginning in the second half of the nineteenth century, the relatively new Beirut municipal council initiated urban improvements and projects based on a legal corpus that was the product of late Ottoman reforms. Aysha's home, like many other homes in the city, was caught up in the feverish rush to reshape Beirut as a modern city, with wide avenues and a well-ordered urban fabric. From within, domestic life reorganized itself around new commodities streaming into the city, with its growing prominence as an Eastern Mediterranean port city and first point of contact for many of the ships coming from Europe. At a time when consumption was politicized in terms of the changing economic and political balance between the Ottoman Empire and the European powers, these commodities often elicited reactions such as that of the judge in Hasiba and Yusuf's court case. At that same historical juncture, a group of educators and writers based primarily in Beirut spread novel ideas about the home in cities and towns across the region, using the lecterns of societies and the pages of the press as their fora. For the first time, "home" was being discussed as a building block in society and the educated woman was being seen as responsible for that home's management and for the upbringing of future citizens.

An emerging middle class was implicated in these processes through its material and moral investment in the home, as a consumer of domestic fashions, and as a target for a body of literature aimed at shaping a specifically middle-class domesticity. Focusing on the period stretching from the second half of the nineteenth century until World War I, this book argues that middle-class domesticity took form in a matrix of changing urbanity, the politicization of domesticity in public debates, and changing consumption patterns. My aim is to write a cultural history of domesticity that is at once global in the widest sense of the term and local enough to enter the most private of spaces.

Domesticity in Turn-of-the-Century Beirut

The second half of the nineteenth century was characterized by a set of relations between Beirut, on the one hand, and its regional surroundings, the imperial center, and the world beyond the Ottoman Empire, on the other, that had particular effects on domesticity. Ottoman reforms during the latter half of the century redefined the meaning of "public" and instituted a new dynamic between domestic space and its urban setting. Beirut's growing importance as an economic and intellectual hub and port city also entailed rapid changes on the level of daily decisions taken by people in their private lives.

Old and new classes who had access to the city's newly acquired wealth and to the new array of commodities brought forward by the industrial revolution in European countries, witnessed a change of lifestyles in their public and private lives alike. One of the most visible manifestations of this shift was the sight of horse-drawn carriages on Fridays and Sundays, the city's weekly days off, carrying the city inhabitants to parks located on the outskirts; these parks were referred to as *muntazahat*, from *nuzha* (promenade or outing).[2] If the word promenade evokes thoughts of the flâneur, this is for good reason. While such retreats outside the city were not an entirely new phenomenon, they fused into modes of leisure that linked to new modes of transportation and new patterns of consumption. Weekend outings to some of those parks were also sexually mixed and developed a reputation for providing the opportunity to exhibit the latest fashions for men and women alike.[3]

Changes in forms of leisure constituted some of the ways the middle and upper classes made an impression on the urban fabric of Beirut, but that impress remained gendered. Even in public places where women could go without an enveloping robe and an uncovered head, particular modes of dress and behavior were expected. When Christian women began to appear uncovered in the souk and to dress fashionably to attend church, this evoked anxiety first and foremost among their coreligionists. Women's behavior in these two settings elicited criticism from moralists in a way that weekend promenades in the park did not.[4] But if these differences were pronounced in some public places, domestic habits and leisure pastimes took place behind closed doors and were, therefore, less amenable to the scrutiny of moralizing members of society.

New standards of living and technologies simultaneously opened up the home and closed it off to its social surroundings in various ways. The new houses built outside the old city were architecturally more extroverted, with open windows and elements of pomp exhibiting themselves to the outside world. During the late Ottoman period, the expanding size of the home and the activities and services brought inside it with the introduction of individual water supplies and indoor toilets meant that more of domestic life was spent indoors, rather than at water wells and spaces shared by neighbors, such as latrines and cooking facilities. But as women became more active participants in social life and sexually mingled gatherings became more common, many homes also became places for literary salons and more lighthearted social gatherings.[5] 'Anbara Salam al-Khalidi recounts in her memoirs that the men and women in her maternal grandparents' family, the Sunni Muslim Barbir family, used to gather weekly in the 1860s and 1870s to read and discuss the latest in periodicals, such as Butrus al-Bustani's *al-Jinan* and 'Abd al-Qadir al-Qabbani's *Thamarat al-Funun*.[6]

Given the impact of new modes of consumption and lifestyles, the changes characterizing turn-of-the-century Beirut have a strong material dimension to them, and changing tastes constituted an important link between the public sphere and the lives the middle class led at home. For that reason, the home stood at the intersection of debates considered central at the time on the topics of public benefit, eastern modernity, and *ifranji* (Western or, more specifically, European) cultural influence. Here, the home was not just a sphere where ideas about modernity were negotiated, tested, and contested, it also took an active part in giving form to these ideas, in general, and to the middle class, in particular.

This took place against an Ottoman modernity that stamped the face of the public sphere, making the home a contested space in terms of both the aesthetics of urban modernity and the commodities within the home. In addition, contemporary debates foregrounded the role of taste in articulating the shape and position of the middle class. What I mean by *domesticity* is, therefore, a constellation of ideas and lifestyles in which the home played a crucial part both as a concept and as an actual material object. Such an approach takes the home beyond intellectual discourses and state reforms, bringing in the question of capital and how it transformed both the way domesticity was thought of and the way it was lived.

Although women do not constitute the explicit focus of this work, the home as a topic of study brings them into the mainstream of history both as objects and as subjects. The central role assigned to women, and articulated by female participants in the discourse of domesticity, integrated women into a modern vision of society where, through their domestic work, they complemented and challenged the transformations in the public sphere. As middle-class women, they were implicated in inculcating children, the future citizens, with ideals of behavior, moderate consumption, and proper taste—all meant to better define the middle class and reinforce its political and economic relevance in society. The topic of home also brings women forth into history as educators, mothers, housewives, consumers, and property owners. Thus, they appear at various junctures in this book as vocal advocates of a new role for the modern woman, active contestants in urban municipal projects, and litigants in court cases involving domestic possessions.

Starting in the 1870s with the burgeoning of the Beirut press, a debate centered in Beirut but drawing in other cities in the region, such as Tripoli, Hama, and Damascus, placed the woman at the center of domestic life as manager, mother, and wife. The result was a vigorous debate on modern woman's position in society through her role at home. Several scholars refer to this body of literature as making a "cult of domesticity"—that is, consisting of a repetitive, mantra-like set of prescriptions put forward in the press and aimed primarily at women.[7] But following the critique of both Afsaneh Najmabadi and Lisa Pollard on the use of the word *cult*, I see the publication of this literature as a process that carved out a larger place for women in public life, not just at home, and as a debate that tied the home to more encompassing discussions of the time.[8] As Pollard argues, debates on the domicile and the family "formed a basic framework through which abstract concepts such as nation and, along with it, loyalty and citizenship were imagined, articulated, and debated," and through which both men and women learned how to be modern citizens.[9]

Modern domesticity constituted part of wider shifts in thinking not only about politics but also about society as a whole and the position the middle class occupied in it. Fresh ways of conceiving of domesticity centered on several main concerns circulating in intellectual circles and in the press at the time: the necessity of educating women; the importance of the family, as the smallest unit of society, to the welfare of the whole; the upbringing of modern citizens; and the cultivation of an ethics of consumption. For the men and women writing and lecturing on the topic, the home was posited as key to bringing together these disparate notions about society. The home became implicated not only in reconceptualizing woman's role in society but also in the very understanding of this society.

The existing books and articles that concern themselves in part or wholly with domesticity in Ottoman Beirut and in the region that later became Lebanon are primarily concerned with the free-standing, central-hall house, an architectural form that developed in Beirut around the mid-nineteenth century.[10] Usually consisting of one or two floors, these houses featured several rooms and services arranged around a central hall. As this design came to be seen as an ideal and as an embodiment of riches, many of the elements of the central-hall house were widely copied, both in the city and in the region, even though the fully realized form remained beyond the means of the majority of the city's inhabitants, including the middle class. As some of the examples architectural historian Ralph Bodenstein analyzes show, the typology was far from being a static or finished product. Rather, it developed and transformed over time according to changing needs and transformations in family structures.[11]

However, rather than focus on the central-hall house, this book concerns domesticity as a category of analysis, tying together its various material changes, of which the physical form and appearance of the house was one aspect among many. In the case of migrants returning to Mount Lebanon, Akram Khater argues that the central-hall house typology was a way by which the middle class communicated and affirmed a position in its peasant surroundings. The central-hall house functioned as a status symbol in Beirut as well. But the home, both as an idea and as a physical form, went beyond signaling a class position, it also responded materially to its surroundings in ways that often escaped a straightforward identification with class. Particularly in a port city affected directly by Ottoman reforms and by a growing influx of commodities, middle-class domesticity was a product of its local as well as its regional and global contexts. The middle class, in that sense, can be said to have been shaped by the home even as it distinguished itself through the home.

Equally important is the position Beirut occupied culturally in its regional setting. Intellectually, the city was a magnet for a new generation of intellectuals, educators, and readers in the region who were finding an outlet in the Beiruti press.[12] Thus, the debate around women and domesticity does not reflect a sense of Beiruti provinciality but rather of the city as a melting pot for ideas and with the towns and villages that constituted its urban peripheries also taking part in the conversation. This was also true of other main cities in the region such as Cairo, Alexandria, and Istanbul, where the peripheries were intellectually active contributors to the urban center.[13] With its rise as main port city during the course of the nineteenth century, Beirut became a regional trendsetter, looked to by other cities and towns in the region for the latest ideas and debates, as well as for the latest in domestic typologies and furniture. If we are to better understand how Beirut functioned on different geographical scales, it first needs to be placed in the context of late Ottoman reforms and the attempt to forge a new Ottoman identity, or *Osmanlılık*.

An Ottoman Urban Modernity

The entanglement of the different levels of the city, the region, and the Ottoman Empire took form through the changing position of Beirut within the overall matrix of Ottoman governance, not least on the urban level. Within the larger setting, Beirut's relationship with the imperial center was recast by the Ottoman reforms of the nineteenth century. Although Beirut had already been transforming intellectually and commercially by the mid-nineteenth century, the political and administrative changes brought on by the reforms accelerated and underpinned the process that eventually led to its promotion by the Ottoman Sultan to provincial capital in 1888. In that promotion, Beirut benefited from a comparatively new conception of rule that brought the techniques of governing the population to the forefront of technologies of rule, placed greater emphasis on fostering closer relationships between the imperial center and the provinces, and sought to address the inhabitants of the empire as citizens rather than subjects.

In discussing the birth of political economy in Europe and the shift away from a sovereign-based notion of rule, Michel Foucault points to the centrality of "the problem of the population" to the art of modern government.[14] The demographic expansion of the eighteenth century coupled with the new science of political economy enabled a form of governance that for the first time in Western political history took the welfare of the population as its end. Eighteenth-century institutions such as schools, armies, and factories served not only their immediate practical ends but also aimed at managing the population in its details. They contributed to the production of subjects who internalized discipline and reproduced it on a daily basis in their relationship to their bodies, society, and authority. In that sense, modern state institutions are directly linked to the kind of relationship forged between the state and its citizens.

The Ottoman Empire faced similar challenges in its regeneration as a state, and many of the reforms undertaken were at least inspired by modern state institutions in the rest of Europe, particularly France. In the process of "stretching the short, tight skin of the nation over the gigantic body of the empire," to borrow a metaphor from Benedict Anderson, the population increasingly became a category of political management.[15] Whereas earlier reforms under Sultan Mahmud II (r. 1808–1839) focused on strengthening the army and increasing state revenue through taxation, towards the mid-nineteenth century, reforms began to deal more directly with the population as a category to be mapped, molded, and managed.[16] Although the financial difficulties standing in the way of implementing these reforms consistently throughout the empire meant that they had a limited effect in homogenizing the population into a national entity, they did contribute to shaping the terrain on which the inhabitants of the empire, both Muslim and non-Muslim, could talk about themselves as Ottoman citizens and as modern.

This new form of governance instituted a dynamic in the relationship between the imperial center and the peripheries of the empire. A rising concern for the imperial capital was tying far-flung regions directly to the center through administrative and bureaucratic hierarchies.[17] Both the vocabulary that entered the language of Ottoman policymakers and many of the reform efforts in the provinces took shape in conjunction with local visions of modernity, with the result that this more modern governance was most successful where twinned with a local desire for self-governance and an appetite for forging a localized modernity capable of living up to the challenges posed by a world knit tighter by new technologies, modes of transport, and trade patterns.

The development of provincial urban centers became the material expression of a constructive tension between bureaucratic centralization and the forging of a common Ottoman identity on the one hand and the manifestation of such an identity on the urban level in collaboration with "enlightened" Ottoman subjects on the other hand. Cities were important in the Ottoman polity, both as provincial centers of rule and as faces of the empire's modernity. Urban management brought together the earliest forms of political representation, new technologies of transportation and services, and the management of urban population growth.

The natural starting point for urban reforms was the imperial capital, Istanbul, which served as the model later implemented in the rest of the empire. The loose regulations implemented in the capital in the 1820s and 1830s were revamped into a system of municipal government and a coherent set of urban management laws. These were first applied to areas of the city inhabited by large numbers of Europeans and therefore, it was reasoned, most amenable to their application. In 1858, the first municipality established under the control of a municipal council was designated as the *altıncı daire*, or the "sixth district," after the affluent *sixième arrondissement* in Paris. The regulation of construction, streets, and the water supply was eventually turned over to an autonomous building council.[18] As this form of urban management spread, it became directly linked to the centralizing logic of the Tanzimat, as the Ottoman reforms of 1839 to 1876 are collectively known. It also became constitutive of an urban modernity that created new dynamics of citizenship between Istanbul and inhabitants of cities as diverse as Izmir, Salonica, Jaffa, Jerusalem, and Damascus.[19] The gradual extension of this system to the provinces by 1876 placed cities as far from the center as Baghdad under the authority of municipal councils, which answered to provincial councils, which in turn answered directly to the Sublime Porte.[20] That same year, Sultan Abdülhamid II ascended to the throne.

Although the coming of Abdülhamid II to power and his suspension of the newborn 1876 constitution signaled the end of the Tanzimat period, his reign of more than three decades constituted in many ways the culmination of some of the guiding principles of preceding reforms. It was under the autocratic paternalism of Abdülhamid II that the role of the state in the management of everyday life underwent a qualitative expansion. In contrast to the late Tanzimat reforms, which had concentrated power in the hands of the provincial governors, under Abdülhamid II the Ministry of Interior developed a highly centralized system, ensuring adherence to regulations issued in Istanbul and requiring approval for the smallest expenditure or action in the provinces. The sultan also often moved to centralize control over provincial governors by establishing direct lines of communication between them and the palace.[21]

The focus on the category of "the population" blended well with Abdülhamid II's autocratic tendencies. Education and urbanization, coupled with tight control over the press and the provincial bureaucratic structure, expanded governance further in the sense expounded by Foucault. These approaches were aimed at monopolizing the representation of the state and at shaping citizens who recognized legitimate rule in the figure of the sultan. Their effects remained limited, though, particularly given the competition from missionaries on the educational front, but they did succeed in "generating new categories of collectivity and subjectivity."[22]

Under Abdülhamid II, the forceful hand policy towards the hinterlands, particularly those populated by unorthodox groups, contrasted sharply with the position of provincial cities in the late Ottoman period.[23] Seen from Istanbul, the latter were relatively integrated into the Ottoman bureaucracy and served as centers for the surveillance and administration of their surroundings. To reinforce this relationship, the Ottoman government executed an array of projects seeking to inscribe the imperial presence on these cities and educate their subjects in the language of citizenry—what historian Selim Deringil calls the public image focusing on the school-mosque-barracks triangle.[24] This approach bolstered cities as centers of governance from which the hinterlands could be controlled and surveilled, but it also reinforced cities themselves and their inhabitants as showcases of Ottoman modernity.

As historian Jens Hanssen shows, with its proximity to the Ansari Mountains in the north and to the unruly Mount Lebanon, and with its burgeoning intellectual and commercial life, Beirut was fertile ground for the kind of modern urbanity nurtured by late Ottoman rule.[25] It had been under the authority of Damascus since the formation of the super-province of Syria in 1864. At the time of Abdülhamid II's ascension to the throne, local personages in Beirut were campaigning for the removal of this authority. Consciously employing the language of reform, Christian and Muslim dignitaries sent petitions to Istanbul arguing for the city's commercial and intellectual importance and asking for it to be made a capital. Whereas the strong European presence in the city had previously been cause for hesitation, the balance of fortunes tipped under Abdülhamid II. In 1888, Beirut became the capital of a noncontiguous province of the same name.[26]

From Town to Port City

The "long nineteenth century" and the dynamics it generated between Istanbul, its provinces, and its imperialist competitors left an indelible stamp on the modern rise of the city of Beirut. At the onset of that century, Beirut was still a small Mediterranean town of six thousand inhabitants ensconced within medieval walls.[27] A combination of circumstances triggered Beirut's development into a main commercial gateway for Syria in the first half of the nineteenth century and, by World War I, into a vibrant city with a population of one hundred and fifty thousand[28] (see Map 1). Beirut's merchants played an important role in the promotion of their city before the age of the Tanzimat. By defying fines imposed on them by the ruler of Acre, Sulayman Pasha al-'Adil (r. 1804–1818), the merchants of Beirut challenged Acre's monopoly over trade in the region.[29] In the words of historian Thomas Philipp, it was precisely the city's "undefined political situation . . . at the beginning of the nineteenth century, a certain vagueness as to political authority, that provided the conditions if not for a 'république des négociants' then certainly those for a merchant community to flourish and do business."[30]

Even into the 1830s, however, speculation was still rife about which city would play the leading role of main entrepôt on the Eastern Mediterranean coast, with the historical ports of Tripoli to the north and Sidon to the south being Beirut's strongest contenders.[31] It was under the brief Egyptian rule (1831–1840) over Syria that Beirut first began to consolidate its centrality through a reorganization of administrative districts, the setting up of a police force, and the instituting of hygienic measures. For example, the ordinance requiring all vessels headed for the Eastern Mediterranean coast to first be inspected at a newly founded quarantine station in Beirut constituted an investment not only in the expansion of capital along epidemic-free trade routes but also in the city itself as a fixed point of exchange along these routes.

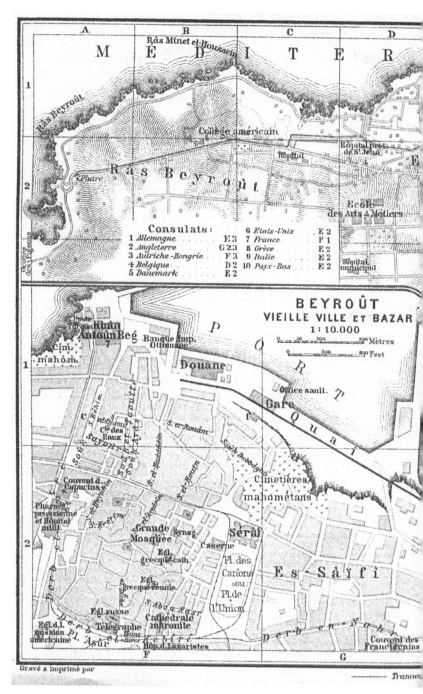

Consulats:

1	Allemagne	E 3	6	États-Unis	E 2
2	Angleterre	G 2.3	7	France	F 1
3	Autriche -Hongrie	F 3	8	Grèce	E 2
4	Belgique	D 2	9	Italie	E 2
5	Danemark	E 2	10	Pays -Bas	E 2

BEYROÛT
VIEILLE VILLE ET BAZAR
1:10.000

Gravé & imprimé par

Map 1. Map of Beirut from Karl Baedeker's *Palestine and Syria: Handbook for Travellers,* 5
edition, 1912. The inset shows the location of two souk clusters: one around Suq al-Tawi
north of the inner city, and one around Suq Abu al-Nasr, by the southwest corner of t
Places des Canons, also known as Burj Square. Source: University of Texas Libraries.

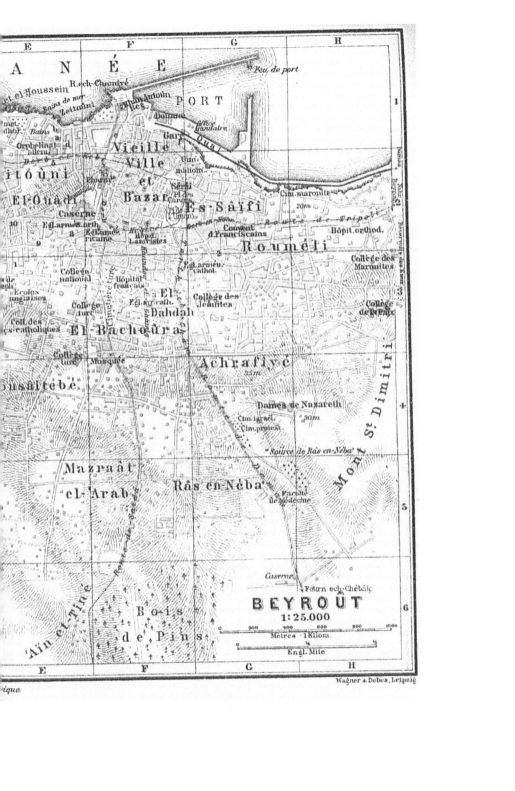

BEYROUT

1:25.000

Métres 1 Kilom.

Engl. Mile

Wagner & Debes, Leipzig

Such investments created "natural conditions" that attracted further investments, thereby further reinforcing the city's position as a fixed node in the
expansion of capital.[32] Further development in the second half of the nineteenth century of the Beirut-Damascus carriage road, the Beirut port, and
two railway lines centering on Beirut seemed "natural" only after initial investments had consolidated the city's role as a point of transit in a network of
global routes of commerce.[33]

After Ottoman forces regained control of Syria in 1840, they adopted
many of the reforms instituted during the Egyptian reign. The Ottoman
government retained the primacy of Beirut, establishing it as the seat of the
vilayet (province) of Sidon in 1841. The emphasis on coastal trade routes and
on Damascus as a political center had made Beirut the uncontested port of
Damascus, and the short-lived Ottoman *vilayet* of Syria (1865–1888), which
placed the two cities under the same provincial administration, reflected this
new reality.[34]

Ottoman governance began to inscribe its presence on the urban fabric of Beirut during the Tanzimat. Following the introduction of building
regulations for provincial cities in the 1860s, the Ministry of Public Works
in Istanbul assigned an engineer to Beirut to ensure correct application of
the law.[35] This constituted the first concerted Ottoman effort to instill into
Beirut the rhythms and order of governance. But it was only after Abdülhamid II took the reigns of power that the concern with the population took
off in a bid to transform the public image of the city into that of a modern provincial capital. However, the school-mosque-barracks triangle that
constituted the foundation of the Hamidian public image was tempered in
Christian-majority Beirut by the primarily civic nature of public monuments.

Beirut's intimacy with Istanbul found expression in such physical structures as administrative and military buildings, public spaces, and monuments.
In addition to the Petit Serail, which was commissioned in 1881 to house
subprovincial offices, the development of the government complex in the
Qantari quarter reflected the city's rapidly changing position. Overlooking
the city and dominating its skyline, the hilltop complex contained civic and
military functions. In the spirit of competition with the missionary establish-
ments, the government complex was endowed with a large, chiming clock
tower showing "Islamic" time on two of its faces and "Western" time on the

other two, to provide an alternative to the various clocks belonging to foreign institutions and showing only Western time.[36] Thus, the project reflected the two systems of measuring time regularly in use in the city.[37]

Other building typologies reflecting the Hamidian concern with education sprang up across the city. They included the Ottoman College in Zuqaq al-Balat (in 1895) and the Sana'i' educational complex west of the city (in 1907). Through their curriculum and their daily rhythms, such institutions instilled a sense of Ottoman identity intertwined with a sense of Islamic morality and discipline centering on obedience to the sultan.[38] Given the much greater number of religious and missionary schools that had been operating in the city for decades, Hamidian educational institutions created but an ideological dent in society at large.[39] The college, however, did contribute in introducing to the city the language of citizenry and Ottoman identity and in educating individuals who went on to become influential bureaucrats and politicians and to play leading roles not only in Beirut but also in the region.

By meshing with urban developments through the system of business concessions granted by the Ottoman authorities, foreign investments also shaped the public face of the city and its relationship with its surroundings. Law ordained that concessions be granted only to locals, but the latter commonly sold them on to mostly European entrepreneurs, with the result that between 1888 and 1914, 72 million francs of European investment were pumped into the city.[40] This included major investments furthering Beirut's position as an entrepôt—such as the port—as well as investments that reconfigured the city's relationship with itself and its surroundings—such as the railway, tramway, water, and gas companies. While the former investments consolidated Beirut's economic position and opened it up to a greater flow of commodities, the latter altered the relationship between the city's inhabitants and the various geographies encompassing them.

The Middle Class and the *Nahda*

In terms of class, the historiography of Beirut emphasizes the dual roles of intellectuals and of the mercantile bourgeoisie in transforming the city starting in the mid-nineteenth century, but the same period saw the rise of teachers, professionals, wage-employees, and government employees equally invested in the new order.[41] Such new groups eventually came to form a driving force in the politics of the French Mandate period.[42] Still, very little is known about their emergence in the late nineteenth century. Avenues of economic and cultural interaction with industrialized countries with imperial ambitions, like Britain, Belgium, France, Germany, Austria-Hungary, and the United States, opened up the doors to new educational systems, commercial ties, and modernization projects and to new reserves of intellectual vocabulary. But equally central were local and imperial projects in education and governance. Many of the disparate groups included under the economically descriptive umbrella of "those of middling means" rose on these changes and were invested in them.

A look at the second edition of *Dalil Bayrut,* a commercial city guide published in 1889, one year after Beirut became the provincial capital, brings some of these new groups into focus.[43] The names in the guide reveal a sectarian cross section of the city: Christians of several denominations, Muslims, and Jews. In addition to sharing the same economic bracket, the various groups of the emerging middle class held several characteristics in common: education, upward mobility, and an investment in the city's position. The introductory pages of the city guide are followed by lists of employees in the expanded bureaucratic structure of the province and the city. The members of this new generation of employees were spread across new institutions brought forth by Ottoman reforms, such as the municipal council, the telegraph service, the customs office, the postal service, the tobacco monopoly, and the police. Their ranks were supplemented by other white-collar and technical employees in concessional projects such as the gas company, the waterworks, and the Beirut-Damascus carriage road.

Dalil Bayrut goes on to list members of the new professional class: doctors, dentists, pharmacists, lawyers, and bankers. Bankers shared their professional field with entrepreneurs on the fringes of the professional financial economy, those offering banking services, commissions, credit, and import. Other entrepreneurs were adapting to the new technologies and a changing economy to produce commodities that catered to growing consumption appetites in the city. They populate the pages of the city guide as dressmakers, cabinetmakers, gilders, and small-scale manufacturers. Also constituting part of this new middle class is a group that appears only indirectly, in the guide's sections on periodicals and educational institutions.

Intellectuals, educators, and journalists not only left an indelible mark on the emergence of the middle class but also often spoke on its behalf. Whether through direct education or through didactic writings in the press, they put forth their conceptions of how this class should behave and hold itself in relation to its surroundings.

Beirut's role in the region was intimately linked with the *nahda*, the late nineteenth- and early twentieth-century upsurge in the production of vibrant intellectual and cultural works in the Arabic language that centered on Egypt and the Levant. Together with its rise as a commercial center, Beirut also developed as a hub for publication, debate, education, and scientific and literary societies. A multilingual generation educated in modern schools shaped what it meant to be modern and middle class in late Ottoman Beirut. At the turn of the century, the wide mixture of educational opportunities in the city contributed to a spectrum of overlapping civic identifications among its inhabitants: Syrian, Oriental, Ottoman, Beiruti.[44]

Missionary interest in the Syrian region had begun after the founding of the American Protestant Syria Mission and the arrival of the earliest missionaries to Beirut in the early 1820s. Even before Abdülhamid II's educational reforms, education was one of the main pillars of proselytization for those missions. They had commenced educational initiatives, aimed at both boys and girls, around Beirut only a few years after their arrival, followed by initiatives in the city itself in the 1830s.[45] Missionary schools were soon competing with local efforts at education, the earliest of which was Butrus al-Bustani's National School, founded as an initiative to promote secular unity after the civil strife in 1860 in Mount Lebanon and Damascus.[46] Al-Bustani's school was unique for its emphasis on nonsectarianism, for even if not exclusively frequented by people of the same sect, most other private schools in Beirut were sectarian initiatives and stamped with a sectarian character.

The education of girls also attracted the attention of local educational endeavors, such as the Greek Orthodox Zahrat al-Ihsan, founded in 1881. Commenting in 1921 on the impact of schooling on the region, historian, politician, and Beirut notable Muhammad Jamil Bayhum remarked that as a result of the "teaching chaos" that reigned during the late Ottoman period, "the Syrian scientific *nahda* matured primarily with Christian women, graduates of the free schools, and was thus the foster daughter of the two classes:

the middle and poor."[47] In pointing to this class dimension, Bayhum is underlining the entry into educated circles of women who came from modest families and who came to be invested in the opportunities their education gave them and others of their sex. The women listed by Bayhum—Salma Abu Rashid, Mari Yanni, Najla Abu al-Lamaʻ, Mari ʻAjami, and Julia Tuʻma Dimashqiyya (as she was known after her marriage)—went on to found women's periodicals where the meaning of home and modern domesticity was debated and articulated.

A spirit of productive intersectarian competition and a concern about the number of Muslim and Jewish girls attending missionary and Christian schools enlivened the educational scene. In the same year it was founded, 1878, Jamʻiyyat al-Maqasid al-Khayriyya al-Islamiyya (the Maqasid Islamic Benevolent Society) opened a school for girls, followed by another school for girls and two schools for boys in 1879.[48] That the first school founded by the Maqasid was a school for girls is not without significance. Despite the opposition they faced from both laymen and religious figures, the founders of the society shared with a number of others of different religious backgrounds a belief in the necessity of educating girls. The Jews of Beirut also initiated their own efforts to compete with European organizations, particularly the Church of Scotland Mission. Since the local Tiferet Israel school remained a school for boys, however, modern female education for Jews remained mostly the province of mission schools, other community schools in the city, and the schools of the Paris-based Alliance israélite universelle (Universal Jewish Alliance).[49] In this respect, numbers tell a poignant story about girls' education. In 1889, there were slightly more than fifteen thousand school pupils in a city with an estimated population of one hundred and seven thousand, a number that saw a steady increase over the next decades. Remarkably, more than six and a half thousand of those were female pupils.[50]

Woman's changing position in society was tightly bound with the outlook of the emerging middle class and did not manifest itself only in education. The vibrancy in the educational system was reflected in the city's burgeoning press and the wider degree of participation in it. What was referred to as *mas'alat al-nisa'* (the women's question) was taken up by the press almost as soon as it started to be discussed in the 1870s in journals such as Butrus al-Bustani's *al-Jinan*, where that question soon came to dominate many of its pages. In addition to the issue of education, contributors to this debate addressed woman's role in managing the home and raising children and her status as a measure of a society's degree of civilization and progress. Muslim, Christian, and Jewish men alike picked up on these issues, and Muslim, Christian, and Jewish women joined the debate as active participants soon after.

Such debates extended to other fora, including literary, cultural, and philanthropic societies founded, run, and attended by women. Like their male-run counterparts, these societies presented podiums for lectures, meetings, and debates. Not all women had equal access to the meetings and lectures held by these societies. 'Anbara Salam al-Khalidi recounts how in 1910, when she was thirteen years old, she had to cancel her plans for a literary evening when she was recognized at the door by Muslim men. That the daughter of the Sunni notable Abu 'Ali Salam was attending a mixed gathering was a piece of news sensational enough to make it into the papers the following day, under the headline "Muslim Girls at Evening Society."[51] Despite such limitations for Muslim women, like al-Khalidi, they still had access to the lectures when they were published in the press. In this way, the press and other publications helped to shape a common language and a common set of concerns that crossed spatial and social barriers.

Another characteristic of the middle class was a newly found social mobility, often tied to the virtues of education and the ethics of hard work. Jurji Zaydan, who classified his family as being "of middling means," is an example of this upward mobility.[52] Born in Beirut to an illiterate father who had emigrated as a boy from a village in Mount Lebanon, his trajectory was radically transformed within one generation through life in the city, his father's hard work, and Zaydan's own proclivity for intellectual interests. Zaydan's case is exceptional only in his ensuing renown as an intellectual and the founder of the Egyptian newspaper al-Hilal, and there were several in the circle of Beiruti intellectuals who traced a more or less similar trajectory, such as Julia Tu'ma Dimashqiyya and Shahin Makariyus—to name two figures central to shaping what it meant to be a member of a new middle class. Education specifically played the role of catalyst in social mobilization, both as a status symbol and as a means of acquiring skills for social advancement.

Many members of this emerging middle class were invested in the position of Beirut as a provincial capital within the Ottoman Empire, major port

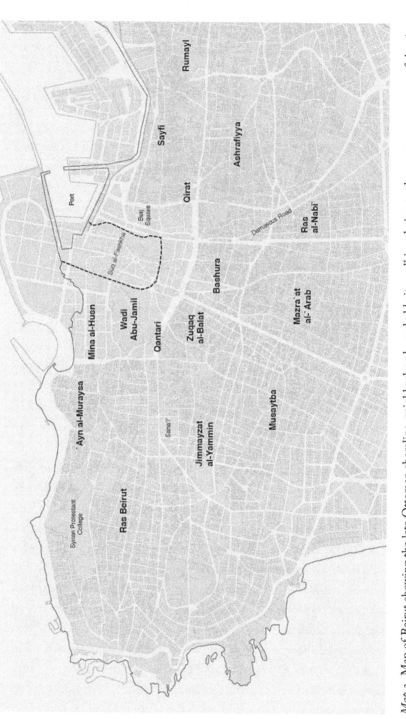

Map 2. Map of Beirut showing the late Ottoman shoreline, neighborhoods, and old city wall in relation to the contemporary map of the city. Source: Børre Ludvigsen, based on data from Jamal Hisham Abed and from Davie, "Maps and the Historical Topography of Beirut."

city on the Eastern Mediterranean, and symbol of an evolving modernity. As merchants with small businesses in the city; as small manufacturers adapting their production to cheap, industrialized imports; and as intellectuals, professionals, educators, public employees, and bureaucrats, their social position was interlinked with the tripartite development of the city as economic hub, provincial Ottoman city, and intellectual melting pot. As pointed out earlier, given the city's various educational systems and intellectual currents, debates on civic identity naturally flourished. Overlapping identifications such as Syrian, Oriental, and Ottoman became an integral part of the debate on being modern and had a profound effect on the understanding of middle-class domesticity.

Neighborhoods and Suburbs

With Beirut's urban growth, middle-class families began moving out into the city's new neighborhoods and contributed to shaping their character. Beirut's old walls were already beginning to crumble in the 1830s and all but completely disappeared as dwellings for the well-to-do spilled out into new neighborhoods and expensive villas dotted the hills of new suburbs. The expansion beyond what was then referred to as inner Beirut (*batin Bayrut*), changed the proximity and distribution of social groups within the city. Until the 1830s, people of different classes and confessions lived altogether within intramural Beirut, with only a few occupying outlying, scattered houses. Even where confessional quarters existed within symbolic or physical boundaries, their inhabitants remained close to the other residents of the city, with whom they also shared communal and commercial spaces. In a rectangle of about 350 by 550 meters, the six thousand inhabitants of Beirut lived, socialized, and shopped; only at death did they take up residence outside the old city walls, where the cemeteries were.

Differentiation along class lines became more pronounced with the development of new neighborhoods and the exodus of the better-off from the inner city. Change started in the 1840s with the mushrooming villas of the suburbs of Rumayl, Zuqaq al-Balat, Ashrafiyya, and Qirat, where the new literary and mercantile elites of the city took up residence (see Map 2). In the space of two decades, urban growth expanded beyond these wealthy suburbs to include less well-off areas to the south and southwest such as Bashura, Musaytba, Ras al-Nabi', Mazra'at al-'Arab, and Jimmayzat al-Yammin.[53] Immigrants from Mount Lebanon after the 1860 civil conflict inflated these outlying neighborhoods, some of which remained destinations for the less affluent well into the twentieth century.[54] The quarters bordering the inner city—Sayfi, Ghalghul, Bashura, and Qantari—took on a middle-class character, but certain members of the middle class, particularly intellectuals and professionals, were also attracted to the newest suburb furthest west: Ras Beirut.

Both the transformation of the inner city and the development of the new neighborhoods were structured by urban projects carried out by the municipal council of Beirut. Even before the promulgation of the 1882 Building Code, there were shy attempts at applying the principles of hygiene, order, and aesthetics, which had come to be regarded as guidelines for urban development. Already in the late 1870s, the municipal council had begun a campaign for cleaning up the inner city, moving tanneries outside the city, introducing regulations for underground sewage holding tanks, and controlling the entry of livestock and flammable material.[55] Apart from regulating commerce in inner Beirut, the council was also concerned with cleanliness in the city as a whole, granting bidding contracts for cleaning the town and its suburbs.[56] In an attempt to introduce visual order to the streetscape, the council issued announcements ordering shops, coffeehouses, and taverns to keep their activities off the streets or pay the requisite fines.[57]

These halting attempts paved the way for a more fundamental reordering of urban space in the 1890s, no doubt finding renewed vigor in Beirut's newly acquired position as provincial capital. Armed with the Building Code, the provincial government and municipal council overhauled the inner city and transformed it along modern conceptions of urban planning. A number of markets and houses were demolished and new avenues cut to embellish the city and improve its traffic circulation. One such major project was that of Suq al-Fashkha (literally, Step Souk), a narrow, crooked street running east and west through the inner city and renamed Shari' al-Jadid (New Street) after its widening.[58]

In the long-term view, these projects fueled an urban expansion that had been launched back in the middle of the nineteenth century. Although the new neighborhoods were not strictly homogeneous when it came to religion, they were characterized by majority confessions, a pattern reinforced by the tendency of migrants to settle near their coreligionists. Roughly, the area west and south of the inner city was majority Muslim and the area to the east majority Greek Orthodox or Maronite, representing the three largest religious groups in the city. Even among the latter two there was a differentiation, as Rumayl took on a Maronite character, fueled by the settlement patterns of refugees from Mount Lebanon after 1860. Ras Beirut and areas closer to the city center, such as Zuqaq al-Balat and Wadi Abu-Jamil, did not witness the same confessional homogenization, but generally maintained a well-to-do profile. The lower class neighborhoods to the south also remained more confessionally mixed and, stamped by the confessional politics of the time, sites of occasional sectarian tensions between their Sunni and Greek Orthodox inhabitants.[59]

Most neighborhoods were far from confessionally homogeneous, however. A case from the Hanafi court registers illustrates the difficulty of determining the religious character of one such neighborhood in Beirut. A customs employee took his wife to court in 1916, demanding that she join him at their marital home, which was located "amongst Muslim neighbors" in Jimmayzat al-Yammin. The wife's representative refused, stressing on two separate occasions that the home was located among Christians and Druze, with only a few Muslim homes out of about two hundred.[60] It remains unclear how seriously the court took the religious composition of the neighborhood in reaching its ruling, since the inspector sent to verify the claims mentions only that the home is located among "good neighbors."

What the case does illustrate is not only that perceptions played a role in the religious classification of some quarters, but also that immediate neighbors mattered just as much as the neighborhood's overall character. In this case, the wife seems to have left the marital home due to a conflict with her neighboring sister-in-law, and thus representing the neighborhood as non-Muslim served the defendant's purposes. Like the inspector sent to investigate the litigants' claims and counterclaims, the judge did not make any direct reference to the sectarian character of the neighborhood, and he ended up ruling in the husband's favor.

In addition to being a matter of perception, the sectarian composition of the neighborhoods also varied with their economic and cultural profiles.

In the wake of the 1860 civil strife in Mount Lebanon, religious sect was consolidated as a political identity that was used to negotiate a religious community's standing with the Ottoman state.[61] But this overlapped with the burgeoning of the *nahda*, which often brought intellectuals from different religious backgrounds together in educational institutions, scientific societies, and other such endeavors. The activities generated and fueled by the educated middle class influenced the character of various quarters and, in some instances, became a catalyst for urbanization.

The Zuqaq al-Balat quarter, lying on a hill on the southwestern edge of the inner city, was an early point of concentration for schools as well as for various intellectual associations, societies, and clubs. What was already a growing, well-off area of private houses developed into a focal point for the city's intellectual life and, starting in the second half of the nineteenth century, began attracting some members of the urban middle class.[62] What mattered to this kind of activity was the cultural and economic capital invested in the quarter, rather than its sectarian character. The various social classes in the neighborhood were mixed when it came to sect, and the mansions of Zuqaq al-Balat continued to attract new constructions, homes for upper-class residents of different religious backgrounds.[63] In addition, the quarter had residents of more moderate and even humble means, especially among the Druze and Sunni Muslim residents.[64]

Further afield, to the west of the inner city, the quarter of Ras Beirut presented a more drastic example of the link between urban and cultural regeneration. Until the 1860s, the quarter was largely rural and sparsely populated, with houses scattered among its fields and orchards. The bordering 'Ayn al-Muraysa, a small fishing village, had a higher population density than Ras Beirut. The choice to open a college in Ras Beirut in 1867 initially raised local eyebrows at the eccentricity of the American missionaries' decision to build "among the coyotes."[65] Within the space of three decades, the presence of the Syrian Protestant College had attracted intellectuals, middle-class professionals, and eventually, in 1907, a tramway, transforming the area into a vibrant quarter with a multiconfessional character.[66] Here, again, the example of Ras Beirut illustrates in a very direct way how education, urban planning, and the cultural space of a new class came together in the formation of a new neighborhood stamped with its own distinctive character.

Researching Middle-Class Domesticity in Beirut

Middle-class domesticity in the late Ottoman period does not readily give itself to research. This work uses a variety of archives, read in light of each other, to glimpse the contours of the home in Beirut in this period. The Ottoman archives in Istanbul and published legal codes provide information on the effect of Ottoman reforms on the urban fabric. Communications between Istanbul and the provincial government in Beirut show which urban reforms affected Beirut and the contestations they engendered. Nevertheless, it would have remained difficult to see how these influenced the home if it were not for an essential supplement: the archive of minutes from the meetings of the municipal council of Beirut. Assumed to have been lost or destroyed during the Lebanese civil war,[67] the archives of the Beirut municipal council have not been used before for research purposes. Starting with the year 1902, specific cases from this archive concerning the extension of services and the implementation of urban changes on the ground provide the previously missing link between Ottoman urban modernity in the making and the home. They also nuance our view of the reforms; rather than top-down impositions, they were effected through a negotiated process that actively involved the inhabitants of Beirut.

Hanafi court records are an invaluable resource on domestic life, even given their limitations in providing statistical generalizations.[68] Hanafi was the official school of Sunni Muslim jurisprudence that was practiced in the Ottoman Empire. But in addition to the Hanafi, or *shari'a*, courts, the late Ottoman court system included confessional (*millet*) courts, commercial courts, mixed courts, and criminal courts. The Hanafi court remained the most frequented for dealing with property disputes, but as more confessional courts were being instituted as part of Ottoman reforms, the Hanafi court was gradually losing its role as a place for Christians and Jews to settle "personal" or "family" matters—that is, those involving inheritance, marriage, divorce, custody, or alimony. Nevertheless, during the period under consideration, many non-Muslims continued to seek the court for such cases, either out of preference or to override rulings in other courts.[69]

I use three types of cases from the Hanafi court records. The first are inheritance, marriage, and divorce cases that include inventory lists of possessions, either as part of an inheritance or a dowry. These are cases that involved

Christians, Muslims, and Jews, and, examined over a long period of time, they show which objects were becoming popular and who could afford them.[70] The second case type I use involves marital disputes, primarily between Muslim couples. These show how negotiations over contested objects took place and, thus, what meanings these objects held in the context of marital disputes. Finally, court cases from the 1860s to the 1880s give examples of how domestic space was dealt with in the Hanafi court, in contrast to the home being dealt with as property in general in the minutes of the municipal council.

Whereas Hanafi court records in which objects appear do contain descriptions of popular domestic items, they do not always provide information on the market value of these objects, exactly what they looked like, or their importance to the way domestic life was conceived.[71] Drawing on typical sources such as the press and published lectures and other works reveals debates on domesticity that show how specific objects related to an idealized conception of the middle-class home. French consular correspondence gives detailed reports of imports, exports, and local industry, giving an idea of the extent of the popularity of certain domestic objects. Furthermore, advertisements provide information on local production and distribution as well as on popular objects of consumption. Apart from occasional images in advertisements, I draw on extant buildings, photographs, and commercial trade catalogues from the late Ottoman period for visual material. Taken together, this archival evidence provides information on what commodities were popular, where they came from, who could afford them, and what meaning they held for domesticity in late Ottoman Beirut.

Before going into more detail in the later chapters on how the home was transformed in its urban context and in relation to the middle class, I present the main arguments of the book in Chapter 2, exploring the notion of *taste* and how it challenged the divide between public and private and between the interior and the exterior of the culture. I elaborate on these ideas in relation to the global production of taste, the culture of class, the position of the middle class between tradition and modernity, and the quest for authenticity. Engaging postcolonial theory, Pierre Bourdieu's work on class, and recent literature on the middle class as a global phenomenon, I argue that even as it functioned as a mark of distinction in contemporary debates on class, taste linked the Beiruti middle-class home to urban, imperial, and global contexts.

Focusing on matters of hygiene and urban aesthetics, Chapter 3 looks at how Ottoman urban administration and the daily workings of the Beirut municipal council reconstituted the relationship between the home and its urban context. Drawing on nineteenth-century global modes of knowledge that privileged rectilinear urban forms and sought to manage daily lives in expanding cities, new bodies of Ottoman law introduced an understanding of *public benefit* that tied domestic habits and individual lives to the public collectivity of the city. The implementation of these laws by the municipal council of Beirut also brought capitalist changes into the home, redefining it as property with a value linked to urban beautification projects. But in the absence of a clear understanding of the relationship between public benefit and the home, the latter remained an open site of contestation, amenable to interpretation as a link between people's private lives and the larger project of modernity.

Chapter 4 looks at ways in which objects that entered the middle-class home in the late nineteenth century generated a new kind of domesticity. Although its relation to public benefit remained ambiguous, the home was indirectly transformed by its changing urban environment and by new spatial ideals. In addition, Beirut's prominence as port city and its growing appetite for the new exposed it to a stream of new domestic objects that were often adopted, adapted, and embraced. Domestic things, the meanings embedded in them, and their potential to communicate social positions contributed to giving the middle class its identity even in the most intimate of spaces. The impact of new items, such as phonographs, on life at home as well as on the course of marital disputes in the Hanafi court, shows the potential for new objects to redefine social relations, making taste more than just an individual matter.

In Chapter 5, I explore modern domesticity as articulated by men and women in the pages of the press and on lecture podiums, arguing that this project carved out an economic and cultural place for an emerging middle class. As industrial production in Europe and the United States brought wider swathes of society into contact with new commodities, articles on the use and disposition of objects at home attempted to differentiate the consumption habits of the middle class from the tasteless riches of the upper classes. While these debates functioned to culturally distinguish the nascent middle class in its social surroundings, the chapter argues that they went beyond that, emphasizing the importance of distinguishing the attitudes of the Beiruti middle class from what the authors called *ifranji* modes of consumption and attempting to ground modern domesticity in "Oriental" or "Syrian" authenticity.

Looking beyond the anxiety over *ifranji* influences, Chapter 6 turns to the ways that popular domestic items were marketed, the outlets where they could be acquired, and the labor, materials, and styles that went into their production. This chapter shows how advertisements in the press promoted the latest fashionable imports at the same time that they tried to further local industries. In addition, the modern and the old inner-city souks were not set apart by stocking imported and traditional goods, respectively, but rather by a growing separation between areas of production and areas of consumption across the city. Finally, the most popular domestic items involved labor, raw materials, and stylistic influences that cut across local, regional, and global levels. This crisscrossing not only rendered the line between *ifranji* and Oriental difficult to trace in reality but also complicated the intellectual project of middle-class modernity.

(CHAPTER 2)

THE GLOBAL INTIMACIES OF TASTE

See how the *ifranja* [Westerners], who are ahead of us in

knowledge and science, have turned taste into a separate topic

of science known as "aesthetics" in order to investigate beauty in

nature and industry, whereas the topic is rarely mentioned amongst

Arabic speakers.

Yusuf Shalhut[1]

In Butrus al-Bustani's encyclopedia *Da'irat al-Ma'arif* (The Scope of Knowledge), published in 1884, the entry for *taste* is limited to its definition as one of the five senses and as a sense for literary appreciation.[2] But less than a decade later, *nahda* authors also saw in taste a link to nature, science, industry, and the production of categories of knowledge. Partly drawing on a history of writing on the topic, partly inspired by new ideas on taste, *nahda* writers now saw taste as a quality that could be refined, reformed, and cultivated in both old and new fields of knowledge. With the richness of the concept and its ability to bring together salient topics of debate at the time—education, progress, politics, and science—taste also soon became entangled with the notion of middle-class domesticity.

Nahda discussions linking the home to its urban context, Ottoman reforms, and changing consumption trends often took on a very material form, addressing taste in an aesthetic and in a political sense. The privileged place the home occupied in considerations of the nature of the private and public spheres turned it into a model for an emerging middle class attempting to create a cultural niche for itself and seeking greater influence in society. Due to its currency as a concept, taste provided a natural bridge for understanding how changes in the public sphere influenced and corresponded to changes at home. But the arguments presented in this book are as much about the contradictions within middle-class domesticity as they are about what that domesticity entailed. For at the same time that the home was forwarded as a model for society in general and the middle class in particular, this model was in no way hegemonic and domesticity remained open to contestation.

The home was affected by both the reshaping of its urban setting as well as by the imported and locally produced commodities transforming it from within. In both instances, taste constituted a link between the home and its wider context: its urban environment and an increasingly global chain for the production of commodities. Participants in the late nineteenth- and early twentieth-century public debate on domesticity in Beirut put forth a vision of an idealized middle-class home where modernity could be localized, an "Oriental" identity could be cultivated, and an ethics of consumption focused on appropriating the means of production could be instilled. But even as a sense of authenticity became anchored in the home, the ways in which tastes were changing introduced tensions into what this middle-class modernity entailed.

Domesticity between Public and Private

In writings on the new domesticity taking shape in Beirut, there were several coexisting, sometimes contradictory conceptions of the home's relationship to the public sphere. It was the space of the conjugal family, at the same time that its salon was a space for socializing with the outside world. It was women's shield from the vagaries of the market, at the same time as it constituted a site for reform and progress. It was the kingdom where the woman ruled supreme without any outside interference, at a time when the press was replete with prescriptive advice on what a woman should and should not do in her home. It was the place where a sense of cultural authenticity could be nurtured, even as it was put forth as an object of reform. Finally, it was the place to cultivate a "proper" ethics of consumption, at the same time that even its most private of spaces was opened to popular commodities through didactic prescriptions in the press as well as advertisements.

These conflictual ways of thinking about the relationship between public and private disguise an even deeper tension. This tension comes out most clearly between the need for maintaining a sense of difference and that need itself being the product of the imperialist encounter. The domestic setting became a place for the production of knowledge about an Oriental, or local, modernity precisely because the middle class in the Ottoman Empire found itself imbricated in globalized cultural shifts even as it needed to establish for itself a specific place within these changes. Because their changing position in society was articulated through the home, women were enmeshed in these attempts at localization, making them more visible in the public sphere and more involved in the ongoing debates on the nature of progress and modernity.

In his discussion of the bourgeois "public sphere" in the Euro-American context, Jürgen Habermas makes the point that the line between public and private went right through the home in the eighteenth and nineteenth centuries, separating the realm of the family from that of the salon. Rather than being the realm of the private as opposed to the public, the bourgeois home became the place where the two met. A notion of familial intimacy developed around this home, one that set it apart from the market.[3] But despite this desire to perceive the two spheres as separate, Habermas argues, the sphere of the home was dependent on labor and commodity exchange.[4] The wider point to be made in relation to Habermas's arguments is that in its modern context, domesticity can only be understood as part of wider transformations in publicity, privacy, and related socioeconomic conditions.

It remains important not to subordinate domesticity to a history of the public sphere. Looking at domesticity in late Ottoman Beirut in relation to urban reforms, economic shifts, and intellectual trends places private life at the heart of what it meant to be modern. That Habermas's model of the public sphere is specifically a liberal, bourgeois space of mediation between society and the state means that it is built on a number of exclusions, not least among them gender.[5]

Historically, the unequal relationship between the two spheres and the correlation of the *public* sphere with the world of men and the *private* sphere with the world of women instituted what Leonore Davidoff refers to as the "great divide."[6] This public-private split has been critiqued by feminist literature as a product of late eighteenth- and early nineteenth-century patriarchal liberalism, predicated on a division of functions that sets the logic of the market apart from the passions of private life. Measuring Beiruti women's impact on the public order through such yardsticks as their participation in public debates, high level of education, and physical visibility, continues to define that impact in terms of women's involvement in what remained at the time largely a world of men in which a limited number of women participated. An approach that de-provincializes domesticity and sets it parallel to the more visible changes from today's point of view highlights how both women's *and* men's private lives defined the "greater" project of modernity.[7]

One of the crucial ways in which the home in Beirut contributed to the project of modernity was through its economy. Woman's envisioned role as manager of the house limited her involvement in economic questions to the private sphere of the home. At first glance, this maintains a separation between private and public by conceptualizing the sphere of domestic life as separate from civil society, what Mary Poovey calls the "ideological work of gender."[8] Simultaneously, the actual consumption habits of the middle class politicized consumption, tying the home and woman as its manager to more encompassing economic questions. Domesticity was, therefore, not merely a reflection of the emergence of the middle class and its related consumption habits but was also regarded as an economic field that could be managed in order to, in turn, better define the middle class. This is particularly relevant in contexts such as the Ottoman Empire, where the industrial relations of production upon which narrowly Marxist definitions of class are based did not prevail. The task is then to bring economic transformations in labor, manufacturing, and domestic consumption to bear on an understanding of domesticity that goes beyond the confines of the home.

The public sphere's link to liberal democracy also raises the question of what happens to the public-private relationship outside the Euro-American context in which it is theorized to have developed. Many of the transformations Habermas addresses—such as the erosion of feudal powers, the growing influence of trade capitalism, the traffic in commodities and news, the centrality of cities to governance, and the institutionalization of regular contact and communication—are all changes that, collectively, began to have a marked influence on the Ottoman Empire starting in the eighteenth century. Yet, these very same changes structured an unbalanced economic and political relationship between the Ottoman Empire and its European competitors. Reduced tariffs on imports to the empire, for instance, were a result of this imbalance and served to further underline the economic ascendance of nineteenth-century industrialized capitalism. Given the link between liberalism and empire, this places the middle class outside the Euro-American template in the unsettled position of laying claim to aspects of modernity while trying to emphasize what it is about that class that makes it specifically local.[9] Isolating the home as a location of cultural difference and understanding it separately from changing economic, political, and social conditions risks placing domesticity at the periphery of modernity. When the question is shifted from locating a site of difference to understanding how such a site is actively produced, however, a new set of questions emerges. Instead of taking the issue of difference for granted, the question then concerns how, during a time of burgeoning imperialism, differences were produced, not as a sign of provinciality but precisely because the need for marking out a distinct location becomes acute in an imperial, homogenizing mode of history writing.

In postcolonial studies, the relationship between public and private often remains the place where scholarship maintains a sense of difference and challenges the categories of a putative Western modernity. Speaking of the private in Gandhi's political practices, for example, Dipesh Chakrabarty describes it as "nonnarratable and nonrepresentable."[10] In *Provincializing Europe*, Chakrabarty further develops privacy as a critique of historicism. Challenging a stagist view of history, where some societies are said to be "not yet" at a properly modern stage, he uncovers privacy as a location where difference can be located, not as an authentic or premodern remnant but precisely in the ways that it makes the limits of an all-encompassing modernity visible.[11] Although Chakrabarty complicates the notion of private by underlining its continued relationship to the public and, thus, to modernity in the case of colonial India, the structure of his book betrays a rift between the larger questions of history and capitalism and the smaller questions of the transformations of everyday life. Questions of capital, appearing in the first part, "under the sign of Marx," remain divorced from the second part, "under the sign of Heidegger," where he deals with middle-class transformations in sociality, domesticity, and the link between the public and private domains.

This persistent problematic lies partly in the tension inherent in surrendering even the home to a homogenizing modernity, often imposed by force of conquest and arms. The way domesticity was thought of in the words of the men and women giving it form in contexts as varied as India and the Ottoman Empire further reinforces the sense that this sphere was cultivated as a place where a sense of control can be maintained. Particularly in the face of rapid changes in the public sphere, domesticity took on the guise of a jealously guarded cultural privacy where a middle class could formulate a localized identity.

Even as the home discursively took on being the place for localizing difference, it remained linked in various ways to its urban, imperial, and global contexts. Perhaps for this very reason, the relationship between the inside and outside remained conflicted for many commentators at the time. As the home opened itself up as a space for consumption, not only was it bound to larger economic transformations through commodities but also the choice of these commodities and the meanings they carried with them helped to define the relationship between the Beiruti middle class and modernity. The home acquired special significance in this regard because it allowed for a closer shaping of what it meant to be modern, both on the personal level and, through the unit of the family, as part of society.

A Global Production of Taste

Scholarly works on Istanbul, Mount Lebanon, Cairo, and Damascus show how in the eighteenth and nineteenth centuries the Ottoman Empire and Egypt experienced changes in household composition, emigration, consumer culture, and shifts in political power from the household to the state.[12] On the one hand, these works hint at the ways in which wider political and economic changes affected the way domesticity was both understood and lived. On the other hand, they leave out how domesticity and the politics surrounding it were ever more tightly imbricated with global transformations, particularly capitalism and industrial production.

During the period economic historians refer to as the *first globalization* (1870–1914), the openness in trade and finance also meant a constant search for new markets to accommodate increasing levels of industrial production.[13] The flow of imported commodities into the Ottoman market not only weakened indigenous manufacturing, but also, by introducing domestic items into everyday life, turned the home into a node in global consumption patterns. Ottomans participated in this as they took the home as a site of reform of the individual and of society at large. Use of new commodities at home constituted part of a conception of the home as an efficient and rational space. Because of their important position in trade networks in the eastern Mediterranean region, cities such as Cairo, Istanbul, Izmir, Alexandria, and Beirut became entry points for these new commodities. This not only altered public life in those cities and their surroundings but also touched areas we normally think of as private, such as lifestyle choices, homes, and social and familial relationships.[14] The increasing velocity of communication and transport meant that it did not take long before Parisian fashions appeared in Istanbul and other large cities of the empire.

Greater uniformity in the world economy expressed itself most forcefully in the industrial realm, but with greater uniformity also came complexity. This went beyond the sphere of consumption, with production chains involving different fashions, styles, and materials stretching across the globe. The hybridity C. A. Bayly discusses in terms of late nineteenth-century art trends can also be found in production processes.[15] This involved more than the non-Western world adapting to and absorbing Western forms of modernity. From Chinese ceramics to Oriental textile motifs, hybridity was endemic to industrial production. Many of the Oriental forms that were marketed back to the Ottoman Empire and other locations on the globe took form at the intersection of World Fairs, new conceptions of Islamic art, and the industrial production of consumer goods.[16]

The Beiruti middle class, like its counterparts elsewhere, was at the forefront of the changing consumption habits of the nineteenth century. With the growing economic power of middling groups and the introduction of cheaper, mass-produced commodities owing to industrialization, to invest in objects was to signal one's socioeconomic position. Due to Beirut's growing prominence as a port city, industrially produced commodities were increasingly imported there, and this had a significant impact on consumption habits. Many of the commodities that made their way to the city were intended for domestic consumption, and, together with a burgeoning literature on home advice, turn-of-the-century advertisements addressed the home as the natural place for new commodities. This transformed domestic life in a very material sense by changing daily habits around the new objects introduced into the home: beds, chairs, dining tables, decorative elements, and the like.

The formation of popular tastes, thus, had to do with changing production and consumption patterns in both the markets of the Ottoman Empire and those of Europe. Although not new items in Beirut, textiles, utensils, construction materials, and domestic elements such as roofs and windows began to blend together artisanal work with the production of the industrially leading countries of Europe—namely, Britain, France, Austria-Hungary, and Germany. Artisans in the Ottoman Empire were adopting industrially produced raw materials as well as new popular styles into their work, just as industrial production was turning to the East in search of new forms. These very same "exotic" forms then made their way back to their sources of inspiration, competing with the very products that had inspired them to begin with.

At the same time, local production also took an active part in molding new tastes. Like their peers in other parts of the Ottoman Empire, artisans in Beirut and its immediate surroundings adapted to survive. But their techniques also went beyond survival. Through an innovative blending of materials and fashions, they became participants in creating taste both at home and abroad. The popular tastes that were prevalent in Beirut at that juncture were configured as much by changing modes of consumption as they were by industrial production and local and regional artisans and manufacturers. The designs, motifs, and materials of the objects brought into the home integrated those different forms of labor that brought together disparate geographical entities.

Taste also bound domesticity to its urban context through the nineteenth-century shift in thinking about the relationship between the urban environment and society. Growing populations and migration to cities meant that cities needed a system able to manage the pressure of growing urban density and the popular agitation it sometimes fomented. In other words, the complications brought on by urbanization were also a part of what Michel Foucault refers to as "managing the population." While the Haussmannization of Paris remains the most striking example of this nineteenth-century urbanism, new urban forms and the institution of urban management introduced a uniform urban vocabulary from Istanbul to Tokyo.[17] In the context of Ottoman reforms, the aesthetic assumptions of this urbanity were influenced by the reformers' experience of European cities. Particularly influential was Ottoman statesman Mustafa Reşit Pasha, who—inspired by his diplomatic missions to Paris, Vienna, and London—advocated as early as 1836 an urban planning philosophy based on "scientific" principles and privileging geometrical rules in street layouts.[18]

The urban modernity introduced into the cities of the Ottoman Empire as part of the overall reforms undertaken by Istanbul brought in a set of aesthetics and rules of spatial organization that affected the home both directly through legislation and indirectly through the concepts of aesthetics, order, and hygiene that were becoming current among the educated classes of the city. The introduction of public services, hygienic measures, and a new kind of urban aesthetic through the urban code redefined the home's material relationship with its immediate context. These new aesthetics signaled a departure from the introverted, courtyard-oriented residences of the old city, where façades had small openings and the home turned its back on life outside its walls.[19] The new residences outside the old city walls articulated a different kind of material and social relationship between domestic space and its context. The home gradually became both physically more open to the outside world through its façades and windows and socially more involved in the city's intellectual and cultural life through new modes of domestic socialization and entertainment.[20]

Notwithstanding contemporary attempts to locate a sense of authenticity at home, the changes of the late Ottoman Empire opened the home up in new ways through notions of taste and their relationship with class and capital. From the point of view of the modes of production and consumption that permeated the home during that period, the separation between inside and outside, the intimate and the global, did not hold in the face of these sweeping changes. This is not to imply that even the private does not escape the grasp of the homogenizing forces of modernity. The more interesting question is how the category of taste itself is generated in this global encounter and what role taste played in defining the middle class and its imagined place in the modern world.

Taste, Class, and *Ifranji* Culture

With late nineteenth-century shifts in consumption, taste became a central trope in defining a middle-class authenticity, not just at home but also across a wide spectrum of everyday activities that centered at least in part on fashion, behavior, socialization, food, and the like. This took place at a time when debates on community and civilization thought of behavior and emotions as fields to be modified in order to correspond to current conceptions of civility.[21] As everyday activity entered regimes of civility and taste, it did so as a domain amenable to reform. Thus, shaping everyday consumption habits was meant to generate new categories of perception by which to appropriate and localize the new modes of living associated with imported tastes.

The fundamental changes brought by the industrial revolution to production processes worldwide transformed tastes and, in the process, shaped a variety of new attitudes about them. This global element weighted taste with the onus of trade relations between industrialized economies and their markets, giving a political dimension to debates over what to consume and what not to consume in the late Ottoman Empire. As broader sections of the population became invested in questions of national identity, calls to consume patriotically became part of widening forms of political participation. Boycott emerged as a political weapon under new modes of mass politics and growing nationalist sentiments.[22]

Talking about taste in modern France, Bourdieu points to its tightly interwoven relationship with class. Taste, as it expresses itself in the choice of music or art, is indicative of symbolic positions in society occupied according to cultural capital—a fund built on the cultivation of such tastes through education and upbringing.[23] Bourdieu himself is careful to point out a common misunderstanding when it comes to his work, and that is confounding the term *distinction* with the delineation of a normatively distinguished position. Rather, as he explains, distinction is about "a *difference*, a gap, a distinctive feature, in short, a *relational* property existing only in and through its relation to other properties."[24] This *difference* takes form through the choices individuals make in diverse areas of daily practices and the related symbolic struggle over shaping a distinct cultural space that defines the contours of class.

While Bourdieu's more concrete findings on modern France hold little relevance for the late Ottoman Empire, aspects of his theory are useful for unpacking middle-class taste in other contexts. To begin with, the Marxist critical approach to class means that its normative dimension, a narrow definition of class according to economic conditions, is displaced by an understanding that class includes people within the same social *space*. It becomes possible to define the middle class on its own terms, according to what its various members themselves recognize as significant and relevant. In that sense, we are not talking about a group mobilized for struggle, but a probable class, one defined

by its members' occupying similar social positions and having similar disposi-
tions and interests.[25] While not excluding the possibility of looking at groups
organized along ethnic or religious lines, this offers the further possibility of
looking at practices that cut across those lines. This is particularly interesting in
the case of the Ottoman Empire, where studies on the members of the middle
class often emphasize their dimension as ethnic or religious groups.[26]

There is also a political dimension to Bourdieu's understanding of the
relationship between taste and class. The struggle over the classification of
tastes is at the heart of the symbolic and political struggle to impose a vision
of the social world, one linked to the positions various classes occupy in it.[27]
Again, in the case of Beirut, not only were participants in the public debate
self-identifying as middle class, but the project of middle-class domesticity
was a project for how daily life *in general* was to be materially and socially organized. Especially given that municipal, provincial, and educational reforms
under Abdülhamid II expanded the reach of the state while curtailing political participation with his suspension of the 1876 constitution, home became
an arena where politics could be discussed and articulated in its general sense:
as a vision of a world where the middle class plays a central part. Objects and
commodities held significance in this regard because the ability to discern
what one consumes and how one consumes was seen as one of the characteristics that the members of the middle class should cultivate if they were to
develop a political outlook and to preserve their socioeconomic status. That a
lot of the debate on domesticity can be read in political terms becomes apparent after the Young Turk Revolution of 1908 and the end of Abdülhamid II's
censorship of the press. Monarchies and republics became explicit metaphors
for the modern home and relationships between husbands and wives.

In the abstract and ahistorical dimension of Bourdieu's scheme, however,
the question of capital in the economic sense is withdrawn altogether. The
global dimension of the production of taste is subdued to the element of
class as it is understood within a national context. For Bourdieu, it is primarily within enclosed social systems that each class strives to distinguish itself
from the class below it, such that the lower class becomes the basic reference
for all classes.[28] In the case of Beirut, the middle class strove to distinguish
itself not only within its own social setting, that is, from the class *above* it, but
also from a putative "Western" or "European" culture, referred to as *ifranji*. In

that sense, the middle class saw itself in a middling position both geographically and socially.

As the Ottoman Empire and Egypt became debtors to a finance market with centers in Paris and London, the question of *difference* became increasingly loaded with questions of national identity. The economic situation in Egypt, for example, contributed in no small measure to shaping the revolt of 1881 in that country, a revolution that forwarded the slogan "Egypt for the Egyptians."[29] These struggles also took place on a more mundane level and on a daily basis through, among other things, attempts to cultivate an ethics over what to consume and how to consume it, and to tie the question of the consumption of imported goods to national economic interests.

The Middle Class between Tradition and Modernity

Positioning the middle class between tradition and modernity has a lot to do with the way the middle class conceived of itself. Often faced with the charge of inauthenticity and the adoption of Western habits, members of the middle class strove to fashion an image of themselves as modern yet rooted in tradition. These claims should not be taken at face value, particularly since the very definition of what it is to be traditional, modern, or authentic is unstable and often contradictory. Rather than take Westernization, Europeanization, and lack of authenticity as starting points of analyses, these concepts themselves need to be unpacked. This holds true particularly for the areas of life where these concepts were often deployed as accusations, such as lifestyles, fashion, and other spheres of consumption.

Given the importance of taste in tying the middle-class home to its urban and global settings, I take the material culture of the middle class not as epiphenomenal and a consequence of imitative or adaptive lifestyles, but rather as an integral part of the experience of modernity. Recent works of history expand on the "white, male, and middle class" hegemonic identity, exploring the variegated formation of the middle class across the globe.[30] Rather than think in terms of "variations or deviations from the original,"[31] recent scholarship calls for a view of the history of the middle class that is tightly linked to an understanding of global modernity. Studies of places as diverse as Zimbabwe, Chile, India, and Japan draw a picture of "transnational historical formations through which the meanings, subjectivities, and practices of being middle class were mutually—and coevally—constituted across the globe."[32] As such, tensions within the formations of the middle class in any context should not be taken as evidence of falling short of some idealized model, but as an integral part of the experience of modernity. This includes a consideration of the contradictions and fractures that characterize modernity and the middle class, not just on the "peripheries" but even at the prototypical English point of "origin."[33]

In the context of the Ottoman Empire and the Eastern Mediterranean, the rise of the middle class is understood as part of the experience of modernity that is in tension with tradition in various ways. In the context of Syria, what Keith Watenpaugh calls "middle-class modernity" refers to Western-educated, middle-class intellectuals located between traditional politics that derived legitimacy from a class of notables and politics drawing on the wider participation and active involvement of the modern-educated middle class.[34] Other studies on Egypt, Mount Lebanon, Istanbul, and Izmir locate the rise of the middle class in the second half of the nineteenth century, and, like Watenpaugh, find the negotiation between traditional and Western one of its defining features.[35] Notably, Akram Khater's work on migrants returning to Mount Lebanon not only argues for a link between tradition and modernity but also points to an inherently gendered aspect of this modernity. In its global formation between its peasant context and its experience in the Americas, the middle class in Mount Lebanon sought to distinguish itself from its peasant origins and surroundings, but this distinction also hinged on a new role for the middle-class woman.[36]

At the same time, changing relations of capital turned issues of tradition and modernity into highly charged fields, not only in the ways members of the middle class chose to present themselves through consumption but also through the global conditions of production. The question of the relations of capital to the formation of everyday life is crucial to the understanding of the middle class as a global phenomenon in any context, yet in the context of the Middle East this understanding remains restricted mostly to questions of identity and the self-positioning of that class. Bringing relations of capital to the home opens the door to understanding the contradictions in what the middle class was imagined to be, particularly in light of changing modes of production and consumption. True, taste stood central to a system of classification of consumption practices, but even as taste became an object to be molded and defined, global conditions of production also meant that taste escaped any attempts at a consistent definition.

Another point of tension that comes up when looking at the middle class in the Ottoman context is its division along ethnic and religious lines. Rather than take these issues as indicative of the impossibility of talking about a middle class, it would be more fruitful to view these tensions as part of the experience of that class's formation. Bringing class dynamics back into the picture de-emphasizes the dominant sectarian dimension of late Ottoman history and, more specifically, of Beirut in that period, and allows for the exploration of cultural dimensions and relations that would otherwise be obfuscated by the use of *sect* as an analytical category. That is not to say that sectarian identity did not matter, but that beyond politics narrowly defined, it has its analytical limitations.[37] For this reason, rather than take sectarian differences as a starting point, I have elected to indicate them as they arise in the events and issues under discussion.

Beirut is an interesting case in this regard because its mixed religious makeup seems to suggest bifurcations in the formation of the middle class, and this was true in certain aspects, such as mixed-gender socialization in public, where different groups had different experiences. Concurrently, life in the dense community of Beirut also generated common experiences. An emerging middle class was gaining wider access to modern education, brought about by schools that catered to different religious groups and linguistic preferences. Inhabitants of Beirut shared the same commercial spaces, had access to the same consumer products, and experienced the same urbanization and urban beautification movements. Higher levels of education meant that a growing readership had access to a common cultural language, partially shaped by debates in the press and in literary and scientific societies. Last but not least, many of the debates on the changes in everyday life reflected a cross-sectarian anxiety about the influence of *ifranji*, or Western, culture.

Finding Authenticity

After Beirut became a provincial capital in 1888, the series of urban projects that had been implemented timidly and piecemeal since the first half of the nineteenth century picked up with ferocity, spurred on by Ottoman reforms as well as by the inhabitants of the city, who saw urban regeneration as a way to promote their city and its regional role. Municipal management was increasingly regarded as a necessary tie between the personal and the collective, and the municipal council's range of tasks now brought it into touch with more areas of daily life. New parks provided new places of leisure, street lighting transformed the city's nightlife, trams and horse-drawn carriages rumbled through newly paved and widened streets, government made its presence palpable in new monuments and buildings, and placards announcing free vaccinations against smallpox were posted in streets and alleys as the city expanded and rose with suburban houses and Italianesque mansions.[38]

In the face of these wide changes, the home gained added significance for those speaking on behalf of the new middle class in Beirut, as elsewhere, as the place where this class could formulate its own ideas of modernity. In an article on domesticity in British Bengal, Dipesh Chakrabarty remarks: "In nationalist representations, the colonial experience of becoming modern is haunted by the fear of looking unoriginal."[39] This fear stems from the perception of standing face to face with hegemonic notions of progress, civilization, and modernity that impose themselves, whether by coercion or brute force, on one's understanding of history, oneself, and one's society. Although not colonial per se, the late Ottoman experience in Beirut shared some of these anxieties, often cutting across religious differences in the city. The middle class was particularly haunted by the issue of authenticity. As modern changes took hold in the public sphere, in a political system modeled after the nation-state, and in the invasion of daily life by signposts of imported cultural norms, there was a marked need for finding a place where authenticity could be anchored.

The home appeared insulated from state reforms, in the sense that the late nineteenth-century body of Ottoman legal codes dealt only superficially with domestic space. Concomitantly, the home was gaining particularities in the way the middle class thought of domesticity. The intellectual discourse on domesticity rose in parallel to the overhaul in urban space and often in explicit challenge to it. In the face of the homogenizing changes that were taking place in the urban environment, the home became, in the intellectual diction, a site for grounding the particularities not only of an emerging middle class but also of a local and "authentic" culture.

The centerpiece of this domestic edifice was the woman. Women functioning as repositories of tradition is a familiar trope in postcolonial studies. Faced with the destabilizing effects of imperialism on public life, mostly male intellectuals posited women as the guardians of tradition, a domain to be protected as that of cultural authenticity. That is not to say that women were removed from discussions on reform and progress.[40] In places such as Cairo and Istanbul, women entered the domain of progress both as its objects and as its actors, and the question of women, and their education and improvement, was actively debated by members of both sexes. In those discussions, the home was regarded as closely associated with women, whose domestic tasks included safeguarding a sense of authenticity in the face of *tafarnuj*— that is, becoming Europeanized or Westernized.

Many commentators on the topic saw the home as the place where an Oriental modernity could be grounded through a new ethics of consumption and an aesthetics of order. As managers of the home, women were deemed significant for implementing those ideals. Additionally, these notions involved the home in wider questions of what constitutes authentic progress and how the cultivation of daily behavioral patterns of consumption, dress, and talk served as the home's constituent parts. Domesticity, in that sense, is part of the wider regional debates of the *nahda* on proper upbringing, or *tarbiya*. As Omnia Shakry argues in the case of Egypt, both nationalist and Islamist writings on motherhood and child rearing underscored the importance of *tarbiya* to national progress and the need to redeem women from their "backwardness" so that they could perform the task of raising future citizens.[41]

These ideas came together around the politicization of consumption. Many daily domestic habits involved a variety of commodities that had become newly available to a wide section of the city's inhabitants. New pieces of furniture and new forms of leisure had an immediate effect on people's daily socializations—visiting, playing cards, or displaying new fashions—which then became the object of prescriptive literature. As the place where much consumption took place, the home became embroiled in the question of a "national economy," a term used to refer to either Syrian or Ottoman production. Several observers writing in the press at the time tried to prescriptively shape new modes of consumption in a way that reinforced a project of appropriating and localizing modernity. Some even saw the question of guiding consumption habits as a question of economic and cultural survival in the face of European imperialism.

Given the apparent fascination of the new class of consumers with the fashions and fads of Europe, *tafarnuj*, or imitating European habits and fashions, became problematic. It was regarded as dangerous both because adoption of imported fashions and habits threatened people's sense of cultural authenticity and because consuming imported items undermined the local economy. The adjective *mutafarnij*, meaning "Europeanized" or "Westernized," became inscribed into behavior, dress, food, furniture, haircuts, and a myriad other daily habits. Even as they were being adopted by the self-styled, nascent middle class, many of these changes were being inscribed through public lectures, in the pages of the press, and even in advertisements into the geographical difference between East and West. Not least, this difference was impressed on objects.

During the period in question objects mattered and mattered greatly to the formation of a specifically modern understanding of the world. Not only did greater access to consumption turn the home into a major target for consumer items, but things—their forms, their provenances, their positioning in space, their influences on the human character, and their various other characteristics—became topics of debate in the literature on domesticity. That is, from the cultural history viewpoint, objects' significance does not stop at how they were used to convey social messages of class, progress, and modernity, but extends to how their very materiality *shaped* the home and the ideas forged around it.

Leora Auslander's work on furniture production in modern France shows how changing modes of production and distribution, particularly industrialization and capitalist relations, mattered just as much as consumption in defining nineteenth-century bourgeois tastes.[42] In the context of the Ottoman Empire, where industrialization remained limited and experienced primarily indirectly through imports, the focus is often on the adoption of imported objects and styles. In many scholarly works, clothes, furniture, decoration, and other aspects of material culture stand simultaneously as evidence for and proof of Westernization.[43] Yet, local processes of production and distribution add a dimension that is overlooked when the focus remains on consumption. This dimension not only opens up an understanding of commodities that looks across traditional/modern and Eastern/ Western concerns, it also highlights the role of local manufacture in affecting consumption practices. Labor processes illuminate how the production of popular commodities cuts across common conceptions of Europe and the Ottoman Empire as producer and consumer, respectively. Ottoman labor in the industrial age wove together, sometimes literally, imported and local materials, in some cases to the extent that local products were able to compete with imports.[44]

Bringing artisanal labor and local manufacture into the understanding of domestic commodities is particularly relevant in the case of Beirut, a city predominantly regarded as a place of consumption par excellence and whose nineteenth-century rise is closely linked to the importation of mass-produced products. A French trade report written in Beirut in 1868 claims that "[there] is neither factory nor industry. . . . The majority of inhabitants in Beirut are merchants or shopkeepers; when commerce slows down, the city withers."[45] This view of Beirut appears both in contemporaneous accounts and in modern scholarship focusing on Beirut as a city of intellectuals and merchants. Given that consumption plays a large role in defining Beirut as *Westernized*, demystifying that term can clarify the impact of changing modes of capital on daily life in the city. Both artisanal production and the mechanized production that developed on a small scale in Beirut and its suburbs incorporated imported forms and materials to forge entirely new fashions and contributed to shaping popular tastes.

The ways with which taste was globalized at the intersection of these processes complicated a conception of middle-class domesticity predicated on the ability to separate local from *ifranji* commodities. Marking out an area of *difference* was contingent on the ability to discern and separate the authentic from the inauthentic in consumption habits, a project that proved itself difficult, if not impossible, given the nature of popular domestic commodities.

Paying attention to both consumption and production investigates the work of capitalism through domestic objects and the tensions inherent to class formation. The point is not to highlight resistance to intellectual projects, but rather to explore how the conditions for authenticity set by discussions around domesticity paradoxically prepared the ground for authenticity's own negation. Framed differently, the question of *difference* as it emerges in this context is not just about destabilizing the forces of globalization and capitalism and opening them up to heterogeneity, as Chakrabarty suggests. It is also about how the globalized capitalist mode of production that emerged at the end of the late nineteenth century—predicated as it was on an uneven distribution between industrialized producers and their markets—occluded any projects for the appropriation and localization of modernity along lines informed by imperial and nationalist productions of knowledge.

In what Ranajit Guha terms "dominance without hegemony," bourgeois hegemony in the colonial state and under the successor nationalist regime is decoupled from the capitalist dominance that characterized the rise of the bourgeoisie in European metropoles.[46] The economic underpinnings of class, in other words, are destabilized by the colonial experience and the imbalance it introduces into the relationship between metropole and colony. In the context of global imperialism, one cannot speak of the Ottoman bourgeoisie either as having any kind of dominance. In the case of the middle-class project in Beirut, there was an attempt to forge a cultural hegemony through domesticity. But the actual conditions of production also meant that the middle-class project remained in tension, precisely because under the conditions of capitalism, the locality itself becomes hinged to global processes of production. As a cultural and political field used to carve a place for the middle class, taste tied the very intimate spaces of the home to modern forms of urbanity and to globalized modes of production.

CHAPTER 3

HOME IS WHERE THE INVESTMENT IS

When you build a house, rent it the first year to your enemy, the
second year to your friend, and the third year move into it yourself.

Syrian proverb[1]

By the time this proverb was recorded, in 1910, one would have been hard
pressed to find a traveler in the region who would describe Beirut as "Oriental." Indeed, in the late 1850s, James Lewis Farley, chief accountant of the
Beirut office of the Imperial Ottoman Bank, had remarked that within the
space of a few years, "a new town," characterized by "the means and appli-
ances of European civilization," had sprung up from the old, "like a Phoenix
from the ashes."[2]

Among the features that made an impression on visitors and locals alike
were the new suburbs. On his visit in 1867, Mark Twain remarked: "The rest
of us had nothing to do but look at the beautiful city of Beirout, with its
bright, new houses nestled among a wilderness of green shrubbery spread
abroad over an upland that sloped gently down to the sea."[3] Resident Fadl
Allah Faris Abi Halaqa, later the founder of the periodical *al-Mahabba* in
Beirut, made a similar remark upon observing the city from the deck of a
ship in 1891: "I was gazing from the boat at this city famous in Syria, with
its shimmering lights emanating from houses stepped down a hill. Some of
these houses were great, high buildings that looked like fortresses or towers
facing the wide sea."[4] These houses stood in the new residential areas that
had started developing with the nineteenth-century expansion outside the
old city walls. In the second half of the century, visitors would distinguish
between the "shabby old city" and the "new portion higher up, with its villas,

embowered in trees."[5] Whatever was left of the Oriental "picturesque" Beirut was being observed only in the old quarters of the inner city.[6]

The promulgation of legal codes from Istanbul governing urban development in the empire, and the institution of an elected municipal council in Beirut tasked with implementing these laws, introduced ideals of urban modernity into the everyday lives of Beirutis. Drawing on nineteenth-century global modes of knowledge that privileged rectilinear urban forms and sought to introduce new standards of hygiene into expanding cities, the council guided the development of Beirut into a city that to its observers was found to be neither Oriental nor quite Western. As the city expanded beyond its medieval perimeter, its tortuous alleys, dead-ends, and blind façades were gradually replaced by gas-lit wide avenues with modern means of transportation, buildings of uniform height and protrusions, and an increasingly hygienic urban environment.

Scholarly works on municipal administration in the Ottoman Empire and North Africa have contributed much to our understanding of the dynamics of urban development and of the relationship between provincial cities and the imperial center. But with their focus on urban management and public life, such studies tend to balk at the outer limits of the home.[7] Studies on the ways municipal reforms reshaped the relationship between the home and its surroundings remain largely absent. This despite the fact that the introduction of sewers, hygienic measures meant to fight off epidemics, the systematized Building Code, and a municipal police force to enforce this new set of urban standards necessitated a fundamental restructuring of the relationship between the home, on the one hand, and municipal authorities and the urban context, on the other.

At the heart of the issue is the changing relationship between public and private. In the late Ottoman urban diction, *public benefit* tied domestic habits and the life of the individual to the public collectivity of the city. Seen as a constituent part of modernity, the relationship between the individual and the city not only reigned in aspects of private behavior to synchronize with changes in public space but also brought capitalism's changes into the home. At the same time, many other aspects of the home, not least its interior, remained relatively free of legal guidance. This left domesticity without any clear legal relationship to the project of urban modernity and, thus, open to legal frameworks that sometimes came into tension with each other. As an

open site of contestation, the home remained a point of conflict between individuals and the municipal council, and amenable to interpretation as a link
between the individual and the larger project of modernity.

Redefining Public Benefit

Understanding the place of public benefit in modern urbanity requires a brief
return to the concept's history. Throughout the nineteenth century, the idea
of public benefit acquired several levels of meaning, many of them connected
to notions of modern governance, while at the same time maintaining a connection to its jurisprudential past. Texts of Islamic jurisprudence dating back
hundreds of years still constituted popular publications as well as reference
sources for debating legal issues in the late Ottoman context. This kind of
inter-centennial debate and commentary constituted a mode of transmitting
knowledge in what anthropologist of Islam Talal Asad calls the "discursive
tradition" of Islam.[8] At the same time, a genealogical reading of the concept
of public benefit does not exclude the ways in which it was deliberately read
against the grain. It was precisely the utilitarian history of the concept that
afforded reformists the opportunity to break away from the tradition they
were embedded in.

Although Islamic jurisprudence and some contemporary Islamic mod-
ernists made a distinction between *maslaha 'amma* (public interest) and
manfa'a 'amma (public benefit), these two terms were often used interchangeably in other relations.[9] In the context of Islamic jurisprudence, seeking
manfa'a is a way for achieving the common good, or *al-maslaha al-'amma*.
Briefly put, *maslaha* means that "the overall welfare of the Community over-
shadows any particular legal consideration, especially of the individual."[10]
Whereas *manfa'a* constitutes the active or moral criteria through which the
common good is achieved, *maslaha* has to do with the way the law (*shari'a*) is
applied and can thus be understood "as a means or a legal criterion through
which the common good is realized."[11]

This was the sense in which the Muslim theologian and jurist Abu
Hamid al-Ghazali (d. 1111), the first to tangibly define the term *maslaha*,
understood the relationship between *manfa'a* and *maslaha*.[12] In *al-Mustasfa
min 'Ilm al-Usul* (Conspectus of the Principles of Jurisprudence) he states:
"Essentially, *al-maslaha* means seeking that which is beneficial [*manfa'a*] or

avoiding that which is harmful [*madarra*]. . . . By *maslaha* we mean the preservation of the objective of the Law, which consists of five principles: the
protection of religion, self, intellect, lineage, and property."[13] Thus, pursuing
manfa'a contributes to the preservation and application of the law, including
the protection of material wealth.

While the constituent elements of al-Ghazali's understanding of *maslaha*
did not change in the following centuries, different models of placing *maslaha*
within the process of legal reasoning developed. The most influential of these
ideas on nineteenth-century reformers came from the Hanbali jurist Najm al-
Din al-Tufi (d. 1316), who reasoned that "anything that brought about *maslaha*
and averted harm was commensurate with the purpose of the law."[14] Al-Tufi's
conception of *maslaha* freed reformers from adherence to legal texts at the
same time that it proposed a legal notion that was "discernible by the intellect
and could be used to extend and adapt the law to new circumstances."[15] In
a similar vein, Dyala Hamzah argues that by establishing *maslaha 'amma* as a
principle of action and confounding it with *manfa'a*, Egyptian Islamic scholar
and reformer Muhammad 'Abduh (1849–1905) is to be primarily credited with
opening the term up to extra-jurisprudential reading and application.[16]

As some understood it, public benefit also came to stand for a link between the material production of the state and the more ephemeral notion
of society. Published in 1869, Rifa'a Rafi' al-Tahtawi's (1801–1873) guide to
Egyptian history and geography, *Manahij al-Albab al-Misriyya fi Mabahij
al-Adab al-'Asriyya* (The Paths of Egyptian Hearts in the Delights of the
Contemporary Arts), explicitly links "public benefit" to the idea of progress
and the worldly aim of government in instituting welfare. Meant as edifying reading for pupils, Tahtawi's book discusses the economic state of Egypt
and the conditions for its prosperity.[17] *Manafi' 'umumiyya* (public benefits) in
the context of Tahtawi's book refer not only to agriculture, manufacture, and
commerce—the three pillars of the Egyptian economy—but also to "production as the habitual process that creates society."[18]

The shift towards the understanding of public benefit, in its modern sense,
as a backbone of civilization (*al-tamdin wa-l-'umran*) was paralleled by decades of putting the category of *manfa'a* into practice within the framework
of Ottoman reform. One such domain of application was urban management,
where municipalities' role in linking the individual to society coalesced with

the potential of *manfaʿa* to define a legal space that used the language of Muslim law without its traditional legal methodology. The inscription of *manafiʿ ʿumumiyya* within a modern idea of progress found a more precise expression in a legislative context with the first expropriation law of 1856, the İstimlak Nizamnamesi. Promulgated two years before the institution of the first municipality, the *altıncı daire*, in Istanbul, the expropriation of property was justified by recourse to "public benefit," as it also was in the first comprehensive Decree of Expropriation in the Name of Public Benefit (Menafi-i Umumiye İçin İstimlak Kararnamesi) issued in 1879.[19] Here, the legal consideration of the individual—namely, her right to a property—is subordinated to the benefits a community is expected to derive through a modern production of its urban environment. Together with the Municipal and Building Codes, the legal framework on expropriation quickly became an important tool for urban management in Beirut and elsewhere in the empire.[20]

Little is known about the urban management of Beirut before the period of Egyptian rule, but a look at other Ottoman cities in the region gives some idea of what sort of system had existed before the nineteenth century. In Syria in general, the neighborhood (*hara*) constituted the basic administrative and social unit, but it was incorporated into larger divisions.[21] In Aleppo, Damascus, and Istanbul, for example, urban management involved a panoply of actors, including trade guilds, religious communities, charitable foundations, and individual inhabitants. Maintenance of the streets and shared services was the responsibility of the residents of each quarter and was largely funded by neighborhood-based charitable endowments (waqf), which contributed to fulfilling quarters' obligations such as government taxes and the maintenance of certain services.[22] Charitable endowments, along with private property owners, also participated in urban development on a citywide scale, guided by a set of laws and official oversight to ensure conformity to imperial standards.[23] The government in Istanbul upheld the institutional framework, while the local court ensured adherence to standards and norms and saw to the resolution of property disputes. While religious and public buildings were regulated through city planning projects, imperial edicts, and head architects, no such ordinances existed for private constructions, including homes.[24]

Historian Jens Hanssen argues in the case of Beirut that urban health concerns precipitated the emergence of a new form of urban governance.[25]

While the concern for public health certainly played an important part in municipal reforms in general, it constituted only one facet of the pressing need for a new form of urban living. As Malek Sharif shows, there was a wider interest in municipalities as modern institutions and, even before the promulgation of the first municipal law for the provinces in 1867, Syria witnessed various attempts at governance at the town and city levels in Dayr al-Qamar, Jerusalem, and Damascus, as well as Beirut.[26] In the same decades that urban governance changed in the Ottoman Empire and Beirut, reformer Sir Edwin Chadwick's work led to the introduction of the Public Health Act of 1848 in England and Wales, prefect of the Seine Baron Georges-Eugène Haussmann carried out his famous renovation of Paris in the 1850s and 1860s, and Tokyo governor Matsuda Michiyuki used the Meiji fires of 1879 and 1881 as catalysts to initiate a plan of urban renewal for that city.[27] Although these attempts are invariably referred to as *Haussmannization*, after Baron Haussmann, and despite the fact that many rulers looked to Paris as a model for modernization, they were all responding—Haussmann included—to new economies and technologies that made labor migration, overcrowded cities, public health, and efficient transportation pressing concerns.

Early legislative attempts in the Ottoman Empire bore a sense of the urgency of dealing with the pressure of urban expansion and the dangers of fire, the latter a particular concern in Istanbul, where wooden structures prevailed and where the first cohesive set of urban regulations was implemented.[28] In 1848, with the aims of increasing accessibility to different parts of the city and minimizing the risk of fires, the first building law, Birince Ebniye Nizamnamesi, focused on parcelization and on widening streets, often taking advantage of locations where there had been fires to do so. Between 1848 and 1882, four other major street regulations and Istanbul-specific laws were passed, until finally the comprehensive Building Code was issued in 1882. Of those earlier regulations, the first empire-wide one, Street and Building Regulation (Turuk ve Ebniye Nizamnamesi) came just a year before the promulgation of the 1864 Provincial Code.[29] As they gradually increased in precision, such codes constituted part of the strategy of urban management in the provinces that placed even the smallest administrative unit within a constellation of embedded hierarchies pointing towards the imperial center.

This complex of laws pertaining directly to urban space emanated from

Istanbul and was gradually applied to the various parts of the Ottoman Empire through provincial governments. An elected municipal council was responsible for ensuring the enactment of the laws and following up on their daily application. As cities were molded by the new ideals of urbanity, notions of urban governance were also transformed and with them the relationship between inhabitants and their material environment. In its practical sense, the concept of public benefit was the legal tool with which the rights of the individual pertaining to property were to subserve the greater good. In a more idealistic sense, the concept mediated the relationship between the individual inhabitants of a city and the greater collective bound together by the dictates of civilization and modern urban life.

To educators, journalists, and their segments of society, the significance of municipal governance exceeded practical considerations. A prominent *nahda* figure and the founder of *al-Hasna'*, the first women's magazine in Syria, Jurji Niqula Baz enjoyed an intellectual career and a range of writings that spanned topics from the public sphere to the role of the family. In an article titled "The Duties of Municipalities," Baz starts with general observations about the concept of society as a construct where each individual has a function and the function of each is determined by his or her capacity. According to Baz, this distribution is crucial for prosperity (*qiyam al-'umran*) and depends on the contributions of various members of society regardless of their gender and stature, and he adds: "while individuals work for their own benefit, the total sum of individual works is to benefit the public [*li-ifadat al-'umum*]." This is where municipalities step in, as indispensable institutions capable of bringing benefits not only to select individuals but to all.

Summarizing an idea entrenched in turn-of-the-century reform language, Baz links together municipal duties and a specific kind of society, namely modern urban society:

> It is an uncontested fact that when people become civilized, crowd into cities, and taste the life of luxury and comfort, their energies fail and their bodies weaken, whereas their necessities increase and their needs multiply. What they had thought to be luxury becomes necessity, and what they used to acquire effortlessly becomes a difficult demand, such as air. . . . That is why when reasonable people became advanced and saw that crowding in cities

leads to the weakening of the human race in body and mind . . . they took the
initiative to assign capable persons to whom they delegated the maintenance
of all that benefits people in terms of health and rest. It is based on this principle and to this end that municipalities were formed.[30]

In other words, Baz argues, given that the link between individual needs and
the social order is a prerequisite for modernity, municipalities played a central
role in linking the two through the category of public benefit.

A similar sense of the core role public benefit played in the constitution
of modern civilization was also shared by practitioners. Municipal engineer
Amin ʻAbd al-Nur expressed the relationship between public benefit and
progress thus: "without [public benefit], the splendor of modern civilization
cannot be accomplished."[31] But practitioners were also compelled to deal
with the complications such a concept generated in practice. Ambiguities in
the urban legal codes persisted for several decades after their promulgation.
Both the Building Code, including the expropriation law, and the Municipal
Code were first translated from Ottoman Turkish into Arabic and published
by Khalil Khuri's press, al-Matbaʻa al-Adabiyya, in Beirut in 1889. Disagreements over the application of the codes led only seven years later to a new,
and this time annotated, translation of the Building Code and the expropriation law by ʻAbd al-Nur. In the preface, he cites the inaccuracy of the
first Arabic translation and the continuing ambiguities surrounding the code
and the expropriation law as reasons for this renewed effort.[32] Even if this
measure resolved some of the conflicts that were arising between affected
inhabitants and the municipal council of Beirut, it also underlined how
the emerging legal framework of the second half of the nineteenth century
became a prerequisite for an urban modernity and reconstituted the relationship between inhabitant and city.

Legal Codes for Urban Beautification

The necessity of introducing a new form of urban management to Beirut
became apparent in the second half of the nineteenth century. The city became a target for centralized urban reforms as building regulations were
introduced to the cities of the Ottoman Empire in the 1860s. Laws and
decrees emanating from Istanbul were communicated to the provincial

council, located physically in Beirut, then from there communicated to the municipalities, which saw to their implementation. Although the legal framework radiated from the imperial center, it gave the provincial administration an important say in matters locally, making its work, together with that of the municipal council, more decisive than the bureaucracy in Istanbul in the daily workings of urbanization.[33] The same impetus behind the expansion of the city after 1860 also constituted a spark for guided development from the center. In 1863, after the influx of refugees from the civil strife in Mount Lebanon turned urban management into a pressing issue, the Ministry of Public Works in Istanbul assigned an engineer to the city in order to "bring about the fixing and building of houses and roads in an organized [*muntazama*] manner."[34]

Beirut's municipal council took on a lot of the functions that had previously been relegated to guilds and neighborhoods, in addition to new responsibilities that adhered to a vision of a hygienic and ordered urban space. Its tasks involved the regulation of weights and measures in the market; the movement and slaughter of cattle; control over the quality of sold meat; cleanliness of the streets and proper disposition of refuse and sewage; general public health; the provision of care for the poor and homeless; and a wide array of daily maintenance routines.[35] In addition, through its agreements with concessionists, the council was responsible for supplying the city with water and lighting. Providing city streets with gas lighting meshed with the municipality's task of ensuring security, a task complemented by the deployment across the city of a police force answering directly to the Ministry of Interior.[36]

The rationale for carrying out this management was framed in the language of reform. The same year Beirut became the provincial capital, a proposal by the council suggested an increase in municipal taxes in order to

> keep roads organized in an orderly and clean fashion and water them [against dust] during the summer; pay the yearly dues ordained by royal concessions to the water company and the gas company, which lights most of the city's alleys and neighborhoods; treat at the hospital the homeless and old, who come in great numbers from outside [the city]; and carry out the necessary reforms and embellishments pertaining to the municipal law.[37]

Order, hygiene, and aesthetics emerge here and elsewhere as watchwords and guidelines for carrying out changes in the urban environment. More interestingly, such terms illustrate concretely how the changing relationship between the inhabitants and their city was rationalized in the language of municipal politics. This language was picked up in the municipal minutes themselves and by members of the council as well as by the municipal inspectors, demonstrating that it constituted an ingrained rationale in the way civil servants and elected municipal council members thought of their work.[38]

The expropriation law and Municipal and Building Codes together constituted the corpus within which the municipal council functioned. Along with the duties listed in the Municipal Code, the expropriation and building laws had the very material effect of molding the city in accordance with changing demands. While fires constituted a dynamic in initiating reconstruction projects in cities where wooden structures prevailed, Beirut, where most buildings were constructed of masonry and stones, was not overly prone to fire hazards. A survey of Beirut in 1894 showed that most of the city's 20,440 structures were of masonry, not built against each other, and seldom constructed with wooden roofs. All these factors made fires in the city less prone to spread.[39] By grounding expropriation in public benefit, the expropriation law became the major tool in the remodeling of a city, independent of its susceptibility to fires. The legal apparatus, thus, constituted a regulative mechanism that allowed municipal authorities to expropriate land, demolish unfit structures, and reproduce space according to their overall vision of an urban modernity.

Under the language of aesthetics and the imperatives of modernity, the inner city of Beirut, with its crooked streets, narrow passages, and blind alleys, began to be regarded as a problem towards the end of the nineteenth century. Whatever little Oriental authenticity foreign travelers were still able to locate in the labyrinthian old town became precisely, for local reformers and provincial governors alike, the location of recalcitrance against progress. With the initiation of urban projects outside the inner city and the growth of the leafy suburbs into residential quarters, most of those who could afford to left the inner city for the better amenities and spaciousness of the newer neighborhoods. The inner city, encircled by its medieval walls well into the beginning of the nineteenth century, did not lose its economic exuberance. But the growth of commercial zones around it and also several of the projects carried out by the municipal council were also pushing people out of the inner city and into the surrounding quarters and suburbs.

Public works all over the city followed the Building Code's classification of thoroughfares into five types, depending on importance, each with its own designated width in architect's cubits (1 cubit = 0.75m): twenty, fifteen, twelve, ten, and eight. Dead-end alleys were set at between six and eight architect's cubits.[40] During the widening of an existing road or paving of a new road, the municipal council was to take half the width required from each side of the street, therefore distributing the burden of expropriation proportionally. As long as the expropriated area did not exceed a quarter of the total property's width, the owners were not compensated.[41] Through the application of the code, the widening and aligning of streets in Beirut starting in the 1880s was directly linked to the idea of public benefit, and through the expropriation of their property, owners affected by these projects became, sometimes unwillingly, investors in the new aesthetic image of the city.

Although the widths were set in Istanbul, decisions on allocating them to specific streets and expropriating areas to the sides were taken locally, with the approval of the provincial council and often in a process of negotiation with those affected by the plans.[42] The practical work of estimating the value and extent of the expropriated property was entrusted to a committee composed of three experts elected by the municipal council, four members of the municipal council, a member of the Hanafi court, and another member from either the Directorate of Endowments (*evqaf*) or the Department of Property Records (*defter-i hakani*).[43]

Following a legally required procedure, any building or land to be expropriated was to be clearly drawn on a map detailing the limits, area, and value of what was to be expropriated as well as its surroundings, the names of the property owners involved, and any natural landmarks in the area. Copies of the map hung for eight days on the doors of houses of worship in the vicinity of the property or on the door of the municipal council's office, as well as on the property set aside for expropriation. During this period, the local police were entrusted with the task of ensuring the maps remained in their location for the entire period. The displaying of these maps was also announced in the local newspapers. Any objections to the expropriation had to be delivered either orally or in writing to the head of the municipal council during these eight days, after which the possibility of presenting complaints was closed and the maps removed.[44]

The daily workings of the municipal council of Beirut followed these guidelines, drawing up plans for intended expropriation and street widening or paving, publicizing the maps, and receiving petitions from owners discontented with the proposed changes. This was true not only in the city center, where the urban fabric underwent the most drastic transformation, but also in the residential neighborhoods around the city. In one instance in the Raml neighborhood, petitions were presented to the municipal council that the area expropriated was taken largely from one side of the street to be widened. Upon reconsideration during one of their routine meetings, the members of the municipal council decided that the objections were justified and asked for the expropriation map to be redrawn accordingly.[45] Other instances in which the municipal council revised maps and expropriation plans drawn up by an expert committee also show the council's responsiveness to petitions and complaints.[46] In this way, the public good upon which expropriation was based took form, in many cases, through a process of negotiation between the duties the council took upon itself and the property owners immediately touched by the changes.

Some of the measures taken by the municipal council in the late nineteenth and early twentieth centuries, particularly when they concerned widening or aligning existing streets, faced considerable resistance, particularly in neighborhoods that were already established. There were property owners who were uncooperative and had enough clout to prevent the demolition of parts of their property, leaving building protrusions into the streets that are evident in the urban fabric of Beirut even in the twenty-first century.[47] But the urban aesthetics adopted by the legal code affected construction on more than just the ground plan level, and other measures, such as extending a sewage network, met with a fair amount of success in the long run. These introductions propagated a new aesthetic language that found its way into the home precisely where private habits came into contact with public streets.

Policing Waste, Domesticating Excrement

In his 1978 *History of Shit*, French psychoanalyst Dominique Laporte places the management of waste, both in speech and in the city, at the center of the generation of modern categories of culture. He argues that waste is the inevitable outcome of what Sigmund Freud pinpoints as the three cornerstones of civilization: cleanliness, order, and beauty.[48] Specifically, when it comes to the domestication of waste—that is, turning the responsibility for waste inwards towards the individual who produces it, rather than casting it outwards as the domain of the street—he claims that the decrees and laws that took shape in France from the sixteenth century onwards had little to do with the actual cleanliness of the streets, given the persistence of offal and foul odors in cities well into the nineteenth century. Rather, the policing of waste entails a shift in the subject's relationship to his excrement, "a relationship that now includes his dangling and dependent position vis-à-vis the absolute State."[49] What is relevant to the case of Beirut in what Laporte underlines, is that rather than being the negative residue of a modern urban aesthetics, waste and its domestication constitute one of the ways in which the relationship between public and private, the local administration and the individual, was negotiated.

Of the long list of works it was entitled to undertake for the benefit of the public, in addition to paving and widening roads, the municipal council of Beirut paid the closest attention to public hygiene.[50] The matter of hygiene touched directly on the home and brought the domestic sphere into direct negotiation with both the text of the law and the practices of local administration. In the interlocking of public and private entailed in the notion of public benefit, the municipal council's infringements and trespasses into private property constituted part of the overall urban management that lent private habits public repercussions. Refuse constituted the link, both literal and metaphorical, between private and public and designated one of the areas where—because private habits often spilled onto streets and into souks—the municipal council had the prerogative to step in and police private habits. For that reason, although public benefit touched on the home only from the outside in the text of the law, in application it constituted forays into the disciplining of some aspects of private space to conform and synchronize with the overall image of the hygienic city.

The clearest references to public hygiene appear in the Municipal Code. Of the duties the municipal council was tasked with, many related directly to matters of public hygiene, such as monitoring the quality of food and drink sold, getting rid of accumulated garbage, ensuring standards for slaughterhouses in places assigned outside the town proper, and taking other measures meant to guarantee the maintenance of "public health."[51] The deployment of the notion of public benefit to explain and justify these sanitary measures in the city comes out clearly in the municipal council's discourse. For example, the minutes at the start of another hot summer describe the upcoming task of watering the streets as one of the "cleaning and purification measures upon which rests the provision of public health." This measure was meant to keep the dust, consisting to a great extent of dried manure, from spreading to passersby and entering houses, thereby carrying diseases with it.[52]

Although hygiene inside homes was not addressed in the Building Code, the requisite of maintaining public hygiene as it appeared in the Municipal Code necessarily drew private lives into the orbit of urban governance. The chapter of the code detailing practices to be forbidden by the municipal council signifies one of the few instances in the municipal, building and expropriation laws where the home is mentioned directly: "[It is forbidden to] let rain and waste water run from houses and shops onto the streets; not to lift the edges of chimneys higher than building rooftops."[53] At the same time, the connection between public benefit and hygiene is clearly made in the daily workings of the municipal council of Beirut. The minutes show that the notion of public benefit could be evoked, for example, for something as seemingly mundane as extending the public sewage network from Nuriyya Square to Suq Sursuq, off Burj Square.[54]

The matter of sewage tied public benefit to domestic space through concern about the effluent that flowed out of homes. Municipal policemen's reports discussed at one of the council's meetings contained the names of individuals who let "waste water that constitutes harm to public health flow from their homes onto the streets." Upon closer inspection, it turned out that forty-three of the persons named could construct cesspits for the waste water to flow into "in order to prevent the kind of damage that affects public health, such as decomposition that results from putrid air."[55]

The language and logic of public health at this time bore evidence of nineteenth-century medical opinion that attributed the transmission of infectious diseases to poor quality air, or miasma. Edwin Chadwick's sanitary reforms for London, for example, were based on the belief that "all smell is, if it be intense, immediate acute disease," and many of the urban reforms in the large cities of the late nineteenth and early twentieth centuries were guided by the principle that sources of disease-inducing miasma needed to be eradicated.[56] As the effects of putrid water on illness became better understood worldwide in the late nineteenth century, the separation of sewage and drinking water became another major concern, driving the installation of sewage systems in cities and efforts to control overflow from homes, among other things.

Taking the sewage systems of Europe as a point of comparison, Benoît Boyer, professor of therapeutics and hygiene at the French Medical Faculty in Beirut from 1889 to 1897, commented on the condition of sewers in Beirut, noting that "[unfortunately], everything needs to be done."[57] In 1897, at the time of the publication of his study on hygienic conditions in Beirut and its environs, what existed were open street gutters, constructed "in the old misguided ways" and in no way watertight. Even the gutters constructed in more recent years, according to Boyer, let their contents escape along the way, thereby infecting the soil and contributing to outbreaks of typhoid.[58]

Implicitly basing its efforts on this body of scientific knowledge, the municipal council of Beirut saw in the effects of private effluents on public health license to impose sanitary modifications on homes. Those who did not comply with the council's requests within fifteen days of notification risked legal prosecution, as did the forty-three offenders mentioned above. The initial phases of laying out a municipal sewage network in Beirut also entailed the prerogative of extending hygienic measures to residences at the expense of the owners. In May 1900, and after repeated complaints from passersby, the municipal council decided to install a public sewage pipe along Damascus road, running straight south through the city and connecting with the main sewer line in Burj Square, a distance of 850 meters. Referring to Article 16 of the Building Code, which stipulates that property owners selling their land in parcels with the aim of turning it into a residential quarter should also install underground piping for sewage, the municipal council concluded that property owners on both sides of the road should bear the costs of this new pipe.[59]

Nor was domestic responsibility restricted to effluents; it extended to cover all waste water that was indirectly caused by a home. In 1909, the municipal council introduced another ordinance that tied homes to the public sewage network. Property owners who had built pavements on the streets were ordered to install gutters with waterspouts connected to carry water from the roofs of homes and from balconies in order to prevent it from flowing from roofs onto the streets. The municipal council authorized itself to carry out the work at the expense of the owners who did not implement these modifications on their own within the allocated time period.[60]

In addition to these general measures, the municipal council's authority extended into the home on a day-to-day basis through individual cases. Two cases from 1904 show how, with a growing rental market, the council could go beyond private property owners directly to their tenants. At the behest of a policeman's report, the municipal council was alerted to a recurrent problem in a residence occupied by a tenant: despite repeated repairs, an earth closet kept overflowing into a neighboring souk.[61] Both the owner and the tenant had been alerted to this fact but had not done anything about it. The municipal council dispatched three of its members, who, upon investigating the matter, concluded that the situation posed a great danger to public health and that it was necessary to install a pipe connecting the earth closet to the nearest main sewer. The council decided to undertake the job and distribute the expenses incurred among the property owners who benefited from the project.

In a similar case where an earth closet was spilling onto the main road and the owner was doing nothing about it despite repeated warnings, the tenant volunteered to repair the pit and increase its capacity on the condition that the council either collect the expenditures from the owner or have the amount deducted from the tenant's rent should the owner refuse to pay.[62] The municipal council agreed to the terms and charged the tenant with doing the necessary changes under the supervision of the municipal architect and the municipal inspector.

Public health was not solely about contagion, pollution, and miasma; there was also sometimes an aesthetic aspect to hygiene. According to a general directive issued by the municipal council in 1904, houses had to redirect their waste water away from the streets and into cesspits "built well and in a way that is not outwardly visible."[63] An aesthetic consideration applied not only in cases where homes threatened public hygiene, but also where lack of hygienic standards in public areas threatened the home. In 1913, Najib Fadil lodged a complaint against Ahmad al-Hut for selling animal pluck and stomachs on a small plot of land owned by the municipal council. Ahmad

slung his goods over a metal fence, thereby letting them hang by the path
that led into a residential building owned by Najib. The concern was not specifically with what Ahmad was selling, but with the way he was selling it. The
council's demand was that he refrain from letting his wares adorn the fence
in order not to disturb Najib's tenants on their way to their homes.[64] Here
again, the link between a clean urban environment and private lives comes to
the fore, even if in reverse.

The Aesthetics of Public Order

If public health constituted an inroad into private habits, the image of the
aesthetic city constituted a disciplining of the home into prescribed spatial
envelopes that corresponded to legal stipulations on street widths and façade heights. Some Municipal Code cases show an overlap between public
hygiene and aesthetics, but the aesthetic imperative manifests itself more
clearly in the text of the Building Code and the attempts to submit the home
to new formalistic ideals. Such attempts were in turn linked to public benefit
through the expropriation law and its frequent use in the paving and widening of streets.

From the public street to the façades of buildings, the Building Code
prescribed a set of spatial delimitations that adhered to an aesthetics of
alignment and order. The paving of new streets and the widening of existing ones established straight lines into which constructions were forbidden
to obtrude. With that, the bridges that connected buildings on either side
of alleys and streets and that were characteristic of the inner city became a
thing of the past. Vertically, a range of allowed heights corresponded to each
of the street widths, with the exact height left to be fixed depending on the
importance of the abutting street. The highest allowable structure reached to
about twenty-six meters.[65]

The Building Code governed minute details of façades, primarily in relation to street widths. Whereas the owner of a building was free to dispose
all other façades as she saw fit, specifications set precise limits, in terms of
both height and protrusions, on façades on public roads. The horizontal limit
of the lowest floor was determined by the street width, as was the allowed
overhang of upper floors.[66] Designated as kiosks or balconies, such protrusions had to be at least 2.8 meters from the ground and were not allowed to

exceed two thirds of the façade in width. Further specifications addressed the
details of protruding door jambs, column bases, window frames, gutters, shop
window panes, and metal shutters, as well as the protrusion and height of
shop awnings, storage awnings, and gas lamps.

Whereas, legally, expropriation under public benefit covered an array
of situations, the majority of cases in the minutes of the municipal council
involving the expropriation law related to street widening and alignment.
Furthermore, with the promulgation of the Building Code in the province
of Beirut, every construction required a permit from the municipal council,
turning an ad hoc system of construction in the hands of master builders into
a coherent legal framework managed by the municipal council. The law also
made a distinction between shops and homes with regard to permit fees, not
only making it cheaper to acquire a building permit for a home but also making permits more expensive for larger homes, since the fees were designated
by surface area.[67]

To ensure the application of the law, the municipal police made rounds
of the neighborhoods, noting any new construction and making reports to
the municipal council should they suspect any violation of the law. In 1903,
due to the city's continued expansion, the council decided to increase the
number of policemen from fifteen to twenty, proportionally representing
Beirut's main sectarian communities: Muslim, Greek Orthodox, Maronite,
Greek Catholic, and Jewish.[68] During rounds in their assigned neighborhoods, they reported owners to be fined for building without a permit or not
in accordance with permit applications or municipal maps, in cases where a
map had been drawn for the area.[69] Although in practice a policeman could
be bribed into silence about infringements, any negligence was punishable in
accordance with the municipal law. When found neglectful of his duties, a
policeman was in the first instance given a warning, in the second instance
he had a month's wages deducted from his income, and finally, after the third
instance, he was relieved of his job.[70] On more than one occasion, the council
followed the proper procedures towards negligent policemen, including the
measure of depriving them of one month's wages or freezing their income.[71]

In that way, the municipal council extended its authority over the aesthetics of the built environment across the city, and in the neighborhoods outside
the commercial center, it was primarily residential aesthetics that were af-

fected. Homeowners reported by the municipal police to have built without a permit were ordered by the council to demolish the new modifications or risk being fined. Such considerations continued to guide municipal work even after the outbreak of World War I. In 1915, a woman who had built a twelve-meter balcony on her home in Bab Idris and then closed off nearly half of it, "knowing full well that this was not allowed," was ordered to open her balcony. As a consequence of this case, the municipal engineer was instructed not to grant permits to anyone who wished to close off her or his balcony, and to immediately stop any similar construction and demolish whatever had already been built.[72] In the case of another home with a wall and entrance protruding onto the street, the municipal council ordered that the protrusions be torn down and that the existing pitched tile roof be replaced with a concrete one, presumably to maintain the building height at the legal level.[73]

Not all cases of alignment and protrusions were strictly aesthetic, given that the dictates of a modern urban image went hand in hand with the demands of recent transportation developments in the city. A tramway, opened in 1907 by the private company Société anonyme ottomane des tramways et de l'électricité de Beyrouth, connected the port to Ras Beirut and the Syrian Protestant College to the west. With the city growing in a westerly direction, it was decided to lay a double track for the tramway so the cars could travel in both directions simultaneously. Accordingly, in 1916, the municipal council decided to expropriate a building containing several homes that stood in the way and to authorize the tramway company to widen the street at that point.[74] In this case, the expropriation "to straighten the road" and the need to widen it for transportation coincided as both aesthetic and technological imperatives in the expansion of the city.

The inhabitants of Beirut became involved in this process of beautification and the resulting forms often took shape in negotiations between them and the municipal council. When it came to extending roads into the various residential areas of the city, it was not uncommon for such extensions to be initiated on the basis of petitions from the inhabitants of a neighborhood who wished to be connected to the main road network. The inhabitants of relatively recent neighborhoods, such as al-Ghaba, at a considerable distance east of the city center, not only petitioned in 1905 for the road network to reach them but also took on the expenses themselves.[75]

This kind of negotiation also took place on the level of individual homes. In one case, a municipal policeman reported a woman in the Basta neighborhood, to the south of Burj Square, for having exceeded the construction approved in her permit. Upon consulting a planned map of the area, the municipal council found that although the construction exceeded the current road limit by 1.5 meters, it was still within the limits of the planned road width. Accordingly, the woman was granted permission to proceed without being fined, but only after paying the difference in permit fees for the additional construction.[76] Another woman, living on Qantari hill, the neighborhood with government buildings that towered over the old city, asked for permission to complete a room on the third floor of her property. Having understood from the municipal engineer that there were plans to widen the street abutting the proposed construction, she offered to sign an official declaration allowing the municipal council to appropriate the additional construction without any compensation when the widening project commenced. For reasons not mentioned in the minutes, the council was unable to commence with the project at the time and agreed to grant the woman a building permit on the basis proposed by her.[77]

Mrs. 'Aysha Goes to Istanbul

One case that stretched over fifteen years reveals how a malleable use of a concept of public benefit that embedded aesthetics in monetary value could complicate the negotiation processes that drove the transformation of Beirut. In the spring of 1895, 'Aysha bint Khalil al-'Aris, an inhabitant of Beirut, was sending signed petitions to the Ottoman government from the Küçük Ayasofya neighborhood near the government quarter in Istanbul. During his tenure as governor of the province of Beirut from January to July 1892, Ismail Kemal Bey initiated urban restructuring projects in the inner city, eliciting protests from affected inhabitants. His successor, Khalid Baban Bey, continued the projects, but went about it more democratically, providing a map of the proposed changes and setting up committees for the assessment of property in an attempt to draw the inhabitants into the process. It was under him that the municipality began the demolitions at Bab Idris, where 'Aysha lived, in a bid to improve the city's connection with the port area. A main east-west artery in this project was Suq al-Fashkha, more commonly known as New Street after its widening. The affected inhabitants staged more protests, claiming the compensations did not make up for the loss of their sources of livelihood. When it emerged that Khalid Bey had made wrong assessments in street widths and the property to be expropriated, he was recalled to Istanbul and Nassuhi Bey was appointed provincial governor in his stead in late 1894.[78] A few months later, 'Aysha began her petitioning.

The trail of petitions left behind by 'Aysha stretches temporally over a period of fifteen years and spatially from the minutes of municipal meetings in Beirut to the archives in Istanbul. 'Aysha submitted at least ten petitions during this period, under four different provincial governors and successive municipal councils. According to 'Aysha, the Beirut municipality had demolished part of her house while she was away on pilgrimage to Mecca, leaving her invalid husband and eleven children, the eldest being a girl and boy of thirteen, on the street. Adding insult to injury, the municipality then expected 'Aysha to pay a one-time *sharafiyya* tax of around 150 thousand piasters, a fee paid by property owners for the increase in property value brought about by urban projects. Since, after its partial demolition, whatever was left of 'Aysha's home overlooked the main thoroughfare, its value had increased, according to the municipal council, but the estimated tax exceeded the amount paid by the council as compensation for the demolitions. Unable to pay the difference, 'Aysha faced the possibility of having her home confiscated by order of the council.

The first two of 'Aysha's petitions reached the Ministry of Interior and the Grand Vezirate in April and May of 1895, respectively, and were duly forwarded for investigation to Beirut's provincial council.[79] Having not received any response, 'Aysha then petitioned through the Ministry of Interior and the sultan's court in the same year, this time explicitly asking to be exempted from the taxes and to receive reparations from the Beirut municipal council.[80] The first response, from the provincial governor speaking on behalf of Beirut's provincial council, came in August 1895, four petitions and four months after 'Aysha had begun her efforts. Having corresponded with the municipal council, the governor explained that in tearing down the expropriated part of 'Aysha's home for the sake of widening Suq al-Fashkha, the municipality was simply acting within the bounds of the law.[81]

Dissatisfied with this reply, 'Aysha petitioned the Grand Vezirate again in December of that same year, this time emphasizing the injustice and greed inherent in the practices of the municipal council, acts of which she claimed to be a victim.[82] To further her case, she pointed out the preferential treatment received by the shops bordering the same widened road, hinting at a municipal council bias that favored prominent businesses over less-privileged homeowners such as herself. The second reply to come through the provincial council was as adamant as the first. Indicating that the expenses to be paid to the municipal council for the work it carried out in Bab Idris had been agreed upon with the property owners, the letter added that the home would have to be seized by the municipality if 'Aysha was unable to pay her *sharafiyya* tax.[83]

There is no evidence of 'Aysha submitting any more petitions until 1902, when she returned with a petition again accusing the municipal council of injustice, this time for refusing to grant her a building permit to rebuild her home when the shops adjacent to her house did not face any such obstacles.[84] The reply from the provincial council was swifter than the last time, arriving a couple of months later and explaining that 'Aysha was not granted a building permit because she did not own property under her name. The provincial governor, Rashid bin Mumtaz at the time, went on to explain that what she in fact owned were shares of a property belonging to 'Umar al-'Aris and that these shares were part of a long-standing dispute with the municipal council. Until the balance with the municipality was settled, she would not be granted a building permit.[85]

The story took a dramatic turn the following year. 'Aysha and another woman, Fatima, resorted to the services of a representative, Shakir Hikmat al-Masri, who submitted petitions on their behalf.[86] While 'Aysha had lost more than a third of the property she laid claim to, Fatima was in more dire circumstances. Of the four separate rooms she owned in Bab Idris, three had been demolished. She owned two of these three rooms together with her brother, and they had rented them out as shops.[87] To argue his clients' case, Shakir used an entirely different language from that found in the previous petitions submitted by 'Aysha: the language of law and justice. He argued that the municipal council's acts were not only illegal but also unjust, claiming that in contradiction to the law, his clients had not consented to the expropriation of their property. Moreover, while the municipal council was demanding taxes from his clients based on the fact that their property had increased in value, it had actually decreased in value such that "they were no longer able to live off its income."[88]

In support of his argument, Shakir attached a document signed by twenty-nine notable inhabitants of Beirut, including the neighborhood mukhtar (headman of the city quarter), the local imam (leader in prayer), purported experts, and members of prominent families such as the Dana, Majdhub, 'Arif, and 'Uwayni families. While they made no mention of 'Aysha, the signatories testified to the decrease in value of Fatima's property after its partial demolition. Not only had the municipal council failed to compensate Fatima for what it tore down, the signatories contended, but the structure had also become dilapidated due to neglect.

The municipal council remained unmoved. The reply, coming from the provincial council four months later, explained again the case against 'Aysha, adding that "she has been made to understand in no uncertain terms that the case is not open to settlement."[89] Similarly, all accusations were denied in the case of Fatima, and the provincial governor, Ibrahim Khalil Pasha, explained that the value of the property had been deducted from the *sharafiyya* tax she owed the municipality. What neither the governor nor the petitioner mentions is that upon inspecting Fatima's home after its partial demolition, the municipal council had deemed it no longer fit for living in. Since Fatima could not afford to rebuild what was left of it and pay her tax, she was assigned a monthly payment of fifteen piasters to subsidize her rent from April 1899 until at least 1905.[90]

In the end, 'Aysha's persistence did yield results. In June of 1905, ten years after her initial petition, she was still in possession of the contested property and had not paid any *sharafiyya* tax. She submitted yet another petition, this time directly to the municipal council of Beirut, requesting a building permit for erecting three shops topped by three rooms on "her property" on what was now known as New Street. The council found no objections to granting her a permit "[since] the part on which she will build is enough to ensure that she will be able to pay the municipality the *sharafiyya* tax she owes it."[91] Similarly, the municipal council, discussing a request by 'Aysha submitted in 1909 for reducing the same *sharafiyya* tax she still owed the council, found

that the amount was "too high for the aforementioned property," and it was
therefore reduced by half.[92]

Not long afterwards, 'Aysha appears again in the archives, this time in
the Hanafi court records, to register a road in Bab Idris as having common
ownership between herself and a merchant of the Da'uq family living in Ras
Beirut. Almost two decades after the municipal council tore down part of her
home, 'Aysha was still living in Bab Idris, claiming the right to property, and
rubbing shoulders with prominent merchants' families.[93]

A striking aspect of 'Aysha's petitions is her co-optation of the arguments of modernity, progress, and public benefit to undermine the municipal
council's claim to be beautifying and ordering the city, and to underline the
council's mismanagement and selfishness. She resorted, among other things,
to the language of aesthetics, arguing that instead of achieving its desired
result, the municipal council tore down part of her home in a manner that
was "outside all art" (hariç-i fann). Here, she adopts the logic of the sharafiyya
tax, but stands it on its head. Municipal projects introducing the aesthetic
principles of wide, aligned streets and urban organization were supposed to
add monetary value to individual property, and such value was translated into
an amount that a property owner paid to the municipal council as an urban
improvement tax. But 'Aysha argued that instead of increasing the value of
her home, the municipal council's project had left much to be desired aesthetically about her home, and had thus in fact reduced its value.

Further emphasizing the removal of municipal actions from any link to
public benefit or aesthetic improvement, petitions signed both by 'Aysha and
by her legal representative placed the "unjust" actions of the municipal council as being outside of "this age" and against the dictates of "civilization."
Together, these arguments strove to scale down the council's actions from
public benefit to the much narrower domain of individual interest—more
specifically, in one of 'Aysha's earliest petitions, the interests of "a number of
wealthy and usurping individuals."[94] In saying that, she challenged the municipal council's claim to be acting in the name of public benefit and carrying
out projects that benefited the community as a whole.

One reason value mattered to 'Aysha al-'Aris was that, as for others in her
situation, income from rentals constituted a sizable family income. Although
'Aysha was not destitute, her socioeconomic position was a precarious one.

She belonged to an extended family of 'Arises, settled for generations in the city, and was one of many who had been affected by municipal projects in the inner city.[95] In the period leading up to aggressive municipal intervention, she and others in her situation had grown accustomed to both living in and living off property that was often inherited. The changing economy of the city opened up even more opportunities for letting space to both businesses and homes. When municipal projects served to add value to property through hygienic and aesthetic transformations, this also meant that individual property owners benefited. 'Aysha's means of sustenance had been reinforced precisely through the acts that the municipal council had started carrying out since the 1860s. Regular maintenance, sanitary installations, and other urban improvements around the inner city were adding capital value to her property.

Rental in a Property Market

The development of market societies throughout the nineteenth and twentieth centuries is linked to the formation of central bureaucracies such as the one that took form in the Ottoman Empire. Through the legal and administrative practices of the central state, property in the capitalist sense was constituted as part of such markets. Speaking of the formation of private property in land, Huri Islamoglu points to the context of power relations that characterized the formation of central administrative states, particularly "the struggles and confrontations among different actors, including administrative ones, for control over the use as well as the revenue of the land."[96] The same can be seen in the case of the housing market in Beirut, which was as much about the formation of private property, as Islamoglu discusses it, as about a process that endowed this property with value specific to an urban context.

Clues to the coming emergence of a real estate market were already embedded in the Building and Municipal Codes. Of the references to real estate value, two stand out: one implicit in the Building Code, the other explicit in the Municipal Code. Article 8 of the Building Code stipulated that when property with street frontage was expropriated in order to make way for one of the five categories of streets, the owner was compensated only when the expropriated depth was more than a quarter of the total depth of the property. Any expropriation exceeding that amount was to be compensated by the municipal council.[97] Article 8, in other words, took for granted that the value of a property would increase as a result of urban improvements and that this increase would be commensurate with the amount of the property's street frontage.

The other, more explicit reference to real estate was the *sharafiyya* tax that was central to the disagreement between 'Aysha and the municipal council. Under the section enumerating the sources of income for the municipality, Article 39 of the Municipal Code states that one of those sources of income is "the [one-time] *sharafiyya* tax paid by those who benefit from municipal organization of streets and thoroughfares."[98] Although the word *sharafiyya* does not appear in the text of the expropriation law, 'Abd al-Nur takes the opportunity in his legal annotation to explain that although the municipal council is expected to compensate for the property it expropriates, it is also entitled to claim some of the value accruing to property due to municipal projects. Hence, the word *sharafiyya* derived from the *sharaf* (honor) endowed upon a property due to urban improvements. As if to underline the capitalist aspect entailed in the workings of this law, 'Abd al-Nur goes on to explain how the *sharafiyya* tax works, through a striking metaphor. Both the property owners and the municipal council can be thought of as shareholders in a company held by the council, where the capital consists of the council's expenses and the value of the property involved. As an owner of shares, the municipality is entitled to a portion of the profit accrued after the completion of the project, a profit consisting of a percentage of the rise in property value.[99]

In addition to the text of the law, local administration also played a crucial role in embedding value in property. The use of the expropriation law did more than reorganize the alleys, streets, and main arteries of the city, it also reorganized the composition of the inhabitants in areas where municipal projects were initiated. Those who were unable to pay the *sharafiyya* tax, or what remained of it after the deduction of compensation, risked losing their property to the municipality. This was the case with Suq al-Fashkha, the east-west artery in Bab Idris that had necessitated the partial demolition of 'Aysha's home. After the completion of the project, the municipal council redivided the lots and charged taxes commensurate with the rise in the value of the properties after widening the street. Those inhabitants who suspected that the council was in collusion with property speculators and businessmen might have found their suspicions vindicated when the tempo of demolition and reconstruction reached an apex on the eve of World War I, and the

Council of State (Şura-yı Devlet), at the time a central body in the Ottoman Empire, dealing with conflicts of administrative jurisdiction, granted a real estate company the concession to erect buildings on empty lots in the center of Beirut and sell them in parcels.[100]

Value as monetary value, brought forth in the case of 'Aysha, can also be seen in the widening and alignment projects that touched on commercial property. One notorious case was the Ayyas family shops in the conglomeration of souks between the old city and the port. Two merchants, from the prominent families of Bayhum and 'Itani, submitted petitions to the municipal council asking that the three shops of Muhammad Ayyas be torn down because they reduced the value of their own shops. They also argued that the resulting connection between their souk and Suq Ayyas would "increase the prosperity of the city in accordance with the Sultan's approval."[101] It seems that the main reason Bayhum and 'Itani submitted the petition was that the demolition of the three Ayyas shops would have given their own shops a better connection to the main thoroughfare, New Street. The municipal council admitted that any settlement was contingent on Muhammad Ayyas's approval, but in its following meetings decided to nevertheless demolish the shops, given that linking the souks with the New Street "is of the best public projects and national benefits," generates income for the treasury, and brings growth and ease to the inhabitants.[102] Despite Ayyas's protestations and his arguments that the municipal council had no right to expropriate his shops given that they were private property in a private souk, the demolition proceeded.[103] Although this case relates to a commercial area, it still underlines the role value came to play in the urbanization of Beirut.

Two additional factors contributed to this process of valorization. First, foreign investments in the form of concessions hierarchized the city along lines of technology and means of transport. Jens Hanssen points out that the concession business differed from previous forms of capitalism in the Ottoman Empire in that it revolved around the exchange of capital and know-how rather than raw materials and merchandise. Projects like the expansion of the port, the railway, the tramways, and street lighting ameliorated value in the urban spaces they transformed and connected together.[104] Second, an Ottoman law promulgated on 10 June 1867 gave foreigners the right to own real property in the Ottoman Empire. The two groups to benefit most from this law were foreign citizens and their local protégés who enjoyed foreign nationalities.[105] While the impact of foreign residents remained limited as compared to the situation in, for example, Istanbul, local protégés benefited from tax exemptions on property.[106]

Regionally, before the emergence of a capital-driven property market, owning one's own home was a realistic and affordable goal even for the lower classes. While some of the destitute might have found themselves out of reach of this goal and thus forced to rent individual rooms, the bulk of the rental market was directed at commercial activities.[107] Inhabiting one's own home, even building it, was not considered a luxury, and the minute fluctuations in prices made it a rather predictable process. The constitution of private property in the commodified, capitalist sense transformed this relationship between inhabitant and home into one mediated by a real estate market. This was also true of Beirut, but especially in the inner city, where tenement-like housing conditions began to arise, and dilapidated buildings whose original inhabitants had moved out, often to the suburbs, were rented out to poor refugees and migrants.[108] Rising rents and living expenses were creating unstable living conditions for many in the city, not just the destitute, and it was not unusual for families to continually move around.

Describing growing up in Beirut in the 1860s and 1870s, Jurji Zaydan sums up his family's living conditions: "The tenant carries his house on his back."[109] His family moved house more than a dozen times in twenty-two years, renting in larger domiciles bearing the names of their landlords. Writing around 1910, Zaydan explains that renting one or two rooms for a family composed of a husband, a wife, and several children was the norm for those with "average circumstances."[110] By the early 1880s, rent was significant enough throughout the Ottoman Empire for the government to introduce legal regulations (*icar-ı akar nizamnamesi*), including a standardized rental contract. Only a small portion of these rentals, in homes or otherwise, can be glimpsed in the Hanafi court records for Beirut. Property owners' requests in the late 1890s for a reduction in rent registration fees indicate more rentals in Beirut than the Hanafi court records reveal. The imposed fees were considered an important source of income by municipal councils. In 1898, however, more than a decade after the introduction of the uniform rental contract, the council was still facing difficulties getting property owners to comply.[111]

Although in his memoirs Zaydan implies that the general prosperity of those of middling means improved as education became their main cultural capital, there is evidence that renting homes continued to be a common practice. Cases dealing with rentals in the Hanafi court were few and far between, but advertisements in the local press indicate the presence of tenants belonging to various strata in society. Both furnished and unfurnished accommodations consisting of entire houses or parts of houses were available for rent in Beirut.[112] Moreover, in addition to the usual fare of storage spaces, shops, bakeries, and mills, waqf property was also rented out as accommodation.[113] More clues to the extent of the rental market are the rent-related conflicts that every now and then made it to court, usually demanding payment of rent. Rentals were mentioned in passing not only in cases brought up during the meetings of the municipal council, discussed earlier in this chapter, but also in Hanafi court cases dealing with inheritance claims, disputes over ownership, divorce cases, or descriptions of property in sales contracts. Although these mentions give scant details about home rentals, the normalcy with which they appear in court cases gives a wider view of the rental possibilities in Beirut at the time.[114]

As investors, the inhabitants of the city became part of the process of constituting the home as property in the abstract sense. Rental contracts are significant not only because they indicate greater urban mobility for an emerging middle class but also because income from rent made it possible to sustain a new kind of lifestyle. In 1910, it was still possible to pay forty piasters a month for a modest, one-room abode in the inner city,[115] an option that those who could afford more had by then abandoned for the suburbs. By comparison, rent for a home consisting of a few rooms in one of the middle-range suburbs, such as Mina al-Husn, was about 250 piasters a month.[116] This meant that a middling wage earner supporting a family on about 850 piasters per month could afford to rent a home composed of three to four rooms, feed his family, and have enough left to partake of the lifestyle that characterized the middle class at the turn of the century.[117]

For those who invested in homes, rent ensured a regular income or, at least, a complementary income that could sustain a lifestyle that went beyond merely providing for necessities. Two business partners who decided to invest in two domestic properties in the suburbs, letting them to four separate families of average means, could assure themselves of a regular monthly income of 300 to 400 piasters a month each at the turn of the century. This would have covered basic food expenses for an average-sized family. There was also the possibility of letting parts of an inherited property that one lived in. Such was the case for 'Aysha. As part of the rental market, the home became more than just a place of abode. It became a commodity on the market with a monetary value subject to change depending on location and urban development. As far as the middle class was concerned, this value was of significance to them both as tenants looking for a home and as owners making use of the real estate market to maintain a socioeconomic position.

From Home to Property

Despite the fact that the new legal codes indirectly led to the constitution of home as property on the market, the home as a legal entity rarely took on a particularity in the late nineteenth-century legal framework. Both hygienically and aesthetically, whatever restrictions the home was subjected to were a by-product of the regulation of the urban environment and not directly related to domestic space. This meant that the relationship between domesticity and its urban environment was only loosely regulated through the notion of public benefit, and the relationship between that benefit and domestic space remained unarticulated. This stands in stark contrast to the treatment of the home in the Hanafi court, where it took on a *domestic* particularity defined in terms of its relationship both to its surroundings in general and to other adjacent homes.

Even as a civil code began to develop towards the end of the Ottoman era, the Hanafi court continued to be used for resolving conflicts around material aspects of the home. In the mosaic of the late Ottoman legal system, the inhabitants of Beirut could choose to take their disputes to their own confessional (*millet*) court, to the Hanafi court, to the commercial court, to the mixed court, or to the criminal court—depending on what the conflict involved and which arena they felt afforded them the best chance of winning. Some disputes were also taken to the municipal council, when they concerned one of the many tasks and duties the council concerned itself with. Despite its shrinking role in handling marriage, divorce, and custody cases involving non-Muslims, the Hanafi court continued to be used extensively for property and inheritance cases by Muslims and non-Muslims alike. Therefore, the court continued to rule on material aspects of the home in a way that did not always coincide with the viewpoint of the municipal council. Cases from the second half of the nineteenth century show how, during the expanding reach of the municipal council in urban matters, the Hanafi court continued to deal with the home as an entity with its own particularities.

Before the institution of the municipal council—within a system of urban management that had involved neighborhood residents, trade guilds, religious communities, and charitable foundations—the Hanafi court resolved day-to-day conflicts over domestic space and ensured that the construction of domiciles proceeded according to set principles and standards. These principles and standards were codified in the *Mecelle-i Ahkam-ı Adliye* (Compendium of Legal Statutes) of 1877, in Book 10, which deals with joint ownership.[118] For example, a section of this chapter titled "Walls and Neighbors" brings together standards relating to visual and material relations between neighboring domiciles and also the principles that were applied in practice at the Hanafi court in Beirut both before and after the publication of the *Mecelle*.[119]

Central to the court's legal framework regarding construction was the concept of "obvious harm" (*darar bayyin*), referred to in the Arabic translation of the *Mecelle* as "great harm" (*darar fahish*) and summarized as all that "hinders the intended benefit of a building, such as dwelling, or causes such damage to a building, that it weakens it and causes its collapse."[120] When it came to property in general, this concept was applied at the Hanafi court in cases dealing with the trespassing that refuse posed to other people's property, especially the effluents of gutters and projecting chimneys. Specifically concerning the home, overhangs over adjacent property also became a recurrent issue with the growing popularity of pitched tile roofs in the second half of the nineteenth century. In order to avoid "obvious harm," it was within the court's jurisdiction to order that rainwater be directed away from the property of others or to rule against the use of shared spaces in a way that disturbed others entitled to them. A man living in the old city, for example, successfully evoked the principle of "obvious harm" to forbid his neighbor from lighting a fire in a space he shared with his neighbors, citing the harm it caused others and the presence of a separate kitchen for such purposes.[121]

The principle of obvious harm could be used in any case, not only those concerning domiciles, but it applied to the home in a specific way when it came to visual relations. Like many other cities in the region, intramural Beirut was characterized by introverted houses opening onto courtyards, but a lot of activities took place on roofs, exposed to the eyes of neighboring onlookers. Many houses put up parapets just for that reason, to shield the domestic activities and socializations that took place in the open air, particularly women's activities.[122] For the Hanafi court, sheltering the women's activities from outside view was a matter of particular sensitivity. Six of the seventeen articles dealing with the characteristics of domestic space in the *Mecelle* concern themselves with the visual protection of women's quarters (*maqarr al-nisa'*), such as the central space or court, kitchen, and well.[123] In practice, the Hanafi court ensured the application of building norms and standards that visually guarded domestic privacy, and it did this with the help of builders, who took care to adhere to these standards during the building process.[124]

The construction boom in Beirut and the growing popularity of more extroverted domiciles put pressure on this system. With the building of additional floors and the use of the popular, large glass window openings, overlooking another building's living quarters presented a problem even in the less densely populated areas outside the city walls. Some cases brought to court to protest visual trespassing involved inhabitants of the suburban quarters accusing neighbors of causing obvious harm by "overlooking the women's quarters where they sit and carry out their business," areas also referred to as *harem*.[125] Litigants included Christians and Jews demanding that their *harem* be shielded from neighbors, who were often coreligionists. The court's usual procedure in such cases was to assign inspectors to evaluate the situation, and in case of infringement, it had the jurisdiction to order people to remove a structure, close openings, or even set up temporary visual obstructions on construction sites to ensure workers' eyes did not precipitously wander in an undesirable direction.

Visual trespassing was not the Hanafi court's only concern when it came to domestic openings; the home also enjoyed specificities in terms of the quality of its spaces. In cases where a neighbor blocked adjacent openings on someone else's property "without legal recourse" (*min dun wajh shar'i*), the court had the jurisdiction to have the obstruction removed. In this case, a *shar'i*, or legal opening, denoted a specific size that allowed enough light to enter the home to permit an inhabitant to read during the daytime.[126] Where this conflicted with the visual restriction of overlooking private space, the court could ordain a window to be cut out above eye level, thereby allowing daylight in while keeping curious onlookers out.[127]

The disposal of refuse, the entry of daylight, and overlooking other people's houses were not fragmented instances under the Hanafi court. Such issues represented a specific constellation of concerns that defined domestic space and constituted part of a body of laws concerned with monitoring move- ment—both material and visual—in and out of the home and with keeping a strict control over the relationships that took place within its walls, including socialization between the sexes.[128] They lent the home a material specificity that distinguished it from property in the abstract sense of the word.

The court's attitude towards municipal procedures remained ambiguous. The Hanafi court and the municipal council were legally entwined through the text of the *Mecelle*, which constituted a reference for the civil courts. But the *shari'a* court had its own procedures of inspection, whereby court representatives assessed conflicts on site and reported back to the judge, who gave the final verdict. In the few instances when municipal council permits or decisions were brought up in court in order to buttress a case, they were simply dismissed by the judge, and the inspection was carried out in accor- dance with the court's established procedures.[129]

Recent scholarship on the Middle East questions the "secularization" the- ory used by earlier scholars to understand the development of the Ottoman state in its later decades. Rather than understanding late Ottoman reforms as drawing a strict line between religious and secular, scholars are showing how these two sides of Ottoman reform continued to be implicated in each other.[130] Similarly, understanding the discrepancies between the municipal council and the Hanafi court as a tension between secular law and religious law distorts the Ottoman legal framework that took shape in the late nine- teenth century. To take this point further, it is important to underline that many of the court cases discussed here were brought to court not only by Muslims but also by Christians and Jews.

It is both more accurate and more relevant to view the tension between municipal and Hanafi procedures as an attempt by a state institution, the

municipal council, to strip the home of the specificities it enjoyed under the
Hanafi court and to submit it instead to a public benefit standard closely
twinned with the dictates of an emerging real estate market. While the
Building Code echoed some of the concerns of the Hanafi court, particularly
when it came to domestic refuse and public health, it remained divorced
from the conception of the home as an entity that needs to be physically
and visually protected. Looking to the interest of a vaguely defined "public,"
municipal politics saw the relationship between the inhabitant and the habitation as one mediated by value rather than by use. Instead of endowing the
home with its particularities, as the Hanafi court did, the council deployed
paradigms of hygiene and aesthetics to underpin this value through, for example, the use of the *sharafiyya* tax.

The category of public benefit cleared the ground, often literally, for re-
configuring the relationship of the home to its context as a relationship that
could be submitted to the exigencies of novelty, order, and productive capital.
These transformations underlay a view of the home, not as a particular set of
relations between inhabitant, home, and surroundings, but rather as generic
property. Concomitantly with the decrease of such cases in the Hanafi court
starting in the 1880s, the municipal council took over the role of adjudicator
in matters of urban space. But without a clear understanding of the relationship between public benefit and the home, this left domesticity and its
relation to the urban and social fabric open to imagination and contestation.

CHAPTER 4

THINGS AT HOME

We all follow what is in fashion: sofas in the living room and high
chairs, half of which stand lined up against the wall. Little do we
care for what is cheap and comfortable to sit on.

Julia Tu'ma Dimashqiyya[1]

In the urban projects transforming the face of Beirut, the position of the
home remained ambiguous, and it was not until the French Mandate period
that a building law with specifications regulating domestic space was introduced. At the same time, the relationships among inhabitant, home, and surroundings were drawn into the changes gripping the city in the late Ottoman
period. Conceptions of urban planning, a real estate market, changes in class
structure, and new status symbols and forms of leisure all transformed the
home both from within and without. More than anything, Beirut's changing
economic position and the emergence of a middle class meant that domestic
things, the meanings embedded in them, and their potential to communicate
social positions as well as mediate social relations contributed to defining the
middle class and giving it identity.

Starting in the late eighteenth century, the military, political, and commercial balance of power between the Ottoman Empire and the "Great Powers"
of Europe (Austria, Prussia, the Russian Empire, the United Kingdom, and
France) shifted in favor of the latter. The Ottoman Empire soon found itself
steadily weakening and in debt. Not only was the empire being reduced politically with every secessionist movement in the Balkan Peninsula, but trade
relations with other countries on the European continent were being fundamentally changed by the industrial revolution and by the ability of the Great
Powers to extract concessions on tariffs for exports to the empire.[2]

As the Ottoman Empire became a captive market for a surging production
of commodities, so, too, the home became an immediate target for exporters
to the region. Beirut's prominence as a port city and its growing appetite for
the new exposed it to a stream of new domestic objects that were often adopted, adapted, and embraced. Through the home and its objects, the middle
class lived out their aspirations to a life of greater comfort and their belonging
to a new world of opportunity and status. Simultaneously, the home itself
was changing as an object. The home was more than a status symbol, it was
the symbol of a modern way of life. In its urban context, it was also subject to
novel spatial ideals as well as directly materially transformed by its situation in
a changing urban environment.

The furniture and decorations that entered the home in the late nineteenth century were crucial to the generation of domesticity as a new kind
of social space. Objects, in that sense, are not mere conveyors of social positions and contemporary ideals—such as class, status, education, progress, and
modernity—they also actively participate in giving form to these abstract
notions from within the home.[3] Materially, the home responded to the new
spatial configurations brought in with imported objects and technologies.
More interestingly, the tastes displayed at home also carried with them traces
of the larger world and industrialized modes of production, endowing objects
with meanings that often escaped deliberate attempts at displaying or conveying social status. A consideration of how the relationship between people
and things was transmitted and shaped in a particular setting, shows how objects reconstituted relations at home and gave form to the emerging middle
class in the most private of spaces.

Hygiene and Aesthetics inside the Home

Despite its increasing involvement in the daily life of the city, municipal authority only brushed against the home's walls, never actually entering its spaces.
The *jawish*, or police sergeant, had the right, by law, to enter and inspect hotels,
bathhouses, warehouses, shops, theaters, game-houses, coffeehouses, and "all
places entered by people for the purpose of commercial exchange."[4] To maintain the bounds of "decency" (*adab*) prescribed for the *jawish*, his jurisdiction
stopped at the boundaries of the home. The only mention of the home in the
Municipal Code concerned what exceeded its bounds, and there were no reg-

ulations for its interior disposition or specifications for its openings and spaces. Yet, the prescriptions relating to hygiene and aesthetics that were prevalent in urban reform found their indirect way into domestic space.

The new home was influenced by the same corpus of nineteenth-century scientific knowledge guiding municipal regulations. The emphasis on sunlight and air, which permeated the hygienic diction of the Beirut municipal council and was also often expressed in the press, found its way into the home, where it blended with the increasing popularity of glazed fenestrations. The contemporary relevance of light and ventilation to domestic life was explicitly articulated in the press in 1881 as part of a growing corpus of articles on domesticity, as in this example:

> If asked what is the most important thing to every home, we would say sunlight and fresh air. If asked what is most beneficial for every man, we would say sunlight and fresh air. And if asked what is the cheapest thing in the world, we would say sunlight and fresh air.[5]

Water was another element contributing to the application of hygienic principles and to organizing the relationship between the home and its surroundings. Water mains were becoming widely accessible in the second half of the nineteenth century. Whereas previously, wells shared by several houses constituted the main source for water, a concession by imperial decree in 1870 granted a private company the right to distribute potable water from Dog River (Nahr al-Kalb) in the north. By providing water in return for a subscription fee, the British Beirut Waterworks both unshackled residential development from the constraint of having a well nearby and brought water inside the home. By 1905, the company was supplying 4,700 out of 18,000 households with water.[6] Many of those who did not get their water through the company, either because they preferred well water or because they found the rates to be too high, could bring water into their homes through being connected by pipe to a nearby well by an independent contractor.[7]

The adoption of new standards of hygiene and aesthetics, both in public and at home, was also a contributing factor in the emergence and spread of a new residential typology in Beirut: the central-hall house. Until the mid-nineteenth century, the most common domiciles in Beirut were the *dar* and the *hara*. The *dar*, on the one hand, was a self-contained, patrilocal residence having an internal court and named after the family that inhabited it. As the home expanded and was progressively divided among successive generations, it continued to carry the original family name. The *hara*, on the other hand, was a less well-off collection of abodes overlooking an internal court and typically inhabited by groupings from the same family branch, coreligionists, or people originating from the same geographical area.[8] As the city expanded beyond the dilapidated city walls, many of those houses, especially the *hara* types, were rented out or sold to less well-off inhabitants and eventually to migrants and refugees from the surrounding region.

In tandem with the urban expansion of Beirut and influenced by the suburban villas of the 1830s and 1840s, what is referred to today as the *central-hall house* began to take form. By the time of Mark Twain's visit to Beirut in 1867, the central-hall house was the earliest sign of the new found opulence of the city's mercantile bourgeoisie, who had been building these Italianesque villas in the eastern outskirts of the city. From the deck of his ship approaching the harbor, Twain could observe the new houses sitting among green shrubbery and dotting the hill of Ashrafiyya.[9]

In the second half of the nineteenth century, the detached central-hall house had established itself as a status symbol. A trade report penned at the French consulate in 1898 comments on its social relevance:

> [This] manner of construction, widespread in the entire Orient, is particu-
> larly prevalent in Lebanon and Beirut. The ambition of every native is to be
> able to own a house of stature. It is certain that many Syrian emigrants seek
> America only to be able to return one day as proprietors in their homeland.[10]

In *Inventing Home*, historian Akram Khater discusses the adoption of the central-hall house by returning migrants as a way to emphasize their modernity and accentuate middle-class mannerisms that distinguished them from the peasant context of Mount Lebanon. Khater argues that constructions of family and gender were integral to the definition of this middle class. In connection with this, he maintains that the privacy and separation of functions ushered in by this new typology promoted separating the mistress of the house from the outside world and focusing her activity indoors.[11]

The ideal of building and inhabiting a two-story, freestanding house with such a degree of privacy was far from the realities of the urban middle class.

Certainly in the homes of the wealthy in Beirut, freestanding, villa-like structures enjoyed gardens that separated them from their surroundings, and the rooms, often spread over two floors, afforded the separation of functions that provided varying degrees of privacy. Such a house was often called a "villa" or a "palace" (*qasr*) and named after its owners, as was, for example, Qasr Mukhayyish.[12] But, particularly with the change in the real estate market discussed in the previous chapter, the urban context meant that restrictions on space and finances put the central-hall house beyond the financial reach of the majority.

Nevertheless, many characteristics associated with the central-hall house did have an effect on domestic life, and the ideal became a desirable status symbol, even if not one within the reach of everyone. Like its equivalent in Mount Lebanon, the central-hall house in Beirut reflected guiding principles used in urban planning, drawing together scientific rationalization of space, hygienic standards of urban living, and the aesthetics of alignment and order. The overall form of the house was rectilinear and freestanding, sporting several façades. This was a radical departure from the inward-oriented, interlocked houses of the inner city. The introduction of several rooms, organized around a longitudinal central hall, also encouraged separation between the different family members and between the private family quarters and the central reception area. The *coup de grâce* for the older style, where there was little separation of functions, was the integration of outdoor services into the house and the disappearance of the flat roof, which had once served as a location for multiple varied activities, including socialization, drying clothes, and sleeping in the summer months.[13] The location of the services (kitchen, storage, toilet, sink) in one corner of the plan allowed for outside access to these areas as well as for piping waste water and effluent to the sewage network provided by the municipality.

Writing on the hygienic conditions of Beirut in 1897, French hygienist Benoît Boyer is full of praise for the conditions the central-hall house provided, particularly in a hot climate, with its ventilation, its cleanliness, and its large and numerous fenestrations.[14] This stands in stark contrast to his condemnation of the level of public hygiene in the city. Although Boyer's representation and accompanying plan were more of a didactic example than a realistic depiction,[15] they still reflected some of the hygienic elements that appeared both in the local press and in actual houses. When placed in the context of Beirut, the ideal north-south orientation of the hall opened up the view towards the Mediterranean as the city sloped down towards it. The desirability of having a scenic view grew with the popularity of larger, glazed windows. The emphasis on sun and air in providing hygienic spaces also found its way into this new form. When oriented in the north-south direction, not only did the central hall constitute an air corridor that ventilated the home, but its floor-to-ceiling, glazed triple arcade brought in the diffused north light during the day and closed out the heat of the sun at its back.

By integrating other contemporary elements—such as red Marseilles roof tiles and wall murals—the idealized central-hall house became the embodiment of the fashionable lifestyle associated with Beirut.[16] The characteristic red tiles that gave these houses their distinctive appearance and made an impression on the passengers of approaching ships, became an important import from France. By the turn of the century, the demand was high enough to warrant the construction of local factories that competed with French industry in supplying the city with both roof and floor tiles.[17]

The growing division of functions within its spaces and the various levels of privacy it ushered in, between the outside world, domestic life, and family life, also turned the central-hall house into an embodiment of modern living. These characteristics of privacy and of separation of the functions of living, sleeping, and eating were taken for granted in lectures and writings on domesticity of the time. Many of their prescriptions on how to properly furnish a home assumed that each function had a room and a set of furniture appropriate to it.[18] By the early twentieth century, organizing domestic life by fixing functions through furniture found a sure echo in advertisements, with specific pieces of furniture listed under the different rooms of the home.[19] The privacy the house could ideally afford the nuclear family meant that the woman—the wife and mother in this family—would be able to administer this social and economic domain in separation from the immediate context and from the extended family. The full range of activities a woman was expected to undertake, from preparing domestic needs to raising children, could now be understood as part of her larger role as a modern woman and sole manager of the home.

Although these changes seem to suggest an enhancement of the conjugal family, as propagated in the intellectual circles of the time, the actual middle-class home continued to signify varying levels of intimacy and different locations within the domestic whole. Two words used interchangeably to mean "home," *manzil* and *bayt*, indicated two separate referents when used together. Whereas *manzil* designated a place of abode that included indoor and outdoor spaces and could be shared by an extended family, *bayt* referred to an isolated quarter within this larger conglomeration.[20] So while a marital couple could inhabit a *bayt* that enjoyed a certain degree of privacy, the space constituting this *bayt* could equally be a separate apartment or part of a larger family home.

This differentiation acquired special significance in the Hanafi court, where a material, legally defined requirement for marriage was the *maskan shar'i* (legal abode). The word *maskan* indicated a generic place of abode, but it also shared a root with *musakana*, the legal term for the consummation of marriage. According to the Hanafi school of jurisprudence, if a man was not able to provide his wife with a *maskan shar'i*, she had the right to separate from him until he did so. The concept of *maskan shar'i* posited the minimum requirements for privacy for the married couple from both their families. It consisted of, at least, a private room that could be closed and access to amenities, such as a kitchen and toilet. It also entailed vaguer stipulations concerning social relations, since both a "decent" neighborhood and the availability of same-sex companionship for women were also requirements.[21]

Outside the context of the Hanafi court, *bayt* could also mean "room," particularly when used in conjunction with *manzil*. An article in the Greek Orthodox journal *al-Mahabba*, for example, explains:

> A [civilized, urbanized person] might take just one *bayt* for himself and his family, where they sleep at night and sit and receive guests during the day. These are the destitute and poor. Others live in domiciles [*manazil*, plural of *manzil*] with several *bayts* and improve their utensils and furnishings. They sleep at night in one *bayt* of the *manzil*, sit and receive people in another, and dine in yet another. These are the well-off people whose earnings cover more than the bare necessities.[22]

Although used more generally to mean home, *bayt* also had more concrete meanings depending on context, class, and familial circumstances. In the core ideal of *maskan shar'i*, *bayt* ensured some degree of conjugal privacy within larger, even concentric conglomerations of varying degrees of privacy and publicity. Used in the context of a larger domicile, it designated a separation of functions throughout the spaces of a home. In both its meanings, *bayt* designated varying degrees of privacy in relation to the nuclear family, the extended family, the immediate neighbors, and the larger neighborhood.

Furnishing a Home

Even as the central-hall house remained the province of the city's notables and commercial bourgeoisie, the middle-class home was also expanding in size and incorporating a wider assortment of furniture and decoration. A few of the most popular items of furniture in the late nineteenth century were affordable, mass-produced imports. Understanding their popularity in economic terms would merely be to echo French consular reports about local preferences for the cheap.[23] The cheapest imported iron bed and bentwood chair remained more expensive than locally produced wooden equivalents. Yet, an increasing number of people *chose* to consume imported pieces of furniture that were advertised as "modern" and as among the "most important *mubilya* for people in general."[24] The popularity of bedroom items is particularly significant because it exemplifies how objects could also constitute part of a self-image, rather than simply part of a projected or social image. Through their role in constructing and stabilizing social categories in a given culture, goods also serve to construct an intelligible universe and to make and maintain social relationships.[25] It is, therefore, important to understand how new commodities transformed the home and how they were integrated into contemporary domestic practices.

The practice of separating different functions at home was becoming more common in Beirut in the second half of the nineteenth century, and it was reinforced by the spread of new pieces of furniture. Such separations were assumed by the corpus of domestic advice in periodicals, but they were a relative novelty in the homes of an emerging middle class with growing access to consumption. In his study of the socio-spatial transformations of the home in late Ottoman Beirut, architectural historian Ralph Bodenstein explores the organization of functions within the central-hall house, their localization in space, and their relationship with each other. He notes that in the 1880s and 1890s, and within the timespan of a generation, upper-class and upper-middle-class houses acquired functional differentiations between reception/living, sleeping, service (including kitchen and storage), sanitary, and circulation spaces.[26] This corresponded to nineteenth-century conceptions of family and household, hospitality, women's domestic role, and domestic service.[27]

Given Bodenstein's focus on the upper classes and the absence of any close reading of the impact of domestic commodities on everyday life, he does not tackle the relationship between actual imports and objects, on the one hand, and the middle-class home, on the other.[28] The differentiation in domestic functions discussed by Bodenstein is still a significant development in late Ottoman Beirut, and one that also affected middle-class lifestyles in a specific way. But in addition to the correct disposition of objects at home in accordance with function, the middle-class domesticity put forth in the press was preoccupied with the consumption of locally produced domestic items and complicated by the ability of certain popular items to unbalance domestic ideals, as the next two chapters make clear. In order to understand these changes, it is important to start by looking at how specific popular imports generated new modes of living and socialization around them.

Prior to the advent of roomier accommodation, the use of space was dictated more chronologically, by the time of day, than by the function of a room. Sleeping arrangements consisted of mattresses that were stacked in a built-in closet or a corner when not in use.[29] The same space was then used for seating and eating purposes during daytime. While raised seating was not altogether unknown, it was not until the second half of the nineteenth century that socialization between people was raised above ground level by the introduction of chairs and dining tables. To distinguish these items from built-in furniture, they were commonly referred to as *mafrushat* (literally, "furnishings") or *mubilya* (probably from the Italian *mobilia*).

With the growing division of functions, living and reception spaces emerged at the center of upper- and middle-class homes alike. In opulent central-hall houses, the spaces meant for reception included the *manzul*, the central hall (*dar*), and the *liwan*, forming varying spaces of mediation within the house and between the home and the outside world. In some cases, it was possible to circulate through surrounding rooms, unseen from the central hall, by means of connecting doors, making the hall an extension of the outside world into domestic space.[30] In the middle-class home, as in its wealthier counterpart, the central hall was also located at the center of the home, with other rooms organized around it. It was the first space one entered, the largest room of the home, and the main space for receiving guests. Given that it was smaller in size than the central hall of a wealthy home and was simply ornamented, the middle-class hall preserved a sense of intimacy even when it gave out directly onto the street, without the benefit of a surrounding garden.

In these reception areas, the very act of sitting was physiologically transformed through new domestic objects that lifted bodies off the ground. Among the most popular imported objects, Austrian bentwood chairs, known as Thonet chairs, were enthusiastically embraced for use in the seating area, at a time when the French bourgeoisie were rejecting bentwood furni-

Figure 1. The central hall of a middle-class home in 'Ayn al-Muraysa (Building 1 on the map in the Appendix). This home occupied the ground floor of a two-story building built between 1900 and 1920. Wall decorations covered by more recent paint consist of two blue bands on a light blue background. Source: Børre Ludvigsen.

ture.[31] Relying on steam for their production, bentwood chairs were based on standardized designs and produced with interchangeable parts. One simple model, Chair No. 14, was composed of six pieces of bent wood, ten screws, and two washers and could be shipped flat in parts and assembled in Beirut, thus reducing shipping costs. Commonly known in its time as the Consumer Chair, this model inaugurated the era of mass-produced furniture, and by 1930 about fifty million bentwood chairs had been sold around the world.[32] This chair's characteristics and the standardized mass production methods used to make it were difficult for both other European and local craftsmen

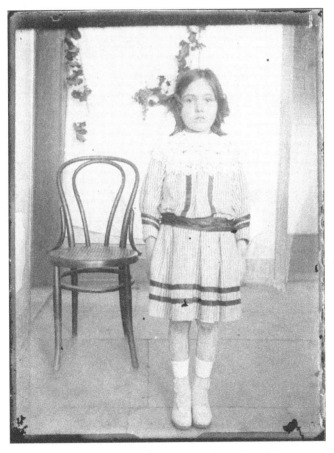

Figure 2. Family photograph showing a child posed with a Thonet chair (Model No. 18), ca. 1915–1920. Source: Fouad El-Khoury Collection, courtesy of the Arab Image Foundation. Reprinted with permission.

Figure 3. Qasr Heneiné, an upper-class foreign home in Zuqaq al-Balat, ornamented in the Moorish style popular in Europe during the nineteenth century, offers an example of divan seating, against the wall in the background, ca. 1900–1920. Source: Matson Photograph Collection, Library of Congress (LC-DIG-matpc-01184).

and manufacturers to replicate, which partly explains why it was a popular import. Another reason for the success of the bentwood chair in Beirut and the wider Levant was its characteristic wicker seat and an assembly method that did not require the use of glue. These features made the bentwood chair suitable for warm weather use and turned Chair No. 14 and the variations on it into an icon whose local equivalents continue to permeate the Beiruti landscape and the rest of the region to this very day.[33]

Other kinds of chairs were manufactured locally, and both chair imports and local production picked up in the 1880s. By 1908, the Nusuli shop had to advertise itself as the sole Thonet dealer in Beirut, presumably in order to fend off competition from others claiming to sell Thonet furniture. Other imported items of furniture for living spaces did not enjoy a similar level of success. Apart from chairs, furnishings in these spaces continued to be dominated by divans, an elevated form of seating where back support relied on cushions set up against the walls.[34] Sofas remained mostly absent from Hanafi court records and only towards the World War I era did they start appearing in advertisements by local manufacturers.[35]

Other movable possessions also contributed to new modes of living that differed from those of the old, intramural Beirut, where it was usual to share cooking spaces, toilets, and water wells. At the turn of the century, there were advertisements devoted solely to kitchens, offering kerosene stoves to housewives who were "keen about their time and money and the cleanliness of their kitchens." By 1911, lighter aluminum utensils began to appear along-side the heavier copper.[36] The spread in the use of kerosene stoves meant that cooking activity became divorced from communal spaces and could be moved anywhere.[37] At the same time, kitchens were filled with imported tinware, porcelain, ceramics, glassware, and faïence, or tin-glazed pottery.[38] With these commodities, the kitchen became more than just a cooking space. Housing such items as porcelain sets for serving coffee and decora-tively gilded trays for offering cigarettes, it was the hidden infrastructure to the reception room's function as the center of middle-class hospitality.[39] Eventually, sideboards entered the scene, introducing a separate space for utensils that showcased a middle-class standard for the reception of guests.

As for the bedroom, domestic advice printed in the press and lectured about on the podiums of societies resonated with its changes to a certain degree. A lecture delivered at the literary society Bakurat Suriyya described the ideal bedroom thus:

> Each bedroom is furnished with a mirror, a commode, a big closet for hanging clothes, a laundry table and its accessories, and one bed if the bedroom has one person. Its floors are covered with mats and beautiful cushions placed next to the bed, in such a way that they do not slip under the bed or chairs. The bedroom should also have pictures, books, chairs, seats, and the like, but only in small quantities.[40]

At the time of this lecture in 1885, this kind of luxury was just beginning to spread to middle-class households. In the 1870s and early 1880s, Jurji Zaydan, his parents, and his siblings rented two- to three-room apartments, using the same room for both sleeping and receiving guests. During the daytime, the family stacked their bed rolls in a niche, called the *yuk*, which was hidden behind a curtain.[41] Although the ideal of having one room per function and one bed per person remained beyond the reach of many, the last two decades of the nineteenth century show a wider adoption of some of the ideal bedroom's individual elements, such as mirrors, commodes, English iron bedsteads, and closets.

The English iron bedstead entered the daily domestic lexicon in the 1880s and persisted in popularity well into the period of the French Mandate. Early on, the most popular model supported mosquito netting and featured detachable legs and a headboard.[42] By 1914, there were four models on the Beirut market, 90 percent of English provenance, mainly from Birmingham. Known for its overcrowded slums, Birmingham's other face was its reputation as the "city of a thousand trades," and along with Sheffield, it was the center for Victorian England's metal industry.[43] Competition and technology in metal production in the English city ensured a supply of affordable beds to Beirut, and on the eve of World War I, the cheapest model was available at 15 francs (about 80 Ottoman piasters), while the more elaborately decorated beds varied in price and size, starting at 20 francs (about 110 piasters). The more expensive copper model of this average range came with four columns, copper knobs, gilded motifs, and supports for mosquito netting.[44]

Like the bentwood chair, iron bedsteads had the advantage of being industrially produced and easily assembled, making their prices competitive.

The availability of cheaper models and the variety of sizes (95, 105, and 120 cm wide) offered indicate that the use of the iron bed had become more widespread towards the 1910s. There were five major stores, including two department stores, selling these beds, and seven import representatives in Beirut, in addition to minor retailers.[45] Metal beds also appear with more frequency in the Hanafi court records towards the end of the century. Yet, unlike the domestic ideal limned in the 1885 speech presented at Bakurat Suriyya, where each person had a separate bed, rarely more than one bed appeared in possession lists presented at the Hanafi court.[46]

Figure 4. Advertisement for metal bedsteads describing metal and copper beds as "among the most important piece of furniture for people in general in this age." Source: *Lisan al-Hal,* 21 October 1887.

Surface Matters

The surfaces of the home also changed, with textiles, images, and colors becoming an integral part of the organizational principle of the home. Wall
colors played a part in lending hierarchy to a new configuration of domestic
space. On the one hand, all attempts at introducing wall paper to Beirut were
met with resistance, most probably due to the mold-inducing level of humid-
ity in the city.[47] Oil colors, on the other hand, constituted a lively import to
Beirut towards the end of the nineteenth century, and most of them came
from England. As an advertisement for Liverpool-produced paint suggests,
these products were specifically marketed to "those who desire to purchase the
best paints and finest oils and varnish to paint their homes."[48] Not surprisingly
so, since people in Beirut and the well-off centers of Mount Lebanon were in
the habit of painting the interiors, and sometimes also the exteriors, of their
houses, with oil colors.[49] Imported colors ranged from the expensive red, to the
cheaper ocher and the most affordable color, yellow, but the most popular hues
varied from light gray to dark blue.[50]

Those who could afford colors employed them so as to mesh with the
hierarchy of rooms in the home, using the most expensive colors and elaborate wall designs in the reception areas. As some remaining examples show,
it was common practice in wealthy homes to decorate walls with colorful
designs and elaborate patterns. Examples from Damascene homes of the
same period show intricate murals depicting views of Istanbul, European
cityscapes, and symbols of modern times, such as steamboats, railways, and
factories.[51] Although its decorations are not as elaborate, the Mukhayyish
house is one surviving example of such opulence in Beirut, with its uses of
color and stucco ceiling ornamentation.[52]

The houses of those of middling means were less ornate, but they still used
colors and stenciled wall patterns to engender similar hierarchies across the exteriors and interiors of houses. Despite being on a smaller scale than the halls
of the wealthy, the reception space still served as a showcase for the best tiles
and most decorative wall paint. Colors, most popularly red, framed windows
on the outside walls and introduced basic, abstract decorative patterns against
the lighter-colored background of the main living space. The expensive red
paint was used more sparingly around the house than were yellow, blue, and
green paints.[53]

In a similar vein, while Italian marble was used as flooring in entire rooms in wealthy houses, in middle-class homes it was used for thresholds or for small columns that supported arches across the main seating area. Again, the focus was on stressing the element of pomp associated with marble in the central hall.[54] It did not take long before local manufacturers began trying to reproduce the popular tile models from Italy and France. An early advertisement from one such manufacturer, Shami and Sha'ya, targeted itself expressly

Figure 5. A home in Furn al-Shubbak south of Beirut showing simple wall decoration, ca. 1915–1920. Source: Fouad El-Khoury Collection, courtesy of the Arab Image Foundation. Reprinted with permission.

at decorating homes, offering tiles "resembling marble" and stressing the company's ability to cater to customers' specific demands by "delivering all that is asked [of us] regarding shape, size, and color."[55]

Images too came to play a pivotal role in decorating homes. Even before the spread of photography, various kinds of images could be found in the home. The use of images by those of average means became a subject of discussion in *al-Muqtataf* as early as 1881. An article, criticizing the bare houses of the rich, posited ornamentation on the wall, such as shelves and pictures, as a necessary part of a home's decoration.[56] Another article assumed the presence of framed pictures, recommending the color green for curtains because, among other things, "it goes with picture frames [*barawiz al-suwar*], which are often gilded."[57]

The presence of images in domestic life increased towards the end of the century as they became more affordable and varied due to newly introduced mechanical and chemical means of production. Syrians and Ottomans rapidly came to dominate the practice of photography, initially carried out solely by European studios. The same was true of postcards, which brought views of the city, monuments, and edifices into domiciles as well. The official photographer of the *vilayet*, Spiridyun Shu'ayb, sold his views to local publishers of postcards—such as Muhammad al-'Ardati and Rizq Allah Sarkis—and Sarafyan Photographers sold postcard views of Beirut and Syria. Advertisers often explicitly directed their products towards decorating homes, especially the reception hall.[58] In addition, various kinds of images were available for purchase in bookstores by century's end. By 1910, Beirut was considered a market for photographic material, and two French companies, one of which was the Société industrielle de photographie, were looking for representation in the city.[59]

There is little indication in the sources of just how widespread portraiture was among the middle class in Beirut before the Mandate period, and available studies look at the middle class and the upper class as one category.[60] But that six of the fifteen studios in the city specialized in portraits suggests that by 1889, taking family and individual portraits was starting to become available to a widening section of society.[61] Living on a tight budget in Beirut in 1898, the Ukrainian Orientalist and novelist Ahatanhel Krymsky remarks that a portrait did not cost much in Beirut, and that it would be cheaper to get several copies of his printed before departing for Russia.[62]

This availability of affordable reproductions indicates an even wider market for photographs in general.

The themes of photographic and other visual reproductions expressed a modern outlook that brought images from the city, the region, and the wider world into the home. Writings on Ottoman photography show its relation to new lifestyles, consumption, and a bourgeois self-image as well as to current notions and symbols of Ottoman progress, reform, and modernity.[63] This underlines how photographs became embedded with meaning through the choice of subject, framing, and representation, with the intention of consciously staging identities. But photography also generated meaning in the contexts in which it was displayed. Specifically in relation to domesticity, images in general not only expressed and represented a modern self but also contributed to constituting it in a domestic setting.

There was certainly an aspect of representation in the images in question, as advertisements suggest that they were used primarily in the main living room or reception hall. Images and photographs were advertised as "home ornamentation" early on, and it did not take long before pictures became an object of concern in advice on home management.[64] But at the same time, photographs were seen as an organic part of the home, with considerable impact on its inhabitants. The content of images in general was regarded as educational material, particularly for the upbringing of children.[65] Consequently, the use of reproduced images became a topic in prescriptive advice about a proper, modern home. Articles in the press criticized the use of images at home in terms of both amount and content, saying, for example: "The pictures [used in decorating the hall] should be of the most valuable and beautiful kind. Two valuable and beautiful pictures are better than many cheap, badly done pictures with inappropriate themes."[66] Other commentators expounded on the subjects deemed appropriate to the overall function of the home as a signifier of taste and as a didactic environment. Preference was given to depictions of famous men, natural scenes, and world locations, due to their instructional value.[67]

At least as far as the choice of subjects was concerned, advice in the press was not completely removed from what was available in Beirut stores. In 1899, Mikha'il Rahmah's bookstore was selling pictures of the four continents of the world, famous people, and the four seasons, as well as themes from

nature and history, "for decorating homes and the reception hall."[68] Around
the same time, Sarafyan Photographers were offering postcards and colored
pictures (photogravures) of historical themes and famous European paintings, whose educational value could scarcely have been criticized.

Entertainment at Home

Changes in the material disposition of the home and its objects were paralleled with new forms of domestic leisure. This took place at a time when a
body of literature was trying to model social activities at home in terms of
a regime of proper and modern behavior. This literature was aimed not just
at new modes of domestic socialization but also at modes that seemed at
odds with civilized behavior, such as prevalent visiting habits. An early article
in the scientific journal *al-Muqtataf* in 1883 criticizes the lower and middle
classes for giving a lot of importance to the refreshments served during visits,
describing coffee, lemonade, and other offerings as incidental for sensible
people, who valued first and foremost good conversation. The article pours
special scorn on the habit of smoking the water pipe:

> What is worse is when the host distracts the visitor with a water pipe or
> the likes of it, sitting across with another water pipe and opening his or her
> mouth only to put the pipe into it, as if the visitor had missed the smell of
> smoke and had come only to get a whiff of it.[69]

Playing card games at home, especially poker, was a form of domestic
entertainment that attracted regular criticism. Along with attention to fashion, gambling elicited anxiety about the economic standing of the middle
class. Concern with poker appears in *al-Muqtataf*, but is picked up more
persistently on the pages of *al-Mahabba*, the Greek Orthodox journal, which
had strong moralizing tendencies.[70] In several articles written between 1900
and 1906, the journal's editorials tie the habit of playing cards to the negative influence of Western civilization, criticizing specifically the middle and
upper classes for being so taken with games such as poker.[71] What was particularly egregious about poker, according to those articles, was that it was
being played at home by women as well as men. Women formed clubs and
regular circles, playing at each other's homes, and gambling their husbands'
hard-earned money to the detriment of their domestic duties and the family

economy. In contrast, one article describes an ideal evening spent at home, where family and neighbors get together, exchanging conversation, engaging in amusing games, and playing musical instruments. Calling these kinds of evenings "old" family evenings, the author contrasts them with the more modern kinds of entertainment that were displacing them, described mockingly as following the zeitgeist and adhering to the demands of fashion (*muwafiqa li-ruh al-'asr wa-mutabiqa li-muqtadayat al-muda*), such as frequenting clubs and playing cards.[72]

Compared to Zaydan's description of his family home in Beirut, writings on entertainment at home at the turn of the century show how within the space of a generation, several new aspects of domestic life were being taken for granted. Domestic spaces tied into new forms of domestic leisure and socialization, and new pieces of furniture influenced how these activities were carried out. Even in *al-Mahabba*'s description of the kind of domestic evening that civilization seeks to abolish, the scene takes place in a home with several rooms, including a reception hall, where guests are welcomed. In descriptions of poker games, players are seated at tables, and they are expected to remain immobile and expressionless on their chairs. Some of the descriptions in these articles indicate sumptuous upper-class settings. Yet, the criticism was directed at the upper and the middle class alike, indicating that the way new spaces and new furniture structured leisure at home also concerned the latter.[73]

One import generating a new space for socialization inside the home was the phonograph. As an announcement in *al-Mahabba* elucidates:

> The use of phonographs has spread to most homes and public places, and people have taken it as a companion in their meetings and evenings. But the modern phonographs brought to you by the store of Jubran Habib al-Shami are preferred over others by those of good taste, and they have come to ask for them with increasing desire [*raghba*]. We have learned that he has received new phonographs of good quality and accuracy. We advise our friends not to miss this chance to acquire one, especially these days when one has to spend evening hours in the company and entertainment of friends and family.[74]

Phonographs occupied a definite place in a constellation of modern practices where taste and class played a defining part. Music as a form of domestic entertainment was nothing new. *Al-Mahabba*'s description of a "simple" evening spent at home in the company of friends, family, and neighbors shows how live music performed by one of the partakers was considered a normal part of socialization.[75] In Ahatanhel Krymsky's description of the domestic entertainment of the upper-class Trad family, there were also improvised musical sessions: "They get together in the evenings and sing Egyptian songs. They sing like a choir with unbearably annoying voices." Krymsky was also present at a more expensive form of this entertainment: "I attended a musical gathering once where an Egyptian singer in Asian clothes sat in the middle of the room with listeners of the wealthy classes gathered around him. They pretended to take him lightly but were learning from him how to sing."[76]

Coupled with the growth of a record industry in Arabic music in the early twentieth century, phonographs brought a kind of entertainment previously reserved for the wealthy classes—one centered on listening to professional singers—to the homes of the emerging middle class. Various outlets offered *ifranji* and Turkish music, but the two most popular forms of music in Beirut were Egyptian and *Shami*, or Syrian, songs. Strongest in Egypt, the regional record industry popularized contemporary Egyptian singers such as Sheikhs Salama Hijazi, Yusuf al-Manyalawi, and Sayyid al-Safti.[77] But the founding of the Baidaphon Company by the Bayda family of Beirut, and the opening of its first outlet on Burj Square in Beirut around 1907, also brought local talent, such as singer Faraj Allah Bayda and singer and buzuq player Muhyi al-Din Baʿyun, to a wider local and regional audience.[78] A 1906 publication of sheet music for the piano, by Wadiʿ Sabra, who would later compose the Lebanese national anthem, lists some songs that were popular at the time, at least among those who could play the piano. They originated from the region and ranged in genre from an "Oriental March" to *muwashshahat* (pl. of *muwashshah*), a musical form based on strophic poetry in classical Arabic.[79]

Between 1900 and 1910, there were at least four stores selling phonographs in Beirut and at least three watchmakers who offered to repair them. The agent for Edison phonographs in the Levant, located in Suq al-Jamil, was suffering competition from other sellers who were passing their phonographs off as Edison machines, and a local singer called Filib Shushani, who had produced records with Edison, had to put out an announcement explaining that his records were available only through the Edison store. Records were available at affordable prices. The same Filib Shushani, along with a busi-

ness partner, Shukri Sawda, started a record-exchange program offering those
"bored with the music they have" the chance to replace their worn-out records
with new ones for one franc, or around five and a half Ottoman piasters.[80]

Many members of the middle class were willing to invest in new commodities that generated a new kind of socialization around them and
indicated an upward social mobility. These domestic entertainments paralleled changing modes of leisure in the public sphere, such as strolling in
parks while decked out in the latest fashion, riding in carriages, frequenting
clubs, and listening to phonographs at cafés. While public pleasures were
subject to criticisms from moralizers, the changes instigated by such objects
at home took on a gendered dimension. In the case of poker, *al-Mahabba*'s
articles focused primarily on how women's poker games came at the expense
of their domestic duties. But the specific vulnerability of the home was that it
was removed from public view and could nurture modes of socialization that
would have been frowned upon had they occurred in public. While authors
of articles in *al-Mahabba* were unfazed by gatherings of men and women,
this was a particularly sensitive issue where the Hanafi court was concerned.
In that context, new objects bore with them the threat of generating domestic socialization that lay beyond the court's purview and upset its procedures.

A Useless Instrument of Pleasure

Many of the new commodities entering the possessions of men and women
appeared in marital disputes and litigation proceedings in the Hanafi court. As
freestanding, as opposed to built-in, items of furniture and other commodities
increased inside the home, many were categorized along familiar gender lines.
A rise in the number of kitchen utensils, linens, and personal items suggests
that women became more invested in their roles as wives, a role underlined by
the trousseaus (*jihaz*) they brought into their marriages. But kitchen utensils
were not exclusively the domain of the woman. The man was becoming more
materially involved in domestic life through the acquisition of fancy objects
for the purpose of fulfilling his role as host, such as porcelain and crystal wares,
as well as bedroom items, such as dressers and metal bedsteads, which were
rarely contested by a wife in marital disputes. Although at the turn of the
century metal bedsteads were a relatively recent entry in a man's list of possessions, they present a case where the gendered division of possessions in the

Hanafi court was actually reinforced through novelty. Before the spread of elevated beds, mattresses could equally well belong to men or to women and were open to contestation at court.[81] With the entry of metal bedsteads, the bedroom remained a mixed space as far as court representations were concerned, but the ownership of some of its possessions was rigidified. Bedding that constituted part of a woman's trousseau was renamed *taqm takht* (bed set) to complement the entry of the bed into the male's possession.[82]

A typical marital case would normally be initiated by the woman in order to demand from her husband her dower, alimony, a legal abode (*maskan shar'i*), or the delivery of her possessions if they were not living together. Although court procedures were fairly predictable, her aim would be more difficult to gauge and could be one of many. She could really be demanding to have her possessions back, or she could be using them in order to push for an improvement in existing marital conditions. She might, for example, have been displeased with the cramped living quarters shared with the husband's family, and opted to use the court to demand the *maskan shar'i* that was her legal right. When not the direct cause of a plaintiff's seeking the arbitration of the Hanafi court, objects were often part of the process of bargaining, claims, and counterclaims. Since many of the possessions brought to court fell along clear gender divides, they often functioned as chips in the bargaining process, brought forth to counter the demands of the other party.

Judges at the Hanafi court were usually open to reaching compromises when they would lead to the restoration of normal marital relations through the payment of dower, assurances of a *maskan shar'i*, or the return of possessions to their rightful owners. In the last case, the judge's job was made easier by the fact that ownership of the objects brought for contestation normally fell along clear gender lines. In the process, both the plaintiff and the defendant were asked to summon witnesses who could testify to their version of the story. This process most often ended by either granting the woman pocket money until the husband supplied a legal home or by supporting the husband's demand to have his wife join him in their marital home should the latter be judged by the court to be up to standard.

But things did not always go smoothly. One case in particular, revolving around a phonograph, deserves specific attention because it ties together many of the various threads of argument in this chapter. One spring day in 1910, a pregnant woman called Hasiba appeared in person before the court to demand that her husband pay the remainder of her dowry, a standard beginning to a standard court case. Her husband, Yusuf, an employee of the tramway company, decided to bargain and demanded that his wife return his phonograph and sixteen records or their value in cash, which amounted to more than he owed her. What normally ensued in such cases was a tallying back and forth of claims and counterclaims, followed by a request for witnesses for the claimant and for the defendant, and culminating in a piecemeal solution.

Yusuf, probably thinking that bringing the phonograph and records in would improve his bargaining position, must have reasoned that his wife would not contest the phonograph, an object that clearly had nothing to do with her claims in the marriage. The court would normally be interested in pursuing this line of development, which is why what happened next was unusual. The judge refused to take Yusuf's deposition into account and ruled categorically in Hasiba's favor, granting her the remainder of her dowry, alimony from her husband, and effectively, by not addressing Yusuf's claim to the objects in her possession, the phonograph and the sixteen records. The judge based this ruling on the fact that "a phonograph is an instrument of pleasure and music [*tarab*] with no value whatsoever, and it deserves to be broken."[83]

In reality, it was neither the phonograph's being an instrument of pleasure nor its uselessness that triggered that moment of institutional wrath. In its dealing with marital and inheritance cases, the court dealt regularly with "instruments of pleasure" such as playing cards and jewelry. Nor was there something intrinsic in the phonograph itself that rendered it inadmissible in a court of law. In a Muslim inheritance case from the same year, an American phonograph together with thirty records was admitted into the case without so much as the raising of a scribal eyebrow. Neither were the phonograph and its records in that case of "no value whatsoever," for they were estimated at 1,700 piasters, a little more than a sixth of the total value of the inherited objects.[84] In addition, while there is no clear interdiction against music, the stronger interdiction against alcohol did not cause a similar scene at court when a set of "alcohol glasses" were entered as part of a Christian inheritance case.[85] Neither was it the phonograph's foreignness that provoked the judge, since other imports, such as sewing machines, caused no trouble at the court.

The judge's objection to the phonograph as "a useless instrument of plea-sure" can be better understood by exploring how the instrument's significance in its social context enabled it to upset the usual procedure of a marital court case. That the case of Hasiba and Yusuf was a marital dispute between two Muslim individuals in a Muslim court of law naturally presents certain limi-tations to using it to understand the impact of objects on the home. At the same time, it would be difficult to fully understand what the phonograph meant for that particular court case without locating it in the larger field of consumption practices revolving around the home. The increase in household furniture as well as the layout and conception of the home itself all played an important role in making the phonograph not just another acquisition but an *instrumental* acquisition. In the context of the court, this meant that in addition to a function or a use-value, the phonograph was sufficiently laden with significance to turn a highly codified, symbolic marital dispute into a real contestation over an emerging gray area.

One of the reasons the phonograph was not easy to pin down at court was the place it occupied in social life. A French trade report from 1901 mentions "the natives' taste for American phonographs, which are widespread, it seems, in the Harems."[86] *Harem* was often used to indicate areas in any household, be it Muslim or non-Muslim, shielded from outside view and from male visitors. But if this observation seems exaggerated or indicative of the availability of phonographs only to the wealthy, there are other indications that in the de-cade before World War I, phonographs were becoming more widespread. Lewis Gaston Leary, who taught at the Syrian Protestant College for three years in the 1900s decade, explains what it was about Beirut that made it feel like a European city if one were coming from Mount Lebanon, Damascus, or Jerusalem: "Gaudy billboards extol the virtues of French cosmetics, Eng-lish insurance companies and American sewing machines, phonographs and shoes, or announce the subjects of the many moving-picture dramas for the coming week."[87] Phonographs, in other words, were being advertised along with some of the most popular commodities of the time.

Moreover, the two cases described here involving phonographs—the marital case and the inheritance case—show that different classes of phono-graphs were available in Beirut. Although the American phonograph in the inheritance case, most likely an Edison, cost 900 piasters, the phonograph claimed by Yusuf cost less. The 838 piasters claimed for the phonograph along with the sixteen records amounted to less than half the advance dowry he claimed to have paid his wife, a standard 2,000 piasters. As an employee of the tramway company, Yusuf probably enjoyed a regular monthly income. The alimony estimated by the court also suggests that his employment with the tramway company was not menial in nature, placing him lower than a high-ranking government employee but higher than a policeman or self-employed grocer on the court's alimony scale.[88] So while buying a phonograph would have been a substantial investment for a man of middling means such as Yusuf, it was not out of his reach.

Phonographs also tied Beirut to a world that went far beyond it. While some advertisements for phonographs placed them definitively in the context of a modern, industrial, and globalizing world by linking them to factories and world expositions, phonographs also had categorical links to their immediate context through the music industry. Due to the involvement of Beiruti musicians and composers in a growing industry in regional and local music, music played on phonographs constituted a cultural product that could be regarded neither as imported nor as local.

This tension between the phonograph's belonging to a wider context and the possibility of domesticating it found poetic expression in the advertisements of 'Abd al-Karim Fadil, announcing the availability of a number of apparently unrelated products:

> He who wishes to please his ears with delightful [mutriba] songs in all languages according to the new model, to learn all kinds of tailorship and embroidery, and regain youth after white hair has set in, let him come to my store, located under the Military Hospital, to find phonographs, [sewing] machines, and the famous Parisian hair dye in all colors.[89]

By advertising these commodities in connection with each other, Fadil transformed their significance from simply domestic objects to signifiers of taste and fashionable imports.

Like phonographs, sewing machines were also becoming more widespread in Beirut in the decade before World War I. But while some advertisements placed phonographs squarely in the context of novelties and new technologies, by the turn of century, sewing machines were already

Figure 6. Advertisements for Columbia and Edison phonographs, the latter warning buyers of imitations. Sold at Au Gant Rouge, the Columbia phonograph is advertised on the basis of the award it received at the 1900 Paris Fair. The Edison store in Suq al-Jamil advertised both Egyptian and *ifranji* records. Source: *Lisan al-Hal,* 30 December 1900, 1 May 1901.

اعلان

من مخزن فونوغرافات
اديسون

اخذ البعض يبيعون الفونوغرافات
منتحلين لها اسم اديسون قاصدين بذلك
ترويج بضاعتهم حذراً من الغش نعلن
للعموم ان كل فونوغراف لا يوجد عليه
اسم اديسون المخترع الاصلي المشهور كما
هو في المثال اعلاه بعد مقلد . وكل من
رام اقتناء فونوغراف جيد جامع بين
حسن الصوت الطبيعي ومتانة آلاته
الفولاذية المكفولة من صنع اديسون
فليشرف مخزن فونوغرافات اديسون في
سوق الجبل قرب البوسطة العثمانية حيث
يجد من الاساطين (سيلاندرات) المأخوذة
عن احسن اجواق مصر ومطربيها و كذلك
اساطين افرنجية من معمل اديسون

"domesticated" and being sold as products intended "for the needs of families," and it was not unusual for them to be included in a woman's dower.[90]
Thus, while the context of the home was a redeeming factor in the case of the
sewing machine, as was its lack of an association with a specific mode of socialization, the phonograph's history in the region reveals a strong association
with the context of the café. Indeed, in order to attract customers, some cafés
bought phonographs. 'Umar Salih al-Barghuti, who as a fourteen-year-old
was sent from Palestine to study at the Ottoman *sultaniyya* school in Beirut
in 1907, remarks on the ubiquitous presence of phonographs in cafés there.[91]

Taking all this together, the phonograph brought into Hasiba and Yusuf's
court case would have appeared to the court to be an ambiguous object, one
that belonged to a valuation system revolving around modernity and taste.
Thus, it was difficult to find a place for it in a marital court case. Equally important, it was also suspected of generating the kind of socialization that escaped
the court's purview and, perhaps, even threatened it.[92] It is within this context
that the judge's description of the phonograph as "useless" can be better understood. Unlike Singer sewing machines and metal bedsteads, it brought into
the court a blend of domestic socialization and consumption for pleasure that
clashed with the existing legal framework governing marital relationships.

In addition to underlining the potential for new objects to transform
social relations around them, the case of the phonograph also points to a
connection between changing tastes and the position of the middle class.
Many of the commodities entering the home served not only to project class
standing but also to negotiate social relations between classes and within the
middle class itself. Changing tastes and new domestic commodities engendered novel kinds of relationships between the home and the city, the region,
and a world increasingly linked by new technologies, economies, and means
of transport. Objects are significant in this regard because they opened up a
field where a body of literature on the home could make use of the possibilities commodities brought with them to put forth an ideal of the relationships
between classes. This is exactly what happened, as we shall see in the next
chapter. Given how laden with meaning some commodities were, taste was
more than an individual matter.

(CHAPTER 5)

A MATTER OF TASTE

No matter how humble and poor a woman is and no matter the
defaults of society, especially in the Orient where woman's freedom
is constrained and her rights are usurped, she is still able to claim
her rule at home and to use her reign in order to spread happiness
and bliss amongst her dear subjects.

Esther Moyal[1]

Historiography usually places the history of domesticity squarely in the context of Western modernity, as an ideal with roots in late eighteenth-century
England and, later, France and North America.[2] At the same time, this localized story of origins is in tension with the rapid spread of ideas about the
home in the course of the nineteenth century, particularly with the rises in
levels of literacy in that period, the development of international markets,
and the globalization of tastes in domestic commodities. From Egypt and
India to Japan and Sweden, a common vocabulary took form and the idea of
"home" became key for an emerging middle class intent on cultivating proper
attitudes that defined it both politically and socially.[3]

Despite the many similarities in a globally constructed discourse of domesticity, the fact that it placed the transformation of society at its heart also
meant that it was open to interpretation, depending on the context where it
was employed. Because of its open-endedness, domesticity became a vehicle
through which disparate ambitions were expressed across geographical and
political boundaries. Middle-class groups, particularly, capitalized on current
notions of domesticity in order to give expression to new ideas about modes
of governance, national aspirations, and women's role in society. Not least,
due to an autonomous vision of the ideal home that was nevertheless linked
to the social order through politics, class, and economy, home had much to
do with articulating a relationship between the public and private spheres.[4]

In late Ottoman Beirut, the ambiguous position the home occupied in the legal system meant that it was an exemplary place to formulate a political project predicated on the participation of the middle class in the modern political order. In the voices of both men and women writing in the press and lecturing at schools and societies, the home acquired a very specific meaning, contrasting strongly with the uncertain position it occupied in the legal framework guiding the city's renewal. As a place where new ideas of citizenship could be formulated, the home brought together ideals of motherhood, the nuclear family, middle-class ethics, norms of consumption, and Oriental authenticity. With wider access to consumption among middling groups, the home was also rapidly filling with new commodities, and ordering those acquisitions along distinctly middle-class lines began to preoccupy the literature on home management. Of the various concepts put forth in the press, *taste* served the most immediate purpose of marking out a place for the emerging middle class that distinguished it from the wealthy, on the one hand, and from European or Western (*ifranji*) influence, on the other.

The issue at stake is not that taste is a construct, but rather how taste and the societal order to which it belonged shaped each other.[5] While the generalized principles of urban planning entered the discourse of domesticity as standards of order, hygiene, and scientific management, taste served to restore particularity to the home. With taste under consideration, the category of class also came to the fore as an object of public debate. The discourse of domesticity was often explicitly addressed to *mutawassitu al-ḥal* (those of middling means). That term was also used in the Hanafi court to determine the financial needs of plaintiffs and defendants in alimony cases. The debate on domesticity layered onto the term's economic aspect the cultural and political characteristics of middle-class modernity.

Following Pierre Bourdieu's view of the intellectual class as the dominated segment of the upper class, I see the attempt by intellectuals and public commentators to reposition themselves at the vanguard of an emerging middle class as a reconfiguration of class difference along new lines.[6] Through governance at home, the home materialized as the place where the middle class could not only articulate a political place for itself but also define itself culturally. This particularity was, nevertheless, defined in connection with a wider global setting.

A claim to a localized "Oriental" identity strove for a particularized modernity at the same time that it continued to embody a wider, late nineteenth-century understanding of progress. The home constituted the arena where such a modernity could be appropriated and practiced.

A Woman's Place

In a speech to al-Jam'iyya al-Urtuduksiyya al-Khayriyya (the Greek Orthodox Benevolent Society) in Tripoli on 3 June 1910, Julia Tu'ma (1883–1954), a schoolteacher in Beirut and frequent contributor to various periodicals, defined her concept of "the first heaven" to her mostly female audience as

> the "home," the miserable hut, if you wish—one room with a kitchen to its side. The abode of the family of which you are at the center. The home whose management has been given to you and the little kingdom over which God made you queen.[7]

Tu'ma urged the women present to demand that their home be called "heaven" from that day on, for what is usually understood by the word "home" is "what the builder builds with stone and mortar and what is added to that by the carpenter, such as doors and wood." To signify what is beyond this physical description of *bayt*, Tu'ma specifically used the English word *home*, to evoke a place that constitutes "a shelter for the woman, a kingdom for the mother, a place of jollity for the man, a promenade for the father, and a pasture of well-being and joy for the children."

Although many of the concepts she addressed in her speech were directly influenced by notions of the Victorian English home, Tu'ma grounded her topic in specificities to which her contemporaries would have related. At a time of increasing emigration she evoked the image of a migrant shedding tears at parting with her homeland and the beauty of its nature:

> [She] pass[es] through Paris and London and see[s] enough of the wonders of the world and the greatness of man to confuse the mind and steal the heart and yet says "despite its lowliness, my country [*biladi*] is more beautiful than all this." In truth, what you mean by your country is your home, and it is more beautiful than all this.

She then addressed the woman who prays and hopes for the afterlife and yet feels a sense of desperation and boredom with her worldly duties, saying: "You, my lady, have been created for a nobler and higher end. You have been created not to dream about the future homeland [i.e., heaven], but to better the first [i.e., your home] in order to inherit the second."

The idea of "homeland" appeared again not long afterwards, linking woman's advancement to a concomitant advancement experienced by the greater homeland:

> Cafés, gaming houses, and streets have become paragons of order and their administrators have made a bizarre art of making them appealing to men. A race and war should be declared between you and those [administrators], in order that you turn the home into a place where your husband and children like to spend time and relax.

At the center of these images of exile, piety, and order stands the mistress of the house, the addressee of Tuʿma's speech. She stands simultaneously at the threshold of her home and the threshold of a world widened by emigration to the Americas and Europe and enriched by an increasing cultural awareness of the capitals of Europe. In the face of this delocalization and the modernization of public life, her task and challenge is to match, even compete with, these changes through her management of the home. The dichotomy between the growing appeal of public space and the offerings of the home outlines the challenge that lies ahead for her and all women living in a rapidly changing Beirut. Tuʿma further stressed this dichotomy by distinguishing between European influence on women's public appearance and the need for them to pursue their civilizational duties at home. Many in her educated audience, she continued, were no longer distinguishable from European women in appearance and dress "in meetings and parties, on streets and roads, and in all places outside the home. But how are you inside your home, O refined, educated one?"[8]

Born in 1882 in the village of Mukhtara in the Shuf region to a family that had recently converted to Protestantism, Tuʿma led a life that challenged the boundaries of gender and religion for her time. Educated by Protestant missionaries, she taught in Shafa ʿAmru in Palestine and Brummana in Mount Lebanon before moving to Beirut, where she accepted Salim ʿAli

Salam's proposal to become academic administrator of the Maqasid Islamic School for girls.[9] At that time, Salam was president of Jam'iyyat al-Maqasid al-Khayriyya al-Islamiyya (the Maqasid Islamic Benevolent Society), which had founded the school, and he was one of the staunchest promoters of girls' education in the Muslim community. In Beirut, Tu'ma also met the man who was to become her husband, Badir Dimashqiyya, member of a notable Sunni Beiruti family and Salam's friend and associate. Given the controversial nature of their cross-sectarian marriage, they took the relatively mixed neighborhood of Ras Beirut, where the Syrian Protestant College was located, as their home.[10] After World War I, Tu'ma Dimashqiyya went on to found the woman's magazine al-Mar'a al-Jadida (The New Woman) in 1921, and between 1915 and 1925, her "salon" formed the base for Jam'iyyat al-Sayyidat (the Women's Society).[11]

This remarkable life exemplified in practice a discursive shift in the understanding of the home in the half century that preceded Tu'ma's speech and an accompanying reconceptualization of women's role in society. This took place in intellectual circles across the region and, as Afsaneh Najmabadi argues, it transformed the house into a social space of citizenship.[12] Initially under the influence of leading reformists and gradually across wider sections of society, an increasing conviction that the education of women was necessary for "progress" and "catching up" with the West reconfigured the woman from "house"—part of a domestic domain subject to the management of man—to "manager of the house."[13] The discursive transition from premodern to modern hinged strongly on the position of women in society, and the home, as the space of the woman and the family and a citizen's "first school," became the target of reform attempts and the subject of textbooks on domestic science and proper education and upbringing (tarbiya).[14]

If the interest in the home in Beirut could be traced back to a specific date, then it would be 14 December 1849, when Butrus al-Bustani delivered his subsequently renowned speech on the education of women at al-Jam'iyya al-'Ilmiyya al-Suriyya (the Syrian Scientific Society). Al-Bustani argued that because a woman was an organic member of society, woman's education brought benefits not only to the woman herself but also, through her influence on the family, to society as a whole. Without an educated wife, "the home would be like a forlorn prairie to the man, his life would be troubled and disturbed, his home without any order, organization, and cleanliness, and his children left to the care of chance and nature." He continued: "For there is no small family or large kingdom where woman does not exert the greatest influence.... What makes people barbarians or civilized, religious or infidels, evil or good, learned or ignorant, etc. is the woman."[15]

Over the next two decades, the debate on women's education and its importance to the advancement of a nation gained momentum. Female writers began to contribute to publications such as *al-Jinan* and *Lisan al-Hal*, and both men and women stressed the need for women's education and its importance to a happy family and a prosperous home. A short story in the very first issue of *al-Jinan* (1870–1886), a bimonthly founded by al-Bustani, presents the character of Maryam, a housewife who miraculously turns the family's life around when her stingy husband, Ibrahim, accidentally gives her a considerable sum of money and leaves her alone with the children for a week.[16] While he is away on business, Maryam pays her debts, replenishes domestic provisions, renews the furniture, carries out reparations, and repaints the house. She goes to the souk and buys clothes for herself and the family, as well as toys for the children, and prepares a nice dinner around which the family gathers happily—a sight sufficient to cure Ibrahim of his miserliness. This and other articles and stories presented models of family happiness revolving around a conjugal family with a housewife capable of managing the home while the husband toiled in the outside world.

Governing the Minutiae of Modernity

The earliest systematic translation of domestic discourse into practice came at the hands of Shahin Makariyus and two young lecturers at the Syrian Protestant College in Beirut, Faris al-Nimr and Ya'qub Sarruf. Not long after they had founded the scientific literary journal, *al-Muqtataf* (1876–1952), they introduced the *fawa'id baytiyya* (domestic benefits) section, which in the space of a few years turned into the long-surviving regular section *bab al-tadbir al-manzili* (home management).[17] This section provided practical advice geared towards scientific management of the home and, together with the *bab al-munazara wa-l-murasala* (correspondence and debate) section, constituted an arena for debating the role of women at home and, by extension, in wider society. The debate drew in an increasing number of female writers, turning *al-Muqtataf* into one of the earliest publications with regular contributions by women.[18] Even after *al-Muqtataf*'s move to Egypt in 1884, the debate continued on its pages, attracting a regular readership from the various cities and towns in Syria, Palestine, and Egypt.[19]

Al-Muqtataf was a trendsetter in more ways than one, and a better understanding of its particular interest in home management can be gained by looking at the overall aims stated in the introduction to the first issue: to make science and industry practicable and attainable to the nonspecialist in order to cultivate the scientific spirit seen as the *sine qua non* of progress and the betterment of the homeland (*watan*).[20] While this idea was not unique to this journal, *al-Muqtataf*'s format and content were particularly successful in turning this abstract vision into a practice grounded in the realities of everyday life in the region. *Al-Muqtataf* did this, first, by providing a didactic explanation of natural and scientific phenomena both theoretically and as they manifested themselves in its readers' everyday lives. It also encouraged experimentation through do-it-yourself science—such as its "home chemistry" (*al-kimya' al-baytiyya*) experiment series—and stimulated reader participation through its "questions and answers" and "correspondence and debate" sections.

Central to the idea of making progress attainable, according to the journal, was the management of the minutiae (*sagha'ir*) of everyday life. An early article titled "The Profligacy of the East and the Management of the West" argued that the success of the West lay in its ability to turn refuse into industry and waste into luxurious products. Rather than focus on scientific and industrious feats that would "throw the reader into despair because of their unattainability," the editors proposed instead to restrict themselves "to showing how Westerners [*ifranj*] and others manage their minutiae, in the hope that it would lead the readers into improving the means of luxury in the country."[21]

The home management section was one facet of these minutiae, on a par with other sections in the journal such as those addressing agriculture, industry, mathematics, and engineering. It provided practical advice based on scientific explanations and on the environmental and actual conditions in which most readers found themselves. What differentiated home management from these other sections was not only that its writers were mostly women but also that its articles were often addressed to the housewife. By looking at the governance of household minutiae and demystifying the scientific processes that surrounded the home, *al-Muqtataf* attempted to introduce women to and involve them in a scientific form of home management that was seen as crucial to the progress of the nation. The audience envisaged for such a section was the well-educated woman who could read; who had a basic grasp of the sciences; and who, through an application of these methods at home, would be able to function as the necessary link between the small unit of the family and the larger societal context. The envisaged female reader was, in other words, Butrus al-Bustani's educated woman.

The reach of such ideas was extended regionally by the burgeoning literary and philanthropic societies found in cities from Beirut to Zahla in the east and from Sidon in the south to Homs and Baynu in the north. These societies included Ghuraf al-Qira'a (Reading Rooms), Bakurat Suriyya (Dawn of Syria), Shams al-Birr (Sun of Righteousness), Zahrat al-Ihsan (Flower of Charity), and Yaqdhat al-Fatat al-'Arabiyya (Awakening of the Arab Girl) in Beirut, Ghuraf al-Qira'a (Reading Rooms) in Bhamdun, Nur al-'Afaf wa-l-Islah (Light of Virtue and Reform) in Homs, al-Khayriyya al-Urtuduksiyya (Orthodox Benevolent Society) in Tripoli, Tahdhib al-Fatat al-Suriyya (Edification of the Syrian Girl) in Shuwayfat, and Yadd al-Musa'da (Helping Hand) in Baynu in the 'Akkar region.[22] Several of the lectures delivered at meetings of these societies were reprinted for the benefit of a larger audience, as were lectures delivered by prominent Syrian intellectuals in Cairo, Alexandria, and Tanta.

The sphere of activities encompassed by literary and philanthropic societies also became a point of entry for many women into the public world of podiums, lectures, and work. One of the earliest of the literary societies, Bakurat Suriyya (Dawn of Syria), was founded in Beirut in 1880 by Maryam Nimr Makariyus and Yaqut Barakat Sarruf, the wives of two of the founders of *al-Muqtataf*.[23] Some of this society's lectures were published in the home management section of *al-Muqtataf*, with topics ranging from furnishing homes and proper manners to the structure of "savage" societies.[24] Bakurat Suriyya's societal engagement also went beyond lecturing, showing an effort, however limited, to extend domestic ideas even to illiterate women. Visiting from Egypt in 1890, the merchant 'Abd al-Rahman Sami remarked on the work done by women-run societies. Commenting specifically on Bakurat

Suriyya, he related how one of the society's women opened her home twice a week to needy women of all religious backgrounds and, together with another society member, educated them in home management and the upbringing of children, also reading to them from articles on such topics.[25]

In the years following *al-Muqtataf*'s move to Cairo, several ideas about the home and women were picked up and promulgated by other Beirut-based periodicals and other publications. In addition, Syrian émigrés in Cairo and Alexandria became part of the network through which there was a regular exchange of ideas with the cities of Syria, most notably Beirut. Authors living in Beirut published in Egypt and vice versa, and Egyptian newspapers and periodicals circulated in Beirut, with many of their articles reprinted in the Beiruti press.[26] 'Anbara Salam al-Khalidi describes in her memoirs how she and her fellow students at the Maqasid Islamic School for girls used to wait impatiently for periodicals from Egypt, such as *al-Muqtataf*, *al-Hilal*, and *al-Zuhur*.[27]

Education on domesticity, particularly for girls, constituted a further link between the intellectuals of Syria and Egypt. The home became a central trope in school textbooks in Egypt and was used "as a symbol through which stories about history, the nation, and modernity were told."[28] Textbooks on morality and home economics, many authored by Syrian Christian men, emphasized the connection between the individual, the home, and the nation and sought to create educated mothers who could actively participate in forging a healthy nation through their management of the family and the household. Although these textbooks were aimed mainly at Egyptian students, intellectuals in Beirut followed these developments and some of the topics found their way into schools in Beirut. Around the same time that the topic of "object lessons" (*durus al-ashya'*) constituted part of the Egyptian Ministry of Culture's curriculum, it was also being taught at the British Syrian Training College in Beirut. A teacher training school for women, the college had 3,108 students by 1914 and provided most of the teachers for the Protestant missions until the mid-twentieth century.[29] Such lessons were aimed at girls expected to become teachers themselves, and were meant to educate them in the proper management of the home and its things.[30]

The home had an explicitly political resonance both for the Ottoman Constitutionalists in Greater Syria and for the nationalists struggling under

the British occupation of Egypt. During the burgeoning period of pedagogi-
cal literature on the home, the intellectual atmosphere in occupied Egypt
allowed for more politically explicit expressions of ideas than would have
been feasible in Beirut under Abdülhamid II. After *al-Muqtataf*'s move to
Egypt, different modes of political governance were used in the journal as al-
legories of relations within the home. The home was frequently referred to as
a kingdom, and one article even compared the woman to a minister of finance
and the man to a prime minister to explain their respective roles.[31] Beirut,
in contrast, suffered under the press regulations of Sultan Abdülhamid II,
which restricted any references to the constitutional models popularly used
in the Egyptian press for elucidating domestic relations.[32]

The relaxation of press censorship following the Young Turk Revolution of 1908 precipitated an explosion in the number of periodicals in Beirut,
including the appearance of the first women's magazine in Greater Syria, *al-
Hasna'* (1909–1912). Its founder, Jurji Niqula Baz (1881–1959), was nicknamed
by his contemporaries *nasir al-mar'a* (champion of women). A doctor and a
graduate of the Syrian Protestant College, Baz was one of the main personages in the intellectual network of the Eastern Mediterranean and a regular
contributor to periodicals based in Egypt such as *al-Hilal* and *al-Muqtataf*.[33]
Before the founding of *al-Hasna'*, he had contributed writings on the rights
of women to various publications, including Labiba Hashim's *Fatat al-Sharq*
in Cairo and the Greek Orthodox *al-Mahabba* in Beirut, and went on to
publish books on women and women's rights, including *Iklil Ghar li-Ra's al-
Mar'a* (Laurel Wreath on Woman's Head), *Nazik 'Abid* (a biography of 'Abid,
a Syrian Muslim woman and activist), and *al-Nisa'iyyat* (Feminist Discourse).

Baz published the first issue of *al-Hasna'* in June 1909, less than a year
after the first elections to the Ottoman parliament since 1877 and a few
months after the deposition of Abdülhamid II. Enthusiasm for the Young
Turk Revolution and the promises of constitutionalism it carried with it became apparent in the speeches and lectures published in *al-Hasna'*, not least in
the use of the home as a model for self-governance and for the participation
of male and female members of society in the modern political order. An address to Jam'iyyat Tahdhib al-Fatat al-Suriyya (the Society for the Edification
of the Syrian Girl) in Shuwayfat, printed in the magazine in 1910, compares
the home to a kingdom where man and woman share the rule, with the man

running the affairs of the exterior and the woman running those of the interior.[34] Another address to Jam'iyyat Yadd al-Musa'ada (the Helping Hand
Society) in Baynu contrasts the despotic times of Abdülhamid II—when "the
man was absolute master, behaving at home the way Abdülhamid II behaved
at court"—to the present-day home where "the family has become a real
constitutional kingdom ruled over by the man and the woman, who lead it according to the rules of council and law, both divine and natural."[35] Here again,
one can see how a political ideal of the home was cemented and propagated
through the mutual reinforcement of the press in Beirut and the regional
societies; al-Hasna' published speeches that were delivered at the podiums of
these societies but that also had a larger, reading audience in mind.

Despite common themes, the opinions expressed on the home and the
position of women within it were by no means homogeneous. There were
disagreements about the extent to which women should be educated, some
arguing that education in home management was being sacrificed to less
necessary mathematical and linguistic skills. While some clamored for
greater equality and engagement in public life for women, there were also
complaints about how woman's growing public role compromised her management of the home. Some went even so far as to place the blame for the
ruin of homes squarely on women's shoulders.[36]

Notwithstanding the variations in this lively exchange, the emerging
contours served to frame the home as an object of debate and as a central
ground where abstract notions of society, civic duty, and progress could be
translated into everyday practice. Various arguments clearly point to the
entry of women into the public debate, both as its objects and as its active
participants. Even when women were not seen to bear sole responsibility for
the advancement of society, their education and their status were often perceived as the sign, the litmus test, by which a whole nation could be judged.
A growing belief in the importance of early education for children only emphasized the importance of educating women so that they could, as mothers,
raise proper citizens. The home became doubly important in that context,
both as the child's first school and as the mirror of society.[37] The result was
that the home became a central site of reform, and the woman, through her
behavior and her responsibilities, was open to constant critique in the press,
more so than the man. As active participants in the public debate, women

would lash back at this, as we will see later in this chapter in the debate on fashion and domestic duties in *al-Mahabba*.

Taste and Those of Middling Means

The consolidation of the home as an object of public debate was linked to the emergence of the home as an object of consumption. As new mass-produced imports and other new commodities began entering the home, ordering those objects in accordance with proper middle-class taste began to constitute an important aspect of the literature on home management. This also went hand in hand with an expansion in the advertising industry. Towards the end of the century, advertisements began presupposing the home was a target for their wares. The ideal home put forth in advertisements was one made complete by furniture and textiles and adorned by ornamentation. As advertisements increased in complexity, they also began creating "needs" for homes and families.

The growing interest in commodities as constituents of an idealized domesticity precipitated giving objects an identifiable order at home. Short articles in *al-Muqtataf* with headings such as "Ordering the Home," "Ordering Photographs," and "Ordering the Dining Table" gave clear instructions on arranging objects. Recommendations addressing the journal's middle- and upper-class readership ranged from the most general, such as overseeing a household with many servants, to the most detailed, such as placing a separate plate for discarded olive pits at the dinner table. Much of the advice was explicitly directed at the middle class, while other articles that put an emphasis on moderation and the fragile family economy implied such a readership. Centering on homemade solutions and supplying technical know-how in household management, they aimed at reducing household expenses for "those of middling means" (*mutawassitu al-hal*).[38]

The notion of order (*tartib*), at once general and specific, became a dominant organizing principle for the management of daily life at home. An article in *al-Muqtataf* is more explicit about what is meant by *tartib*:

[E]very piece of furniture at home should be either useful or beautiful. Nothing should be put in the home unless it serves the first purpose, the second, or both at the same time. Something that is ugly should not be put in the home at all even if it is useful.[39]

An article in *al-Hasna'* gives a similar perspective:

> For beauty and perfection to rule in the management of the home, it is un-
> avoidable to put each thing in its place and to prepare a place for each thing.
> This is also indispensable to any manageress who wants to find what she is
> looking for time-efficiently and to maintain an organization without disturb-
> ing the contents of a home.[40]

Although the Arabic word *tartib* does not have the other meaning the
English *order* has, as in "to give an order," another word often used in relation to the home, *nizam*, does carry the meaning of organization, or order
imposed from above. Used together, as they often were, *tartib* and *nizam*
indicated the kind of discursive relationship between object and person
around which home literature constructed its arguments. As the home grew
in complexity and order became one of its main organizational elements,
it slowly acquired a system of its own which, in turn, worked its effect on
its inhabitants. Thus, order was perceived not as a "contingent" (*'aradi*) but
as "an essential [*jawhari*] matter that influences the character of a home's
inhabitants the way that different regions of the earth influence the natural
disposition of animals."[41] Hence, an ordered home became more than just a
setting for family life, it also became a primary shaper of the relations that
pervaded it and of the individuals it nurtured.

The emphasis on order and organization echoed the general principles of
urban planning current in Beirut at the time. Yet, for the literature on domesticity, order and organization did not capture all the skills necessary for the
management of a home. For example, in a speech delivered at the Egyptian
University in Cairo and printed in *al-Hasna'*, Labiba Hashim, founder of the
women's magazine *Fatat al-Sharq*, stressed the importance of order and organization, adding: "it is not enough for a woman to know about housework, but
capability and taste are among her first duties."[42] Although predicated upon
order and organization, taste (*dhawq*) comes forth in this last example as a category that embodies something more than these two generalized principles.

Many of the concepts constituting the discourse on domesticity, such as
efficiency and rationality, drew on contemporary developments in industrial
society that touched Beirut only indirectly.[43] But home advice also had another history, feeding on a long tradition of prescriptive manuals on manners

from the days of medieval Islam that were still in vogue in the late Ottoman period. Ayyub bin Musa al-Kafawi's seventeenth-century lexicon, still in
print in nineteenth-century Istanbul and Cairo, reveals the various historical
layers implied by the use of the word *dhawq*. In addition to denoting the
physical sense of taste, lived experience, and an innate aptitude for sciences,
the word also related to the aesthetics of literature, or *adab*.[44] Taste also related to *adab* in the sense of manners, for *adab* "in all its uses reflects a high
valuation of the employment of the will in proper discrimination of correct
order, behavior, and taste."[45]

While medieval manner manuals were originally aimed mainly at the
upper classes, in the late nineteenth and early twentieth centuries, with individuals' wider access to modern commodities, increased literacy, and the
formation of a modern public sphere, the focus of social reformers shifted
from the edification of the elite to concern with a wider audience.[46] This
development can also be observed in Beirut, where advice on domestic
taste was often addressed to *mutawassitu al-hal*. As such, the late Ottoman
palimpsest of *dhawq* became inscribed in the intellectual literature with two
related families of meanings: taste towards others, in issues such as manners and behavior, and taste towards the self, in issues such as dress and
food.[47] In the latter understanding, it also came to be understood in terms of
other contemporary phenomena, such as fashion and ornamentation, and in
terms of an idealized middle-class sensibility revolving around a conscious
self-fashioning modeled upon moderate consumption.[48] Although the constitution of the self as a subject of moral conduct was not new to the cultural
practices the educated were familiar with, it now lent itself to the constitution of a particular class and its particular position in the world.

In contradistinction to order, the variation in tastes between different
cultures and different individuals was considered natural. But if taste was
relative, it remained positively so only within certain boundaries. Taste was
distinguished as either good taste or bad taste, and it also was used to distinguish between lifestyles and between social classes. Although it varied with
a person's makeup and surroundings, taste was still something that could be
cultivated or, in the absence of a proper upbringing, corrupted. Proper exercise and refinement of the perceptive faculties led to the attainment of what
was interchangeably referred to as sound (*salim*) or correct (*sahih*) taste.[49]

Taste as a constituent of cultural capital comes to the fore in a philosophi-
cal essay in *al-Muqtataf* in 1892, authored by Yusuf Shalhut. The very absence
of an Arabic word for "aesthetics" was, according to Shalhut, indicative of the
need to develop certain areas of knowledge in which the *ifranja* were ahead of
the Arabs.[50] In order to elucidate what proper aesthetic appreciation entails,
Shalhut enumerates "the provisions of beauty" as "unity and variation, har-
mony and moderation, order and organization, perfection and elegance, and
the agreement of the parts with the whole and the means with the end."[51]
These conditions, the author argues, endow a thing with beauty by making it
more accessible to the senses and more easily perceived by the mind.

Not entirely incidentally, given the prevalence of taste in discussions on the
home, the author compares two homes to concretely illustrate the relationship
between order, organization, and perfection. In the one that is furnished and
ornamented with cushions and curtains and where objects are placed in their
appropriate positions and go together in terms of size, shape, and color, the
visitor is pleased by the appearance of the home and finds it agreeable to sit in.
In contrast, in a home where the objects are gathered upon each other in an
orderless heap, the visitor's sight tires out, and she finds herself hastening to
leave in order to put an end to "the embarrassment of the eye."[52]

This understanding of taste by turn-of-the-century writers recalls an argument from sociologist Pierre Bourdieu's classic work *Distinction* on how
taste's relationship with its social and economic conditions of production
confers different social identities on objects and people. The place Bourdieu
gives to cultural phenomena takes into account how the conscious and un-
conscious struggles for the maintenance of class boundaries create and are
in turn reinforced by objectified cultural capital. The viewer's ability to place
an object in a wider cultural field, to which she has access through education
and economic status, is what gives that object aesthetic value. In the ability to
decode, understand, and appropriate an object, the capacity to see (*voir*) becomes a function of knowledge (*savoir*).[53] This transforms economic capital
into symbolic capital, whereby perceived differences and distinctive properties become self-defining mechanisms by which a class distinguishes itself,
particularly from the class below it. This translates into a set of aesthetic
principles that manifest themselves in choices of things (such as houses, furniture, paintings, books, and clothes) and practices (such as sports, games,

and entertainments).[54] That such a system of separation and identification was employed in Beirut during the period in question is evinced by the myriad articles organizing objects and practices along lines of economic and educational status.

In contrast to this downward self-demarcation described by Bourdieu, where the working class becomes the negative referencing point at the bottom of the class structure,[55] the references to the poor in the discourse on the home (standing out starkly because there are so few them) often appear to view the poor favorably in comparison with the wealthy. One article argues that the tight rooms of the poor might be an eyesore in terms of appearance, but when cleaned and aired out regularly they can be healthier than the beautiful rooms of the rich, where microbes find an abode under the carpets and in the thick folds of curtains.[56] Similarly, commenting on the impossibility of buying taste, Labiba Hashim contrasts a poor hut that is "beautiful because it is well-ordered and everything is in its place" to a castle that is replete with wealthy furniture and rare feathers but that, nevertheless, lacks sound taste.[57]

The category of taste was used to emphasize the dissociation of value from monetary worth and to stress the importance of proper edification, moderation, and a rationalized economy in an idealized middle-class domesticity. A brief return to Julia Tu'ma's speech on the "first heaven" can begin to unravel taste's link to women, to the nation, and further, to a sense of aesthetics prioritizing moderation and comfort over fashionable appearances. Tu'ma's first advice to the woman who wants to make her home "attractive" to her family is to take care of her appearance "not only when dressed for worship or weddings, not only in honor of the guest or the strange man, but also in honor of your husband and children and in order to get them used to order and beauty."[58]

What could be said about a woman's appearance could also be said about the appearance of the home, and this is Tu'ma's second piece of advice. What is important about a home is not its riches and glamor, but that it has "a motto [shi'ar] or appearance that speaks for the personality of the husband and the spirit of the woman." In contrast, she continues, houses all look the same: "We all follow what is in fashion: sofas in the living room and high chairs half of which stand in one line against the wall. Little do we care for what is cheap and comfortable to sit on."[59]

Willed moderation was not only presented as a defining characteristic of the middle class but, more importantly, as a characteristic that separated it from the upper classes. It fit in snugly with the aesthetics of order, which rejected the useless, and with the idea of scientific economy, which granted the woman control over household expenses. The element of moderation was often used to criticize tasteless wealth. Dissociating taste from wealth was stressed simultaneously with the ability to produce good results in the household independently of the use of money. Instead of reproducing a tasteless display of riches, women were advised by newspapers and journals to offer a rich display of taste, and articles presented various tips on achieving this using homemade solutions and sometimes costless methods. Examples of these methods included creating a picture frame from cardboard and using cups, bowls, and vegetables to create an elaborate dinner table decoration.[60]

By contrast, descriptions of homes lacking in taste were accompanied by a thinly veiled sense of "horror" or "visceral intolerance"[61] towards dull interiors that "tired out the vision" and "exhausted the eye."[62] This was particularly so with wealthy homes. Wealth, as it manifested itself in the ownership of large houses and expensive furniture, did not amount to good taste. An early

Figure 7. Illustration for a homemade dinner table decoration. The left-to-right order of the illustration suggests it was adapted from a foreign language publication. Source: *Al-Muqtataf,* June 1885.

article in *al-Muqtataf* criticizes the dreary interiors of local wealthy homes for their monotony and bareness:

> White and yellow dominated the place; the tables, chairs, and seats were of yellow wood, the cushions on the seats and chairs were predominantly yellow *atlas* [cloth], the frames of windows and mirrors were gilded, and the marble on the floor as well as on the table tops was white. The walls were also white and bare, with no photograph, image, shelf, or any other kind of decoration.[63]

Everything, from the furniture to the walls and from the colors to the ornamentation, failed to offer contrast and difference and brought together incompatible objects and colors. This house failed, in other words, to live up to the dictates of good taste. In contrast, the article then lavishes praise on the home of a European that, by constantly offering new things, all arranged in order and taste that "relaxed the eye," was both appealing to look at and invited contemplation. An example of the novelties offered by a European's home in Beirut can be observed in Qasr Heneiné, where the decoration incorporated Moorish and Oriental architectural motifs that were popular in nineteenth-century Europe and had made their way into indigenous displays at World Fairs.[64]

The contrast with a European home is more explicitly tied to the relationship between proper domesticity and progress in another article from *al-Muqtataf*, after that monthly had moved to Cairo. Contrasting wealth and taste, the article evokes the same dreariness of wealthy houses in the monotonous arrangement of chairs and the blandness of walls covered with wallpaper and mirrors, concluding:

> It is well known that Americans and Europeans have exceeded us in ornamenting their houses and organizing their furniture and that their women take a lot of the credit for it. So, we will not be able to keep up with them in this domain unless our girls learn from those experiences and let this disposition possess their spirits.[65]

When coupled with a criticism of local visitation habits and manners, such as offering jam and water pipes (*narjila*), these comparisons connected to new ideas of domestic leisure that valued comfortable furniture conducive to well-mannered, structured conversation.[66]

In contrast to the attack on tasteless riches, criticism of *mutawassitu al-hal* aimed at edification and the spreading of a moderate, modern aesthetic through the double-edged sword of criticism and prescriptivism. Led by a cultural elite, the spreading of an idealized domesticity was an attempt at recasting class difference and carving out a place for a middle-class culture and wider political participation. Given that the class was seen to be in its formative stages, the appropriation of the category *mutawassitu al-hal* can be understood as an attempt at swelling its ranks through reform and edification. As an anonymous young woman who had preached the domestic gospel to a school colleague wrote to *al-Muqtataf*, her colleague had responded positively and "she has become one of us and is determined to write to you soon."[67]

Imperialism and *Ifranji* Effects

Although Bourdieu's theory of distinction goes a long way in explaining the contours delineating the emergent middle-class domesticity that distinguished itself from the culture of the notables and the wealthy, it stops short of explaining the role *ifranji* culture played in articulating this distinction. Particularly towards the end of the nineteenth century, and under the growing political, economic, and cultural dominance of the industrialized countries of Europe, distinction from the upper classes seems to become insufficient for giving a middle-class particularity to the home or for defining its specific cultural characteristics. At the same time, the idea of *ifranji* begins to play a greater role in defining what this middle-class domesticity entailed.

An adjective originating from *Farang/Faranj* (Frankish), *ifranji* meant "European" in the context of the nineteenth century, but was also used more generally in the sense of "Western."[68] Another derivative of this word, *tafarnuj*, meant "Westernization" or the act of taking after the West. In addition, a person pretending to be like a Westerner would be called *mutafarnij* (male) or *mutafarnija* (female), an adjectival form evoking a superficial likeness. These permutations found expression in the changing aspects of everyday life in late Ottoman Beirut. The adjective *ifranji* was used to describe the new ways that people dressed, what they ate, how they behaved, and how they furnished their homes. But these descriptives were not devoid of negative connotations.

Another look at *al-Muqtataf* reveals the stakes involved in the debate on the place of Europe in Beirut's local modernity. Thomas Philipp's claim that this periodical's editors embraced European modernity as a holistic model for their society glosses over the conflicted and changing relationship *al-Muqtataf* had with European modernity throughout its many decades.[69] This relationship often broke out in a trenchant criticism of the very ground this modernity was laid on. "Al-Tamaddun wa-l-Tawahhush," (Civilization and Savagery) an article written in 1885, questions the classification of cultures into civilized and savage and points out the distinction's imperialist dimension:

> It would have been easier had such a judgment been carried out on a scientific basis because scientific judgment changes with time and personal opinions do not degrade the value of a culture. But some states have turned this classification into a tool for their domination of others with the excuse of extracting the latter from the depths of savagery and bringing them into the folds of civilization.[70]

The *al-Muqtataf* editors then proceed to show the civilized aspects of "the Orient" and the damage done to it through the imposition of European civilization: the eradication of ancient civilizations, the decimation of local inhabitants, and the weakening of virtues such as noble-mindedness and sense of honor.

Such proclamations may seem remarkable considering that they were made in the same pages where only a few years earlier an article, also by the editors, urged an emulation of European domestic habits and order. Particularly in its earlier years, *al-Muqtataf*'s self-contradictions can be partly explained by the journal's avant-garde status. European model homes presented an opportunity to break through the existing local order of wealth and privilege and to advance ideas already established as progressive and modern. A European home "constantly offering new things" thus justified novelty, even in the absence of moderation. At the same time, the European model was slowly revealed as deserving of critique in and of itself, for offering a form of modernity that suffocated other cultures in the name of progress.

A Bourdieuan analysis of taste and class applied indiscriminately to the placement of aesthetics within the field of culture precludes an understanding of the role the *idea of Europe* played in this formulation. Several scholars have noted the ambivalence in the intellectual circles of the Ottoman Empire towards a putative European culture—embracing its technical developments while at the same time rejecting its moral content.[71] Using one of the strategies for dealing with such ambiguities, al-Muqtataf was quick to draw a distinguishing line between making use of the fruits of European progress, on the one hand, and having a political and economic opposition to European aims, on the other.[72] At the time of the writing of "al-Tamaddun wa-l-Tawahhush" in 1885, Beirut was only beginning to experience the infrastructural upheavals that would indelibly change the face of the city. The emerging concessions market and the effects it was to have on the region were beginning to be felt in projects such as the Beirut-Damascus carriage road, and one of al-Muqtataf's leading lines during its tenure in Beirut was that the development and management of the *objects* of European modernity, particularly science and industry, should be taken on locally.[73]

Most arresting about these early articles is al-Muqtataf's attempt to forge a local modernity, alternatively described as "Syrian" or "Oriental." Though remaining geographically indeterminate, the appellation Syrian took on a quasi-national character through al-Muqtataf's references to the "Syrian homeland." The journal's reference to "the Orient" were more ambiguous in their use and sometimes expanded to include the Iroquois of the Americas and the Maori of New Zealand.[74] In such contexts, this term served to redeem societies and histories framed as "backward" by European discourse. Implicitly, it referenced a late Ottoman fascination with Japan as a successful model of Oriental modernity that challenged the European one and constituted a point of reference for other "Orientals."[75] The Japanese model served to dissociate what had seemed to be a necessary link between Europe and modernity and to open up the possibility for nations outside Europe to become modern while preserving their integrity.

By the turn of the century, al-Muqtataf's early attempts at localizing modernity through evoking a "Syrian" and "Oriental" identity had wedded themselves to the debate on domesticity in the popular press in Beirut. More specifically, the thin line that supposedly divided Western progress from its objects mapped out a contrast between women's pursuit of *ifranji* fashion in public and the necessity of their focusing on "authentic" and moral values. Positing itself as a counterbalance to the rapid transformations in the public sphere, this discourse sought to localize specifically Syrian or Oriental qualities in the home, within the domain of the woman.

The effect of economic imperialism on local culture took on a decidedly negative aspect in the press. Over the course of the nineteenth century, the relationship between the Ottoman Empire and the industrialized countries of Europe changed from one of equal trading partners to one in which the Ottoman Empire was debtor, a source of raw materials, and a captive market for Europe's surging production in commodities. Although this transformation was a major trigger for the rise of Beirut and the emergence of a middle class, it also made it difficult for local manufacturers to compete with industrialized commodities and to constitute a source of income for the city and the province.

The paradox in the case of Beirut was that the city's success in repositioning itself with respect to global trade was precisely what made it so susceptible to a flow of commodities. This was not lost on a contemporary observer commenting on fashionable appearances: "We meant in the beginning to look like Europeans in order to get closer to them with the aim of facilitating our businesses . . . but we soon outdid them in so many things."[76] Here again, the author expresses a conflicted relationship between the initially enabling aspect of contact with and emulation of Europe for the growth of a middle-class culture, and the perceived detrimental effects this contact was having on a local sense of identity in the long run.

One of the earliest reactions to the local popularity of industrialized imports comes from 1870, the first year of the publication of the bimonthly magazine *al-Jinan*. An article titled "al-Sina'a" (Industry) uses the metaphor of a merchant who eventually loses his capital when his expenses exceed his income to comment on the state of economy in the region:

> Our [Syrian] homeland will soon go bankrupt if we persist in this state we
> are in, and the reason for this is that all our clothes, utensils, furniture, and
> medicines come to us from foreign countries. These countries take our gold
> and silver as payment, whereas what we import in return turns to dust.[77]

This article preceded the consolidation of *ifranji* as a discursive trope, but the author leaves little doubt that by "foreign" [*ajnabi*] he was referring to Europe, whose peoples "cooperate to benefit their homeland." In order to rectify this situation, the article suggests a three-faceted solution: manufacturers should diversify and improve their products, the wealthy should form associations to establish factories, and the public should consume local products.

The last point is one example of how responsibility for the weak position of local manufacture could be placed on consumers' preference for imported over local products. Of more significance to the present discussion, the contours of the home as a space of consumption become clearer in light of the products listed in the article. The author complains that although cheaper and good quality boots, tables, chairs, and cloth were being produced locally:

> It has been implanted in our minds that all foreign products are better than our own, and so people buy based on this reputation regardless of quality or price. Yes, we do not deny that foreign products are generally of better quality, but we regret that although we make some similar products, people remain undesirous of them. They should desire our products, even when they are of inferior quality, because [their consumption] benefits all of us.[78]

To several commentators of the time, understanding and recreating the conditions of production locally was a main method by which they came to understand the appropriation of the modern world. The call for developing local industry in order to achieve progress, prosperity, and economic autonomy emerged in following years on the pages of leading periodicals.[79] These writings share an emphasis on the importance of an indigenous industry for a viable economy. Part of the blame for not having achieved this goal was laid on laziness and lack of industriousness on the part of the inhabitants of Syria or on the producers for failing to modify their products and offer what was more fashionable on the market. Invariably, the articles also brought up the role of consumers in undermining local industry.

With their emphasis on the consumption of products such as textiles, furniture, food, drink, and clothing, these articles indicate that the home had become an important sphere of consumption and, as we shall see in the next chapter, there were various consumption practices and locales emerging around Beirut that buttressed this function of the home. Although the home management literature encouraged moderation and homemade solutions and posited the home as the domain in which to teach proper attitudes towards consumption, it simultaneously assumed such elements of furniture, cutlery, and textiles to be constitutive of the home at a time when their use was not entirely widespread.

The interest in appropriating and localizing the means of production gained more momentum with the loss of Ottoman territory. The intertwining of anxiety over local manufacture, growing nationalistic feelings, and the troubled political atmosphere of the Ottoman Empire culminated in the boycott in 1908–1909 of Austro-Hungarian imports. A Young Turk government seeking to rally Ottoman patriotic sentiments after the revolution of 1908 was instrumental in orchestrating an empire-wide boycott in response to Vienna's annexation of Bosnia and Herzegovina on 5 October 1908. The boycott was successfully implemented in Beirut, where everything suspected of being Austrian was seized by the stevedores.[80] In order to prove his French loyalties, the owner of the department store Orosdi-Back even had to remove the Austrian post office from the premises.[81]

Authenticity and *Ifranji* Excesses

Although the adjective *ifranji* was used to describe furniture, food, behavior, and tailoring, it found its most concrete expression in elements of women's fashion: the fine feathers on a velour hat, the frill on a dress, the tight corsets, the sumptuous hairstyles, and the colors, patterns, and designs of dresses. These elements, evidence of women's supposed obsession with fashion, were regarded as wasteful and, more importantly, as signs of *tafarnuj*, or taking after the superficial appearances of the West. Reactions to *tafarnuj*, did not imply a wholesale rejection of European or Western culture, but rather indicated a fear of adopting only the superficial, sometimes morally loose, aspects of its modernity.

The place *ifranji* culture occupied in the turn-of-the-century debate on modernity is exemplified in a speech delivered in 1902 by ʿIsa Iskandar Maʿluf at the Greek Catholic Oriental School in Zahla, where he taught.[82] Maʿluf was an educator, and his speech is typical of his time's spirit of didacticism, which sought to mold a new, modern generation. Echoing a speech by Butrus al-Bustani delivered more than three decades earlier, Maʿluf enumerates the differences between the habits of "Orientals" and those of "Westerners."[83]

Significantly, whereas for al-Bustani, examples of differences between Arabs and *ifranj* include such things as facial hair, clothing, and culinary and greeting habits, the contrasts take on a more essential and immutable character in Maʿluf's speech: "For the difference between the habits of the Orientals and the Westerners is like the difference between the location of the two continents. . . . And we are located where the sun rises, and they where it sets."[84] After outlining a set of oppositions, Maʿluf then moves on to give advice on which manners to cultivate and which to avoid, including these:

> [Among the things to cultivate] is maintaining the beneficial habits of the homeland, particularly that which relates to food, drinks, and clothes. . . . [Among the things to avoid] is adopting that which does not go with our taste and is not of the nature of our country, by which we mean Europeanization [al-tafarnuj] and false civilization [al-tamaddun al-kadhib].[85]

Similar themes on *ifranji* culture are addressed in the debate on fashion that took place in the late nineteenth and early twentieth centuries in two Beirut-based periodicals, *Thamarat al-Funun* and *al-Mahabba*. Seen as an uncritical adoption of all that comes from Europe, fashion turned into an object of ongoing criticism and was woven into discussions on local morality and "Oriental" nature. These two periodicals stand out for having devoted space on their pages to discussing the question of fashion from various angles. Furthermore, they offer two perspectives colored by each periodical's position within one of the city's two largest religious communities: Muslim Sunni in the case of *Thamarat a-Funun* and Christian Greek Orthodox in the case of *al-Mahabba*. This underlines both differences and anxieties that were shared across the sectarian divide in the city.

By the turn of the century, the reach of novel fashions had expanded to include women. Into the 1880s, advertisements were content to mention provenance and novelty in order to attract customers. In the advertisements appearing in the city commercial guide of 1889, *Dalil Bayrut*, there is no mention of women, despite the fact that a variety of services and commodities for domestic consumption were on offer.[86] This began to change towards the turn of the century as advertisements began to address female consumers directly. The trend was particularly noticeable when it came to fashion, as various merchants began to market silks, wool, broadcloth, lacework, and other textiles to female consumers.[87] The same was true of accessories such as umbrellas and of clothes, both prêt-à-porter and tailored. The reach of fashion was not restricted to Christian women or others who had begun to expose their faces in some public spaces in the city. One tailor specializing in the latest Parisian fashion tried to expand his pool of clientele by offering women the services of a female measurer.[88] Fashion thrived behind closed doors and underneath the black robe (*izar*) and light face covering still worn to the souks by many women, regardless of religion.[89]

Thamarat al-Funun and *al-Mahabba*'s critique of fashion concentrated on the clothes and ornamentation taken up by women, generally perceived to be the most susceptible to the latest trend.[90] The focus on domestic duties and the cultivation of the virtues of simplicity, propriety, and moderation were posited as the remedy to a superficial and morally suspect *tafarnuj*. Rarely did the critique of fashion take hold as a critique of Europe itself; instead, it emerged as the critique of being *overly* European. More importantly for our purposes, various contributors to the debate posited the place of woman at home as the counterpart to her ornamented appearances in public.

Thamarat al-Funun (1875–1908) was a major, biweekly newspaper founded by 'Abd al-Qadir al-Qabbani, who was also one of the founders of the Maqasid Islamic Benevolent Society and mayor of Beirut from 1896 to 1902.[91] In its early years, the newspaper's concession rights were owned by Jam'iyyat al-Funun (the Muslim Society of the Arts), moving to al-Qabbani with the closure of that society.[92] For *Thamarat al-Funun*, the home unfolded as a moral obligation and a given right, as well as a necessary opposite to women's appearances in public space. The editorial team both published original pieces and reprinted articles from other publications under their regular *akhlaq wa-'adat* (manners and customs) rubric to criticize consumer excesses.[93] The criticism of women's transgression of the boundaries of the home was part of this more general debate on correct manners and behavior in the face of a changing material reality.

An unsigned article, which seems to have been originally published in the Egyptian press, was probably chosen because it struck a fine balance between the necessity of educating women and the demand for a practical education revolving around domestic duties. Emphasizing the virtues of the "Oriental" woman who restricts herself to her domestic sphere, the article warns the husband of her Europeanized counterpart (*mutafarnija*), whose excesses transform her into a "public exhibit" for the desirous eyes of others and whose education only serves to give her access to comic literature, fashion magazines, and romantic novels.[94]

The newspaper's own articles often attempted to ground this critique in Islamic *shar'* (law), which was considered "general and sufficient for all people's needs regardless of the degree of civilization and progress."[95] Some arguments for moderation cited the dictum *inna ahsana al-umuri awsatuha* (the middle course is always best).[96] Having women work out of necessity or engage in voluntary work in societies was not deemed to conflict in anyway with Islamic law. In contrast, women's ornamented appearance in public was considered anathema to the very idea of civilization and harked back to the backward days of *jahiliyya*, a derisive reference to the culture and beliefs of the Arabian peninsula before the advent of Islam.[97]

Whereas a woman's appearance in public space, seen as a primarily masculine space, necessarily entailed her ornamentation and her visibility to desiring eyes, the home was regarded as woman's shield from the vagaries and brutishness of the marketplace. In that sense, Islamic law guaranteed a woman's rights and protected her from the hardships a man found himself by necessity subjected to. Even when Islam was not evoked to argue for limiting women's rights to the domestic sphere, the home was still posited as a woman's ultimate right. To organize society otherwise would be to upset the divine order of things and to subject women to an outside world for which they were not suited, argued one Christian contributor to the newspaper, As'ad Daghir.[98]

In its first four years, *al-Mahabba* (1899–1912) was a weekly issued by Jam'iyyat al-Ta'lim al-Masihi al-Urtuduksiyya (the Greek Orthodox Society for Christian Education) in Beirut. During its remaining years, it was owned by Fadl Allah Faris Abi Halaqa, who moved the publication to Haifa in 1912. Its short tenure in Haifa endeared it to members of the Jewish community in Ottoman Palestine, who viewed it as a supporter of their cause.[99] During its years in Beirut, *al-Mahabba* played a central role for the Greek Orthodox community in the city and also in the region. It attracted readership and contributions from Tripoli, Homs, and Hama, all cities with sizable Greek Orthodox populations. One of the regular contributors was Jurji Niqula Baz, who went on to found *al-Hasna'*.

Al-Mahabba's articles, particularly its editorials, were moralizing and edifying in tone. Though the periodical covered the news of the Greek Orthodox community and clergy in the region and its articles made frequent references to the church as public space, the debate on fashion itself did not resort to religiously grounded vocabulary and arguments. Women's appearance in mixed spaces such as churches, clubs, and salons was perceived differently from their appearance in the marketplace, particularly when they appeared there fashionably dressed and made up. Echoing *Thamarat al-Funun*, an article in *al-Mahabba* criticizing women's appearance when they went unveiled in the souks also invokes a derogatory reference to *al-jahiliyya*.[100] *Al-Mahabba* was also concerned with how attempts to appear wealthier than one actually was could potentially upset the social order by reducing whole households of middling means to poverty. Focusing on domestic virtues, knowing one's place as a member of the middling groups, and managing one's expenses accordingly were considered not only morally but also economically redemptive characteristics.

The debate on fashion in *al-Mahabba* bore the heavy imprint of the collapse of gold mining shares in 1895 and the crash of the Istanbul Stock Exchange, outcomes of fraudulent speculation and the Ottoman Empire's integration into world and European financial markets. Having had eagerly invested in the goldmines of the Transvaal, many Beirutis watched as their fortunes were reduced by the workings of international finance.[101] This financial crisis compounded with an already existing economic crisis caused by a bad silk harvest in Mount Lebanon to produce an unstable economic situation that lasted several years.[102] The sense of economic security among this emerging middle class and the confidence its members had in themselves as citizens of the world were deeply shaken by their financial losses. The repercussions were still being contemplated six years later, in an article titled "al-Nahda al-Nisa'iyya wa-l-'Muda'" (The Female *Nahda* and Fashion): "The effect of the latest incidents on our commerce and businesses has demonstrated that we are of the nations least knowledgeable of economy, most keen on appearances, and least attached to the essence of things."[103]

The Transvaal crisis left an indelible mark on the debate on fashion in *al-Mahabba* and consolidated women as its main objects. Although the author of "al-Nahda al-Nisa'iyya wa-l-'Muda'"—most likely Abi Halaqa himself—points a finger at both men and women for their attachment to appearances, it is women who form the primary target of his attack.[104] It is because of their blind imitation and mindless adoption of "what Europeans call 'moda,'"

he argues, that "Oriental women" were not at the forefront of "real progress." This he ties directly to the delicate economic position of the emerging
middle class, where a woman's demands for the latest and most expensive
dresses might exceed the income of her husband or father. Despite the financial crisis, the author continues, "women and families are still running after
the same furniture and feathers," threatening the delicate economic positions
of entire middle-class families.

Disparate critiques linking women's quest after fashion with the precarious position of the middle class culminated in a full-fledged debate opened
in 1905 by al-Mahabba's editor. The thrust of his argument criticized female
members of the middle class whose excesses went beyond their means, making them indistinguishable in appearance from members of the upper classes.
Though nowhere does he substantiate his arguments using religion, he turns
to domestic morality for guidelines on woman's role in society. The focus on
appearances, he argues, compromises a woman's "true" virtues, those revolving around her current or future role as mother and wife. Consequently, by
neglecting to manage her home properly and choosing instead to spend domestic income unwisely, she threatens to push the entire family to the edge
of economic destitution.[105]

Unlike Thamarat al-Funun, al-Mahabba often had women contributing to the debates in its pages, particularly on discussions of women's rights
and duties. The attack on women launched by the journal elicited responses
from several readers, most of whom were women responding in self-defense.
Accusing the editor of exaggeration, they argued that ornamentation was a
right and a necessity for women that need not be a contradiction to their
domestic duties. They also objected to the focus on women, one reader from
Homs even suggesting that the magazine write articles on the more perti-
nent issue of "men and fashion."[106] Two male respondents, perhaps provoked
by endowing women with such agency in societal change, challenged the
attack differently. Since women were followers rather than leaders, they both
argued, women's forays into fashion were a mere imitation of the male example. It was men, not women, who held responsibility for societal ills and
for reforming women by example and by education.[107]

Though most of the respondents contested the editor's accusation one
way or another, highlighting the differences in opinion on fashion, the

exchange circumscribed the limits of the debate. Not once challenging the idea that the home was women's responsibility, they also reaffirmed a moderation becoming middle-class women and, less scrupulously, men. Without reaching a firm conclusion, the debate served to demarcate a woman's outward appearance, particularly in public, by her duties at home and by the ethics of moderation that formed part of her responsibility as a member of the middle class. It also served to unmistakably link the ills in society to the superficial imitation of *ifranji* culture and to posit the focus on the home as the remedy.[108] *Thamarat al-Funun* and *al-Mahabba* were not alone in their criticism of modern excesses, but their focus on fashion called attention to an assumed link between a woman's appearance in public and her duties at home, and emphasized the centrality of the home to the wider debate on consumption and *tafarnuj*. Although they differ in their framing of the issue, the two publications also show how reactions to changes in the public sphere often bridged confessional and religious divides, and elicited a sense of anxiety among Muslims and Christians alike.[109]

Oriental Interiority

The home as an inner sphere of authenticity related to an anxiety about the changing face of the public sphere. This anxiety can be understood as part and parcel of the various responses to the material conditions of the urban cultures of the nineteenth century. Rapid urbanization, the encroachment of an industrialized world, and the accompanying break with familiar norms of interpreting experience expressed itself locally through a tension between *mazhar* (appearance) and *jawhar* (essence) or *batin* (interiority). While the latter came to signify what is particular to a localized sense of the self, the focus on consumption came to stand in for foreign or European appearances. Among the authors cited in this chapter, several draw this distinction between surface appearances and essence. In relation to taste, Yusuf Shalhut ties taste to a cultivation of the ability to discover a secret meaning that goes beyond the appearances of things. Making a distinction between imaginary and real beauties, Shalhut argues that, on the one hand, it is possible for someone to attribute beauty to an undeserving object by "being attracted to its imaginary charms and to apparent (*zahir*) ornamentations which serve no purpose." On the other hand, only a cultivated sensitivity allowed a person "to understand beauty in things not understood by just any eye and to discover in hidden corners details of beauty that no one else is able to notice."[110]

The interplay between inside and outside, between true happiness and appearances, between a localized self and universal changes, structures much of Tuʻmaʼs delivery of the speech cited at the beginning of this chapter. Tuʻma connects this distinction directly to the idea of home. The migrant she imagines to be wandering in London and Paris, stunned by the achievements of those places, on *seeing* these wonders finds herself longing for the inner beauties of her country, which is home. In the same speech, Tuʻma genders that localized self by challenging the cultivated and educated ladies who had become indistinguishable *in appearance and dress* from European women to demonstrate their accomplishments *inside* the home.

A few years before the debate on fashion, Salwa Butrus Salama, writing from Homs, had tackled a similar issue in *al-Mahabba* in an article titled "Fi al-Fatat al-Haqiqiyya" (On the Real Girl). Like Tuʻma after her, Salama refers to young ladies' eagerness to look like European women, and she describes the cause: "It is our nation's [Syria's] ill luck that we are the leading people in adopting the conventions claimed by vain people to be the basis of civilization."[111] Women, she argues, have abandoned the essence (*jawhar*) of their interior duties at home, clinging instead to a display of external ornamentation. They have assumed that a woman's virtues depend on her appearance, unaware of the moral and material damage as well as the decline and corruption behind ornamentation and makeup.[112]

In the face of the concern that adopting *ifranji* appearances would threaten aspects regarded as essential to the definition of local culture, the home emerged as a repository for authenticity and women emerged at its center as guardians of this authenticity. Partha Chatterjee discusses a similar tendency in colonial India to divide the world into a material domain and a spiritual domain. By doing so, Bengali intellectuals removed the woman question to an inner domain of sovereignty and rendered it relatively unimportant in the arena of political contest with the colonial state towards the end of the nineteenth century.[113] In contrast, the division of the world into essence and appearance in the Beiruti context brought the question of women as markers of modernity to the fore. These differences notwithstanding, a gendered inner domain of morality and authenticity took shape towards the turn of the nineteenth century in the region. As was the case in India, such a sphere emerged in response to European economic and cultural hegemony.

However, even if an inner sphere might have been formulated discursively, one cannot assume it actually existed in reality. As Manu Goswami points out in the case of India, the desire for a private sphere untouched by colonial (in the case of Beirut, imperialist) and capitalist transformations does not imply its existence.[114] The porosity of this supposed inner sphere brings attention to an inherent contradiction in the idealized middle class put forth in the pages of the press and on lecture podiums. The model of the ideal home constituted an important facet of a set of responses to the precarious position of the emerging middle class. But even as this home was forwarded as a model for the political participation of this class, it was also posited as a model for society as a whole.

Gendered, middle-class domesticity globalized the home at the same time that it sought to localize it. As the urban surroundings of the Beiruti home were cut through by straighter, wider streets and pervaded by new modes of leisure, the home became the place where a more localized, authentic modernity could take shape. Linked to changing modes of consumption, the home became in the eyes of many the place where proper modes of consumption, compatible with the new dictates of the economy, could be inculcated. Thus, the ability to separate real value from superficial value and to separate what is compatible with local culture from the latest *ifranji* fashion, was central to the attempt of defining a middle-class domesticity. As a new space of consumption, the home also stood central to several suggestions for buttressing local industry as a necessary step towards "catching up" with industrialized economies. The very act of localizing the home, therefore, linked it to changes in urbanity and global trade. This tension in perceptions of domesticity opened up the space for domestic objects themselves to undermine the ideal of the middle-class home and complicate the task of preserving it as a location for authenticity.

CHAPTER 6

LOCAL FORMS AND *IFRANJI* PLEASURES

> This is to let the public know that my trade is *ifranji* cabinetmaking
> and that I make furniture of all the different kinds that are asked of
> me. For in this I claim no virtue just as a potter claims no virtue in
> the creation of a pot.
>
> Yusuf al-Ghoraieb Najjar[1]

The idealized relationship between the emerging middle class and good taste in late Ottoman Beirut regimented the consumption and use of new popular commodities. But the meanings objects carried with them and their potential to change the ways their users presented themselves, behaved, and even perceived themselves also took form in areas beyond the conscious self-fashioning of the middle class. Production, on scales ranging from the local to the global, in its own turn generated ways of conceiving of and talking about objects, therefore suffusing them with yet another layer of meaning.

In her study of the changing meaning of furniture in the lives of modern Parisians, Leora Auslander addresses the importance of production and distribution, in addition to consumption. She argues that taste and style were the crystallization of a complex dynamic where interdependent systems of production, consumption, and distribution interacted with the meaning borne by objects as well as with political, cultural, and economic changes. In this constellation, the role played by capitalism in the nineteenth century in reorganizing production and distribution, and the accompanying shift from a society of orders to a society of classes, gave birth to taste as a political power of social representation where the bourgeoisie could collectively present itself as a class through goods.[2] In the context of nineteenth-century Paris, mechanization and the commercialization of the relations of production and distribution not only made luxury goods more available but also brought with them social unrest and changing relations between the state and the people.[3]

In the same century, changes in the modes of production and distribution had their own effects on the formation of the middle class in the provincial capital Beirut. At a time when the discourse on domesticity sought to articulate an authentic modernity, where the home as a sphere of consumption nurtured local industry, practices of distribution and production upset attempts to define a sphere for this local industry. As new modes of consumption were introduced with the import of mass-industrialized commodities, production of domestic objects also changed. The resulting processes of production brought together local, regional, and global labor, and involved the introduction of fashions and styles that made prescribed attempts at discarding the rotten fruits of *ifranji* culture a complicated exercise of discernment.

In underlining the role of material things in negotiating culture at a time of industrialization and changing consumption habits, part of the task is exploring how the agency of things is enabled by the conditions of production as well as by the conditions for authenticity set by intellectual projects.[4] The ability of domestic objects to determine authenticity becomes possible only in light of the prerequisites for authenticity set by intellectual discourse, particularly those prerequisites stressing the importance of proper consumption. The same is true for the promises of transcending class boundaries that objects may hold for their owners. Such promises became especially loaded within a discursive constellation that warned of the dangers of crossing such boundaries. Historiographically, bringing these objects and their modes of production and consumption to bear on intellectual discourse elucidates some of the tensions inherent in imagining the middle class in Beirut, a class that through its ethics of practice was supposed to embody the ideal of a modern society.

Love of the Glittery and Cheap

Turn-of-the-century Beirut witnessed the emergence of a middle-class culture defined by economic position, education, and a lifestyle characterized by greater access to commodities. A multifaceted group composed of Christians, Muslims, and Jews and including teachers, professionals, wage-employees, and bureaucrats became invested in a form of consumption structured by the importation of newly affordable, industrially produced commodities. Although it is difficult to get a precise idea of consumption trends from the available sources, reading trade consular reports, Hanafi court records, and advertisements in light of each other does clearly reveal the items that became popular in Beirut during the last three decades of Ottoman rule.[5]

Particularly when it came to bibelots—small decorative items and trinkets—one can see in the second half of the nineteenth century the marked presence of imported commodities in local stores in the city, which began to fill up with a myriad of little objects. In other contexts, bibelots were one of the earliest domains of consumption to go beyond a small elite.[6] Bibelots, approximated by the word *tuhaf* (sg. *tuhfa*) in Beirut, were also one of the domains in which wider access to consumption first became apparent. An early mention of *tuhaf* appears in Khuri's *Dalil Bayrut* (1889), in an advertisement for a store selling textiles and "Oriental goods." The advertisement indicates that the word *tuhaf* was also used to refer to trinkets with a *curiosité*, or oddity, value.[7]

Once the popular inclination towards consuming small, inexpensive items became apparent, it elicited negative reactions from several quarters. To the eyes of French officials located in Beirut, the abundance and the choice of objects enjoying popularity among the inhabitants of the city seemed haphazard, even grotesque. Having been used to the secure position of French imports, the writers of the commercial reports penned at the French consulate general struggle to understand and adapt to a new reality where the customer dictates tastes. The interest in cheap objects in the Levant in general was found to be particularly striking in the case of Beirut. The paradox, in the opinion of one consular report, was that despite the city's affluence, its stock of European merchandise was of low significance and quality. The report further complained that the limited number of shops in the souks specializing in European merchandise sold common quality Austrian and German products.[8] French merchants and middlemen were encouraged to understand "indigenous" tastes and to market products well suited to those tastes in order to attain a position for French imports.[9]

Here, taste emerges again, this time as an economic category that needs to be understood and analyzed in order for French commerce to gain a better foothold in a changing market. In trying to pin down what, exactly, this taste consisted of, commercial reports written under the guidance of successive French consuls point out the locals' love of the *clinquant* and *bon marché* (gaudy and cheap) and their preference for articles that were invariably described as *criards* (loud) and with *dorures* (gilding) and for colors that were *brilliantes, vives,* and *voyantes* (brilliant, glittery, and showy).[10]

One such report points out the example of a model store in Beirut in order to urge French exporters to expand their trade in the area of "articles de Paris" and gadgetry (*bibelot, bimbeloterie*):

> It is sufficient to spend a few hours in the store of Mr. D. M. in Beirut to account for this. This wholesale store furnishes all the bazar shops in Beirut as well as the cities of the interior. Its collection is constantly renewed and one can find objects in Moroccan leather as well as card cases, cigarette cases, etc., toys, office articles, perfume, imitation jewelry, watches, knives, etc.—all of very inferior quality, but at such low prices that one can buy a hundred objects for thirty francs.

Explaining the significance of being able to buy so many objects at a low price, the report continues:

> One does not need to have resided in the Levant long to understand that low prices are a perpetual temptation that cannot be resisted by the native, flâneur by temperament and a lover by taste of the gaudy and cheap.[11]

French trade reports may have been prone to exaggeration; nevertheless, the objects that appear in cases that came before the Hanafi court attest to such a trend in consumption, often in objects meant for a domestic setting. Towards the end of the nineteenth century, court cases gradually become populated with sundry inexpensive commodities, such as cups, goblets, tumblers, carafes, vases, chandeliers, lanterns, floor mats, carpets, handkerchiefs, towels, pictures, frames, and small decorative items. Possession lists associated with both probate inventories and marital conflicts expanded for men and women alike to include porcelain, ceramic, and cut glass products and also gilded items, to name some of the most popular imports of the time.

Advertisements in the press make the link between decorative items and the home explicit. Going back to *tuhaf*, for instance, their domestic relevance is explained in an advertisement from 1910: "We have various kinds of precious *tuhaf*, which those of [good] taste would be proud to give as gifts to their friends or to have at home."[12] One advertisement specifically markets *tuhaf* for the living room, while the furniture manufacturer Sioufi makes the decorative aspect more concrete by enumerating some ornaments for homes: statues, vases, bronze planters, pictures, and artificial flowers.[13] Other references to decoration appear in advertisements for precisely those stores that emphasized abundance.[14] Not only was a domain of expanding consumption opening up to classes beyond the elite but, as these advertisements show, such investments were also expected to end up in the home.

What can be gleaned from court records and advertisements is brought into greater relief by the new consumption outlets dotting the commercial areas of the city. Beginning in the 1880s, major department stores in France, such as Au Bon Marché, Grand Dépot, and Grand Magasin du Printemps, acquired wholesale channels into the region, and their emphasis on low prices and abundance found parallels in a similar typology of local knickknack stores, such as al-Kaff al-Ahmar (also known as Au Gant Rouge, the French translation of its name), Au Petit Bon Marché, Magasin Cristal, Makhzan Suriyya (Syria Depot), and Makhzan al-Bada'i' al-Inkliziyya (Depot for English Goods).[15] By 1890, the souks were already selling imported umbrellas and baby carriages, clocks and watches, clothes and textiles, and also "Chinese" and "Indian" commodities produced in European factories. By the time Beirut's first department store, Orosdi-Back, was inaugurated in 1900, about a dozen souks were already stocked with similar wares, and over the next decade they expanded their offerings to include aluminum kitchen utensils, binoculars, phonographs, battery-powered doorbells, sewing machines, hair and skin products, artificial flowers, postcards, and other commodities.[16]

Advertisements for local stores sported long lists of diverse wares, giving the impression of a cornucopia. One long list in an advertisement for Au Petit Bon Marché even ended with "etc.," evincing a seemingly limitless supply of the types of objects advertised: " . . . fans, soap, air-fresheners, fezzes, ornaments, children's socks, etc." The same advertisement, sporting a set of faces from different walks of life, advertised fixed prices, explaining that this signified treating the dim-witted on an equal footing with the clever, who knew how to bargain. Local stores also made a point of catering to a growing range of consumers by advertising low prices.[17]

Figure 8. Advertisement for Au Petit Bon Marché: "We treat the clever and the dim-witted the same." Located in Suq Ayyas, this local store was modelled after the French department store, with an emphasis on low prices and variety. The faces featured from all walks of life appear to be cut and pasted from imported magazines. Source: *Lisan al-Hal*, 4 April 1905.

The opening of the Orosdi-Back department store in 1900 crowned consumption practices already in the making in Beirut, but this store also introduced some new aspects of modern consumerism. To the abundance already constituting the focus of local stores, Orosdi-Back introduced the order of the modern department store. Muhammad 'Izzat Darwaza, accompanying his father on a business trip from Nablus in 1906, describes the sight that met his eyes:

> Among the things I saw that I found wondrous was the store referred to as Omar Efendi Stores, or Orosdi-Back. It was on an avenue on the port road, and it occupied a large building with wide doors, several stories, and many halls and labyrinths [*dahaliz*]. The store sold all a person could need of textile, metal, wood, ceramic, and glass products coming in several kinds, shapes, and sizes. Each kind of merchandise had its own hall and its own sales-employees.[18]

Such promises of abundance, accessibility, and equal treatment for all were meant to invite middle-class consumers into a fantasy world where, through their newly found access to consumption and their desire for upward mobility, they would be able to blur class boundaries.

The informal and personalized tones of advertisements, often written in the first person, created a sense of familiarity between sellers and their intended customers. They frequently invited customers in as one would to one's own private place, asking those interested in the merchandise on offer to "honor my/our store [with their visit]."[19] Initially, in the 1870s and 1880s, advertisements (*i'lanat*, sg. *i'lan*) appeared on the last page of a newspaper and their content tended to match the literal meaning of *i'lan* (announcement). They were placed in the press to let people know about newly arrived merchandise, newly acquired expertise, or the opening or relocation of a business. The occasional images accompanying them were etched drawings that seem to come mostly from trade catalogues.[20] Apart from advertisements for the French department stores, which were usually pasted in as is in the language of origin, the norm was to use only Arabic. Other languages—French, English, or German—usually appeared only when an original logo was inserted.[21]

While these characteristics persisted into the early twentieth century, the content of advertisements changed with the advent of the knickknack stores. The lists of items presented in advertisements did more than just inform, they were also associated with various techniques to attract attention. A store advertising the advent of Parisian fashionable items, for example, placed its text upside down in the newspaper.[22] This need to stand out was becoming more and more necessary as the space taken up by advertisements in the papers increased over the years. Images and the use of foreign languages, especially French, also served the purpose of giving a distinct appeal and identity to individual businesses. The names of some stores and manufacturers, such as Au Gant Rouge, Ghoraieb & Bitar, and Sioufi, began appearing both in Arabic and French, and logos and emblems from trade catalogues or other sources were modified to include those names. As an indication of things yet to become more widespread, Sioufi sometimes used custom-made drawings signed by a local draftsman, Jibra'il Faris al-Khuri, to showcase its own furniture.[23]

These various and changing techniques used local language and referred to well-known persons and locations in the city at the same time as they integrated a personalized appeal with imported imagery and French translations of Arabic store names. The resulting collage of text and imagery started animating the pages of the local press in the 1900s. Advertisements' incorporation of the local and the imported both spoke to and created the needs of an increasingly educated population familiar with several languages, by now at ease with juggling the basic vocabulary of consumption, and constantly attuned to the latest and, not least, imported fashion.

Advertising the Latest Fashion

The irritation displayed in French trade reports over the population's recalcitrant consumption habits geared towards the cheap and plentiful was matched only by the perseverance of the intellectuals trying to change those habits. Many of the popular objects of consumption were destined for the home, but the prescriptive middle-class aesthetics of order and moderation commonly heard in public debates of the time regarded the habits of consumption as excessive. The ongoing indulgence in purchasing large amounts of cheap objects undermined the carefully constructed arguments around good taste and moderation forwarded in the press. As we have seen in the previous chapter, what were regarded as especially detrimental in relation to the middle class were showy attempts at reflecting a social status higher than a person's real one. This flew in the face of calls for the self-preservation of the middle class, regarded as a group with a precarious economic position in its context. But perhaps most disturbing of all to the public debate on domesticity was that these practices ascribed to a pursuit of "the latest fashion," which was often an imported one, thus posing a threat to a posited authentic and moral interiority.

While the intellectual discourse of domesticity found in the well-managed home the antidote for the quest after the latest fashion, advertisements appealed to a desire for fashion and novelty in areas including the home. In advertisements in the press, appearing side by side with prescriptive articles on home management, fashion acquired a new vocabulary and a variety of connotations. In addition to marketing to "those of good taste," advertisements also put forth "the latest fashion" as a desirable commodity in and of itself.[24] Gradually, references to the new shifted from concrete descriptives such as "new designs with every steamship,"[25] and found more abstract expressions in words such as *tarz* and *muda*, meaning "fashion." With this, the appeal to novelty acquired fixed and recognizable words. By the late 1880s, several advertisements were linking domestic furniture to the needs of "this age" and to the "latest arrivals" of "the new fashion" (*al-tarz al-jadid*), explicitly placing the home within a sphere of consumption in constant transformation.[26]

As advertisements increased in complexity, not only did some start addressing women directly, they also began creating "needs" for homes and families.[27] An example of this was an advertisement for the steam-operated washing machine. While the advertisement did not address itself specifically to women, it described the machine as "necessary for families" and included a drawing of a woman and a small girl operating the machine, which left little doubt that the home was at least an important niche. An advertisement for a gas cooker was more direct in addressing women and adopted much of the language of domesticity by addressing itself to "mistresses of the house who value time, money, and the cleanliness of their kitchens."[28]

Figure 9. Advertisement for steam washing machines: "Necessary for families, hospitals, schools, and hotels." Sold both in Beirut and Damascus, the machine was advertised as so easy to use it could be operated by a child. Source: *Lisan al-Hal,* 3 June 1910.

Another example of commodities meant for the home was the sewing machine, an import that took on a specifically domestic relevance in Beirut as elsewhere. By the first decade of the twentieth century, sewing machines of all kinds entered the average Ottoman household as well as small-scale manufacturing.[29] Many brands of sewing machines were on the market as early as 1860, but the success of the Singer company in the region is almost mythical. Its installment payment scheme and offer of free instruction were so successful in the region that they were quickly adopted by rivals. Though the sewing machine was not restricted to use in homes, one of Singer's main marketing slogans was "necessary for families," indicating that the primary users were envisaged to be women.[30] Perhaps in an attempt to compete with

Singer, the European sewing machine manufacturer, Naumann, was promoting itself in the same direction, not only visually through the use of female users in its advertisements but also with the offer of free in-home instruction with each purchase, a marketing effort presumably aimed at women who preferred not to leave their homes.[31]

Although advertisements for domestic commodities resonated with intellectual concerns in their appeal to those of "good" and "sound" taste, they also stood in tension with them. While intellectual literature on home management primarily linked good taste to an ethics of moderation concerned with managing the household economy and preserving a postulated "Oriental" authenticity, many advertisements linked good taste to the latest fashion and the latest import. "Europe" often emerged in advertisements as a marker of modernity, rather than as a counterpoint to authenticity.

The language of authenticity and of valuing local labor eventually entered advertisements in *fin-de-siècle* Beirut, as local manufacturing expanded after the turn of the century. Advertisements for local producers drew on the ethics of consumption put forth in the press, emphasizing the "national" aspect of their production. An advertisement for the furniture manufacturer Sioufi claimed that "the patriot [*wataniyy*] has the right to, even should be proud" of the level manufacturing had reached thanks to "our patriotic owner Ilyas Afandi Sioufi and his vitality."[32] In addition, 'Abd al-Basit al-Unsi's commercial guide for Beirut, published in 1909–1910, lists textiles under two headings: European merchandise and national (*wataniyya*) textiles.[33] In contrast, the power of labels such as "Parisian," "English," or "*ifranji*" to attract is evidenced by their persistent usage as catchwords in advertisements. Such labels were so effective that they even found their way into describing locally produced commodities influenced by imported fashions.

The wedding of taste to novelty and *ifranji* imports in advertisements was often in tension with the prescriptive aesthetics of moderation and authenticity propounded in the popular press. But at the same time, predicating an authentic interiority on moderate consumption and discerning middle-class taste in public discourse had already introduced the possibilities within which domestic things can act upon the lives of their modern subjects. In other words, the discourse on domesticity and related ideas about reform had already highlighted things, their disposition, and their consumption as

Figure 10. The wall behind this cake seller on a Beirut street (ca. 1900–1920) features advertisements in Arabic, Ottoman Turkish, French, and German. Source: Matson Photograph Collection, Library of Congress (LC-DIG-matpc-02215).

central to the construction of a modern everyday. At the same time, both advertisements and the debate on domesticity delineated "*ifranji*" and "Oriental" as categories used for understanding and reacting to commodities, their provenance, and their consumption.

Sites of Production and Consumption

The late nineteenth century in Beirut was the age of the souks. This dominant commercial form was to Beirut what the arcades were to Paris in the early nineteenth century. They emerged in response to an expanding market economy and the opening up of consumption to wider sections of the population. Souks not only sold but also exhibited imported wares, with advertisements sometimes encouraging consumers to come and take a look, since "looking is for free" (*al-firja bi-balash*).[34] The way the souks took form was influenced by the growth of Beirut outside the confines of the historical city and by the accompanying urban projects that sought to control and shape that growth. Before Beirut's expansion, the intramural souks were organized around professions—such as blacksmiths, carpenters, or cotton stuffers (*haddadin, najjadin,* and *qutun*)—and combined production and consumption on a single site. Walking down the souk of the blacksmiths, for example, fused the commercial transaction with the smell of hot metal and the sweat of the blacksmiths. In the 350 by 550 meter rectangle that constituted intramural Beirut, it was possible to perform all the diverse errands of the day in the various souks, pausing for a leisurely break in one of the small squares that punctuated the dense urban fabric, in close proximity to one's home.

This way of life started changing in the 1870s, when clusters of souks began to emerge, mostly on the peripheries of the inner city, organizing commercial functions around new economic zones directed at the changing patterns of international trade. One prominent cluster extended from the port southward and contained Suq al-Tawila and Suq al-Jamil. In the early 1890s, provincial governor Ismail Kemal Bey ordered that these two souks be aligned perpendicularly to Suq al-Fashkha, in a bid to improve the connection between the port, which was enlarged around the same time, and the rest of the city to the south.[35] As related in Chapter 3, later municipal interventions included the expropriation and demolition of three stores owned by the Ayyas family, against objections voiced by the owner, in order to improve the connection between the souks and New Street.[36]

Together with the souks of Ayyas, Bayhum, and Siyur and the khans (caravanserais) of Fakhri, Antun, Barbir, and Shuna, Suq al-Jamil and Suq al-Tawila coalesced into an economic zone incorporating the commercial activity taking place in the wharfs. In some cases, such as that of Khan Bayhum, the khan stretched over to include parts of the surrounding souks.[37] Suq Ra'd wa-Hani and Suq Abu al-Nasr coalesced into another economic zone to the west of Burj Square (see the inset in Map 1 in Chapter 1).

Formalistically, the souks ascribed to the sense of aesthetics and order pervading the Building Code, modeled along straight lines and assigned street numbers that were sometimes used in advertisements. The part of the intramural city south of New Street and west of the new souks had been identified as a problem area since the 1870s. By the turn of the century, its narrow streets and sharp angles contrasted even more starkly with the surrounding souks. Several travelers made a clear distinction between the "old" town and the new emerging souks. This conception reflected on how the souks themselves were perceived both by contemporary reformers and by later historians. A French trade report from the turn of the century distinguishes between the "souks" and the "bazaars," explaining that "souks sold European, not Turkish products," presumably referring to the clusters around the port and west of Burj Square.[38] Contemporary historians echo this claim by setting a marked distinction between the modern souks, which "specialized in deluxe items and European imports," and "the old Arab souks of the historical center of the city."[39]

Neither the commercial city guide (Dalil Bayrut) of 1889 nor that of 1908 makes a distinction between the old souks and the new. Both kinds of outlets are listed under "souks," indicating that things were somewhat fluid between the two. Moreover, as the two commercial city guides reveal, neither were the items sold in the souks divided along these lines. One could find European and "national" textiles side by side in both the "old" and the "modern" souks. Most importantly, the correlation between deluxe items and European imports was no longer straightforward by the time the souks started to dominate. In fact, it was precisely the spread of industrially produced, affordable items and their ability to compete with local production that enabled the wider mode of consumption embodied by the new souks. The proposed utopia of accessibility and transcendence of class made the souks fashionable, and many merchants tried purposefully to market to as large a section of the population as possible by advertising low and affordable prices.

What fundamentally distinguished the souks of the late nineteenth century from the older souks was the separation of consumption sites from production sites. Apart from small-scale producers such as tailors, shoemakers, watchmakers, and soapmakers, the new souks were primarily spaces of commerce and consumption. Some of the older sites of production persisted, such as Suq al-Rasif to the west and al-Dabbagha to the northeast, but most other production sites were located on the edges of the city center, mediating between the increasingly commercialized core of the city and its new suburbs. Damascus Road to the south, Nahr Road to the east, and Bab Idris to the west attracted a number of industries, such that by the eve of World War I, they had acquired a manufacturing character. While several of these new production sites were also consumption outlets, the souks of the late nineteenth century organized themselves predominantly around ready-made objects, not around either *ifranji* or national production.

While there was a tendency towards specialization in the textile sector, most stores in the souks advertised themselves by catering to variety rather than specialization.[40] The souks grouped commercial activities that took form with Beirut's rise to a port city together with older forms of commerce. Walking through one of the turn-of-the-century souks, one was likely to encounter tailors, watchmakers, and shoemakers side by side with textile, clothes, and furniture stores, such as was the case in Suq al-Tawila. At the same time, any one store could offer commodities as diverse as baby carriages, clocks, gloves, and binoculars, as was the case with Makhzan Suriyya, also in al-Tawila.[41]

The Sioufi furniture store exemplifies the tendency towards separating production from consumption. Owned by Ilyas Sioufi, the business was one of the largest furniture manufacturers in Beirut, and its advertisements were featured regularly in the press. Around 1900, the store was located on the road to the Wheat Wharf in the port area, and it advertised itself as "Sioufi Factory," an outlet for producing as well as selling furniture.[42] The manufacturing facility expanded over the years, boasting around sixty steam-powered machines. It also sported in its storage spaces a wide variety of woods: oak,

rosewood, mahogany, nutwood, and diverse types of Norwegian wood. Together with the expansion in manufacturing, the relationship between the
production and retail parts of the process changed as well. By 1910, Sioufi was
no longer inviting its clients to the factory but rather to Qasr al-Mafrushat
(Furniture Palace), its commercial outlet in Suq al-Tawila. The advertisements referred to the outlet as the "exhibition hall" (*salat al-'ard*), once again
stressing the element of exhibition that souks often boasted of and the centrality of finished objects to their function.[43]

Ifranji Cabinetmaking

The separation between local and imported items was not any easier to trace
in the production locales emerging on the edges of the city than it was in
the souks. Whether it was through the imitation and collage involved in the
making of furniture or the use of raw materials imported from various places
in the making of textiles, producers were changing their modes of production
in order to withstand the competition from cheaper, mass-produced items.
In that process, the models and products they incorporated into their trade
transformed it and contributed to the creation of new popular tastes.

Whereas the word *ifranji* was employed in advertising and public discourse
as a counterpoint to a localized modernity, it served very different purposes in
the process of production of domestic objects. As trade with the industrialized
countries of Europe expanded and imports increased, provenances attached
new meanings to imported objects. Debates in the press also contributed to
constructing *ifranji* not as a specific referent to places with their own realities
and problems, but as an idealized adjective embodying immorality, corruption, and oppression from one point of view, and superiority, progress, and
modernity from another. In advertisements, the non-homologous designa-
tions "Paris," "England," and "Europe" rang as solid in customers' ears. The
French were facing particular difficulty placing their furniture on the market
as "Made in France" and "Made in Paris" became labels subject to forgeries,
and not only in Beirut. In 1896, the French consul reported that a large number of nutwood chairs, painted in various colors, were imported into Beirut as
products of Marseilles when in fact they were manufactured elsewhere.[44]

Fetishizing commodities as Parisian, English, or European eventually
extended itself to local labor processes as producers adapted their trades to in-

dustrialized imports. Even as production in and around Beirut began to supply the city with some of its most cherished goods, the constant need to compare these goods to European imports persisted. For local manufacturers, "in the Parisian style" and "comparable to the best factories of Paris" (or England or Europe) were common catchphrases for advertising the quality of their products.[45] Just as in the case of sites of consumption, labels such as "national" and "*ifranji*" gave the appearance of surface uniformity and a process of Westernization, whereas in fact they obscured complicated processes of production.

As in other cities of Syria, in Beirut local industry continued to provide the local and regional market with most of its furniture. Apart from the iconic bentwood chair and the iron bedstead, little furniture was imported to Beirut.[46] The growing popularity of new types of furniture in the late nineteenth century generated a category of producers who adapted their trade to changing trends with innovative vigor. Many of the twenty-nine cabinetmakers advertised in the city's commercial guide of 1889 specialized in imitating furniture models popular in Europe. Their work included common imitations of specific furniture imports and "objets d'art."[47] These local cabinetmakers adapted to imports by using furniture catalogues from manufacturers in Europe as sources of inspiration for their own work. Their wares were explicitly marketed as *ifranji* and their form of cabinetmaking as "*ifranji* cabinetmaking" (*nijara ifranjiyya*).[48]

Yet, local production of furniture was not restricted to imitations. With the proliferation of product catalogues from international companies and the spread of printed images, local carpenters enjoyed more flexibility than industrialized imports in catering to their clients' preferences. Comparing two cabinetmakers, both describing themselves as specializing in *nijara ifranjiyya*, gives an idea of the range of possibilities available to furniture makers in Beirut. While the carpenter Nakhla Mughni offered ready-made furniture as well as models copied from drawings, Yusuf al-Ghoraieb's advertisement reveals a wider range of possibilities:

> I guarantee those of [good] taste and with a love for precision to present of my work what matches the best products of Parisian and English factories in terms of exactness, durability, and precision. In addition to the French, English, and German designs I have, I receive at the beginning of each month an

industrial journal from Paris containing strange designs and types of furniture.
Those who desire exact replicas will be pleased with the result, and for those
who want new designs, I can design and draw whatever is demanded of me.[49]

The length of the advertisement and its mention of a dining room buffet Ghoraieb had made for the home of the wealthy Bustrus family suggest
that he catered to the more well-off inhabitants of Beirut.[50] Nevertheless,
it shows the range of possibilities both clients and carpenters had at their
disposal. With the increasing popularity of Austrian products towards the
end of the century, some carpenters also began copying Austrian models. The
copies were heavier and had a rougher finish, but had the advantage of being
cheaper than the originals.[51]

That is not to say that it was not possible to purchase furniture produced
in European factories in order to furnish one's home. French factories established in Egypt were exporting furniture to the Levant. In 1908, when
Michel Ibrahim Sursuq, the scion of a wealthy merchant family, wanted to
furnish his house in the upper-class neighborhood of Ashrafiyya, he ordered
all his furniture from the French furniture-maker Maison Krieger's Egyptian branch.[52] There was also a limited offer by the Beirut-based merchant
Karl Altans of living room sets "made in Europe."[53] Every now and then, an
advertisement would appear in the newspapers announcing a moving sale,
and it is reasonable to assume that these often included imported pieces of
furniture sold at more affordable prices.[54]

Local labor employed in producing furniture for the home blurred the
lines between local and *ifranji* through the use of an additional finishing
layer, that of gilding. Gilding seems to have been particularly popular during the last two decades of the nineteenth century, when it was listed in
advertisements among other products of "the latest fashion."[55] When, in 1881,
al-Muqtataf complained of the dominance and monotony of the color yellow
at home, including the gilding of window and mirror frames, it referred specifically to the houses of the rich.[56] At that time, the use of gilding had not
reached full-blown proportions. Within the decade, however, gilding was no
longer confined to the domain of rich homes and ecclesiastical settings, and
it became widespread enough for some artisans to advertise gilding services
as their main activity. Of the three gilders listed in Khuri's *Dalil Bayrut*, only

one, Khalil Qurm, also sold domestic furniture and church decoration and accessories.[57] Furniture producers also expanded the possibilities for gilding by offering the option of decoratively gilded furniture. Applications went beyond the initial offerings of gilding window and mirror frames to include several items used at home, such as beds, candlesticks, chandeliers, lamps, and copper, bronze, and cut glass wares.[58]

As gilding grew in popularity, merchants began to use European or French provenance to market their gilded objects, and artisans used comparisons with Europe to market their skills. An advertisement by one artisan who specialized in gilding copper, Milhim al-Hunud Sa'igh, not only places gilding squarely as a European practice but also, curiously, refers to the surface quality of the gold paint as "the original color":

> With God's grace, after my travels in Europe I have been able to master painting copper with a stable and beautiful golden color using the method that is used in Europe. Whoever wishes to paint their copper vessels from beds, candlesticks, chandeliers, lamps, etc. and return them to their original color is welcome to my store in the souk of Misters Ra'd and Hani, where they can see samples of this paint.[59]

In gilding, as in cabinetmaking in general, local production adapted to changing conditions, new tastes, and industrialization. Local cabinetmakers were able to offer something that finished imports could not: they could take consumer preferences into consideration. Given the small scale of the city and the semi-artisanal nature of its furniture production, the end product was the result of a process of negotiation between what producers were able to offer through the technologies and skills in their possession, the various imported and existing furniture models and materials, and the decisions and adjustments the consumer introduced to existing forms.

The capacity to cater to changing tastes as well as to introduce changes in imported styles is one explanation of why sofas took a long time to catch on. Of the local furniture manufacturers, Sioufi was the only one sporting the entire range of furniture common in Europe at the time, including sofas. On the eve of World War I, other furniture makers and outlets, such as Jubran Karam 'Awn, were adding sofas to their advertised offerings. Curiously, the most extensive advertisement by Sioufi places sofas not in the *salun* (salon),

but under the section for the study/office and for the *dar*, the reception area
in wealthy homes. This suggests that sofas had not yet entered areas of middle-class socialization and were still aimed at wealthier homes' meeting point
with the outside world. The items the advertisement lists under *salun* are
congruent with more widely advertised pieces of furniture: chairs, closets,
and a variety of smaller items such as mirrors, consoles, frames for mirrors
and curtains, hat-stands, and flower-pot holders.[60]

Ifranji Imports, Local Labor, and Oriental Tastes

While wood destined for furniture was primarily supplied from within the
Ottoman Empire, local furniture production also meshed with textiles, a strong
area of import and one where materials, technologies, and labor mixed in innovative ways.[61] Due to the versatility of their use, textiles had long occupied an
important position in decorating the home, but as they became a main import
to the Ottoman Empire with the industrial revolution, they also bore the mark
of economic changes. Still, choice of textiles continued to permeate several material aspects of the home, from bedding and curtains to cushions and rugs.
Particularly when it came to furniture, choice of upholstery became one of the
areas where cabinetmakers were able to tailor their products to different tastes.
Textiles also allowed for the renewal of existing furniture through the services of
upholsterers, of whom there were ten in Beirut in 1909, seven of them Jewish.[62]

With the revival of British interest in Syria in the 1830s, English factory
products began to occupy an important niche among imports into Beirut, and
they did so by undercutting the local textile industry.[63] Before the turn of the
century, British cottons—primarily in the form of colorful calico prints and
white madapolam—proved to be a very popular import and were regularly
used for domestic furnishings.[64] Other nations, notably Germany, Austria,
Belgium, France, and Switzerland, found a niche for their imports in the Levantine market in the latter part of the century.[65] By century's end, Britain still
had a grip on the calico and madapolam products (primarily made in Man-
chester), but Germany, Austria, and Switzerland were competing with it in the
areas of cotton bedcovers and calico prints.[66] As countries such as England
turned to capital equipment production, this opened the opportunity for others, such as Italy and India, to expand into the Ottoman market, the latter
supplying one fifth of Ottoman yarn imports.[67]

These imports may have been marketed as "English" or "*ifranji*," but they were actually referred to by their manufacturers as "Oriental." At a time when World Fairs in Europe and the United States were packaging the exotic into a marketable commodity, industrially produced textiles found inspiration in the products of the East. Popular regional patterns were studied, imitated in European factories—sometimes down to the standard sizes—and these styles were then reexported back to the region.[68] For example, by 1910, bedcovers (*sharshaf*) had nine commercial agents in Beirut, including major importers and department stores such as Orosdi-Back, Bérangé, and Hani and Audi.[69] Described as products "for the Levant," "Oriental," and "Arab," such goods met with considerable success in Beirut.[70] Among textile products, by far the most popular was the genre of "fantaisie," involving busy patterns, often with strong floral overtones.[71]

Some of these products were also meant for sale in Europe, but much of the production ended up competing with the models that had inspired them to begin with, such as products of Damascus, Homs, Hama, and Aleppo. Moreover, production in those cities used imported undyed yarn and cheap synthetic dyes, but the dyeing process itself took place locally.[72] By 1908, the popular, colorfully striped *alaca* cotton, which was marketed in Beirut as a "national" product, used British yarn for the weft and yarn from Adana or India for the warp.[73]

Beirut continued to acquire cloth from Aleppo, Hama, and Damascus, whose production had shifted from silk to cotton in order to respond to the rising importance of English cotton.[74] Foremost among the cottons was *dima*, a striped cloth used for furniture and curtains and produced mainly in Homs but also in Damascus and Hama. Homs's cottons also included Tripoli belts, which came mostly in black and white stripes, and *bayad*, which served primarily for making towels. *Alaca*, which used silk for the weft and cotton for the warp, served in some of its categories for furniture and was produced mainly in Damascus, Hama, and Homs. A consular trade report describes the *alaca* textiles designed for use with furniture as "European in taste and usage, with large stripes." Production in these same places also supplied bedrooms with twilled *sharshaf*, used to cover mattresses and beds. Some of the luxury silk products for furniture, cushions, and carpets could also be supplied on demand from factories in al-Zuq, a considerable distance north of Beirut.[75]

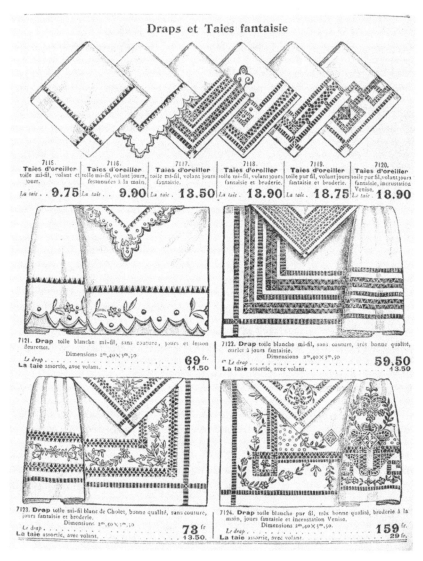

Figure 11. Fantaisie-style patterns were popular in late Ottoman Beirut. The Arabic word *fantaza* is still in use today to denote fineries or attempts to look to be of a higher social class than one actually is. Source: Au Printemps sales catalogue, summer 1919.

Even Beirut itself, seen by many as the place of consumption *par excellence*, developed an industry in textiles for its own consumption, and in at least one instance, it was able to compete on a regional scale. In the 1890s, Beirut was second only to Homs in the production of the popular *dima* and produced enough *alaca* to make a visible presence, at least in its own market. Production also included the *manusa* cotton fabric, used for clothing and furniture, and which Beirut was exporting to Trabzon in the 1890s, undercutting British competitors.[76]

Rather than diminishing, the tendency to integrate imported material into local and regional production picked up over time and acquired a "national" label of its own to compete with *ifranji* even before the Ottoman boycott of Austrian goods in 1908–1909. The increase in the use of yarn, both imported and domestic, over the second half of the nineteenth century points to the vibrancy of this branch of manufacturing.[77] By 1908, and with increasing demand for textiles, there were sixteen merchants in Beirut dealing with "national" textiles and the suburbs housed three silk and four cotton factories.[78]

Processes similar to the ones taking places with the local and regional textile industry also occurred in the construction industry within Beirut itself. The construction boom of the latter half of the nineteenth century increased demand for French roof tiles, flagstones, and glass, and importation of these materials transformed the appearance of Beirut as new construction incorporated them. With the expanding residential suburbs, the pace of construction also made a rapidly setting mortar a desirable product. Yet, one product the French had difficulty in importing to Beirut was hydraulic lime. Given Beirut's climate, this powder had an advantage over previously used varieties of mortar because it set quicker, even in damp or wet weather. But local masons had found a replacement. By combining imported Portland cement with locally produced traditional lime, they had come up with a mixture that set faster than Portland cement alone and cost less than importing hydraulic lime. Bringing together local labor, materials, and knowledge with imported materials, this product competed very successfully with hydraulic lime.[79]

The manufacture of utensils from tin offers another example of how processes of production complicated the proposed line separating local from imported labor. The story begins with the ways Berutis chose to light their homes. Gas lighting had been available in Beirut since the Société anonyme

Figure 12. A Jewish tinsmith in Jerusalem. The workshop shows the raw material, petrol cans, from which kitchen utensils were shaped in the late nineteenth century. Source: Author; Bonfils catalogue no. 1565/643.

ottomane du gaz de Beyrouth began providing this alternative around the same time the city became the provincial capital in 1888. The gas company signed a deal with the municipal council of Beirut to provide lighting for the city's streets. In 1889, six hundred lamps were installed along the main streets, and another thousand were added over the next few years. One reason for the municipal council's eagerness to invest in street lighting was its increasing concern for security, given the threats and vice nighttime brought with it.[80]

While gas lighting met with considerable success on the urban level, this was not the case when it came to lighting domiciles. In 1904, some fifteen years after the city began using gas lighting, only 830 of 18,000 surveyed homes had a subscription with the gas company. This stands in contrast with Beirutis' choices for their water supply. In that same year, the British-owned Beirut Waterworks, was providing 4,700 homes with water from Dog River to the north, in preference to well water.[81] But for lighting, the inhabitants of Beirut continued to prefer kerosene, mostly imported from Russia. Not only was it cheaper than gas, but in comparison with lamps burning animal oil, kerosene lighting produced less soot and burned more evenly. An added value of kerosene lamps was their status as objects of exhibition, representing a new form of domestic technology and giving a stronger light, which meant that lamps could be lifted higher in the rooms.[82] At the turn of the century, there were also stores advertising incandescent lanterns, which gave an even brighter light and produced less soot than wick lamps. An advertisement for such lanterns marketed them as giving "a bright white light like that emanating from gas," indicating the value associated with the quality of gaslight.[83]

More significant to our purpose in this example is a by-product of kerosene imports. After kerosene cans were emptied of their contents, they were cleaned, flattened, and used for crafting tin kitchen utensils, pots, and pans. Because the practice was common, the local profession of *tanakji*, or tinman evolved around it.[84] The continued use of kerosene for lighting at home, thus, not only provided its users with a cheaper alternative to gas lighting but also provided the city with raw material for local labor to transform into utensils cheaper than imported ones.

As these various examples show, claims that buyers dictated taste in Beirut were not entirely unfounded. Rather than submit to the ready-made productions of a mass industry, the city found that the intermeshing of industrial imports with local labor and materials allowed the continuation of a semi-artisanal production that in turn allowed for wider choice. Practices of production as well as outlets of consumption served to blur the line between local and *ifranji* industry. Actual processes of production extended across continents, intertwining industrial with local labor in inseparable ways. "Oriental textiles" were imported, "national cloth" included British and Indian threads, *ifranji* cabinetmaking meshed imported designs with local preferences, and various other products depended on local labor for their transformation into commodities. As artisanal, individualized forms of labor persisted side by side with and accommodated themselves to mass-produced imports, textiles, construction materials, and raw materials merged with local techniques and local forms of knowledge.[85]

Textiles labeled "national" or "European" brought together aesthetic forms that took shape in a process that moved across geographies and blurred the very boundaries of "authentic." Manufacturers exporting textiles and trinkets to Beirut put forth an "Oriental" model different from the one the debate on domesticity had in mind. These products fostered a taste for an indeterminate "Orient" that took form globally. Its popularity did not influence only those styles being produced in Beirut and its regional surroundings. Oriental taste, not least self-Orientalizing taste, was making forays into various parts of the Ottoman Empire.[86] With floral patterns, decorated brush stands and chamber pots, Japanese screens, peacock feathers, and various odds and ends, the "Orient" also found its way in the 1880s into Victorian homes, among other places.[87]

This movement to and fro contributed to shaping prevalent tastes in Beirut during the same period. Local producers were adapting their trade to tastes that were transformed by the popularity of the *ifranji*. They were able to adapt imported styles to suit local preferences owing to the semi-artisanal nature of the local production and the location of production sites within walking distance of the souks. But they were not simply responding to prevalent tastes and preferences. The adaptions, including the materials and techniques integrated, also became an integral part of local production. Prevalent tastes thus emerged at the intersection of production, consumption, and distribution, incorporating popular imported styles but also adapting them to accommodate technological and economic changes.

CONCLUSION

In a speech delivered at the Oriental School in Zahla in 1902, 'Isa Iskandar Ma'luf structured the relationship between Oriental and Western customs as a long list of opposites:

> The difference in the customs of Orientals and Westerners [al-Sharqiyyin wa-l-Gharbiyyin] is like the difference in the location of the two continents. They pride themselves on removing facial hair and we on growing it. We smoke tobacco rolled or in hookahs, and they chew theirs. We drink pure water and they alcohol. We are located where the sun rises and they where it sets. We write from right to left and they from left to right. . . . We greet others by lifting a hand to the head and they by lifting their hats off their heads. Our bedouins eat using their fingers and they with forks. . . . Our bread is thin and theirs thick. Our clothes are wide and theirs tight. We take off our shoes when we enter a place, and they take off their hats. . . . The music and songs we listen to do not move them, and the music they appreciate we do not.[1]

Written at the turn of the century, the speech shows how the supposed differences between East and West could, by that time, be mapped onto various levels of a changing material world—from alimentation and clothing to etiquette and taste. Articulating the elusive boundary between East and West went beyond mere political and economic matters, seeping into lifestyles transformed by growing access to consumption in the latter part of the nineteenth century.

What is most striking about the sets of opposites Ma'luf posits is that many of the objects and customs he places squarely on the Western side of the divide had at the time of his speech become part of daily life in Levantine cities. Hats, forks, and "tight" clothes had entered daily use, if not for a wide section of the population, then certainly for an emerging and educated middle class, of which Ma'luf was part. In particular, his reference to bedouins eating with their fingers is curious, given that forks were widely available and affordable in places such as Zahla and Beirut. But for Ma'luf, allowing "we" the Orientals to slip over into "our bedouins" accentuated the idealized opposites he was tracing and underlined them as natural, rather than cultural, differences.

Among the various ways such discursive work attempted to negotiate the modern world, the middle-class home stood central as a site for appropriating, reinterpreting, and localizing modernity. Public debates, advertisements, and court records recurrently pointed to the role of the home and its objects in shaping the status of women, familial relations, class relations, and patterns of everyday life. Given the increased access to consumption, the home's materiality formed a specific point of concern in the varied attempts of intellectuals, judges, and commercial advertisers to regiment and give meaning to a rapidly changing material world.

The subject of this book shifts the emphasis from the state and its legislative and administrative spheres as sites of formation of modern categories, to domesticity itself as a category. In the context of changing modes of consumption and new ideas about the place of the home in the larger social structure, domesticity and the ideas and commodities associated with it open up a new perspective on Ottoman modernity. Rather than focus solely on how the home was produced through legal categories or through the state's administrative practices, we can turn our attention to domesticity and thus introduce aspects of the home that escape the definition of the state. Similarly, through examining changing habits of consumption, we can bring to light tensions and contradictions in the way the home was imagined. This is especially relevant in the case of Beirut and other cities in the region where the state was weak in its formative and manipulative practices and an intellectual discourse on domesticity and the middle class often did not acquire a hegemonic status.[2]

Focusing on the category of domesticity as a material field and as a site for the formation of the middle class contributes to demystifying the process of Westernization, a term that is often used to describe the changes taking place in turn-of-the-century Beirut and beyond. Despite references to Oriental and *ifranji* differences, those differences were often exaggerated, as Ma'luf's speech exemplifies. In considering a time when the Ottoman Empire was still thought of as part of Europe, it would be more useful to think of these differences as internal opposites that structure each other. In that sense, efforts by Beiruti authors of different religious backgrounds to articulate an "Orient" can be understood as part of the process of realizing the imagined realities of "Europe" and "the Orient." These efforts show how actors in the region were actively engaged in defining "Europe" and "the West" as places of difference, as well as participating in the production of knowledge about themselves as "Orientals," an aspect brought up by Edward Said towards the end of his canonical *Orientalism*.[3]

Although Said was mostly interested in the history of Orientalism as viewed from the West, his text spawned a body of work extending, critiquing, and commenting on his theory. Several of these works discuss the notion of "self Orientalism," or "Orientalism in reverse" as Syrian philosopher Sadik Jala al-'Azm first called it in 1980, two years after the publication of *Orientalism*.[4] Taking this Orientalism of the self beyond the negative ontological connotations suggested by al-'Azm, some of the critique is directed at the way Said's history of Orientalism affirms the very categories of East and West that it seeks to question. Anthropologist Richard Fox, in contrast, underlines how "Orientals could use Orientalism against Western domination," generating nationalist ideologies and identities that challenge Western political and cultural hegemony.[5]

There is, however, a point to be made that cuts across the very idea of "the Orient," and looks instead at how the terms of the imperial and colonial encounter generated a mutual need for delineating differences between East and West. This mutually constitutive relationship is not meant in any way to overlook the imbalance between the militarized and industrialized nations of Europe, on the one hand, and their colonies, markets, and sources

of raw material, on the other. Yet, notwithstanding self-proclaimed Orientals' appropriation of or participation in the production of an "Orient," the
point is rather how a nascent middle class's quest for any authenticity at all
was driven by a homogenizing element viewed as external to its own culture. Taste became part of this homogenization and differentiation process
in as much as it was the material manifestation of difference. But even more
importantly, taste—and the daily choices made on its basis—was itself constitutive of that difference in the way it was constructed globally and in its
ability to find its way into the most private of spaces.

As we have seen in the case of Beirut, the meanings "things" carried with
them and the ways in which those meanings altered the self-understanding
of members of the middle class were not always governable. New modes of
production and new relations of capital intertwined with the production of
taste in sometimes unpredictable ways. Popular commodities became satu-
rated with the relations of production and domination that suffused them
through advertisements, through discourses about the home, through their
daily uses, and through appearing in arenas of contestation such as the
Hanafi court. In the absence of any middle-class cultural hegemony, any attempt at giving a fixed meaning to those commodities was thus wrapped
up in processes that went beyond the mere cultivation of a proper ethics of
consumption.

The very notion of taste, as Leora Auslander argues, is implicated in the
formation of the social order to which it belongs. In France, the shift from
style to taste came with the "shift from a society of orders to a society of
classes, from an absolute monarchy to a constitutional monarch."[6] In this
fundamental restructuring of society that followed the revolution of 1789,
a multiplicity of tastes emerged as constitutive of social meaning. But consumption was not the only field that took on political meaning in its relation
to domestic economy and the social standing of the bourgeoisie. Mechanization, rationalization, and industrialization led to an expansion in production
and distribution that promised a demotic access to goods. The capitalist reorganization of these relations "meant that the bourgeoisie could envision
representing themselves, claiming a collective identity, through goods."[7]

The perception of danger and promise in the increased availability of
"things" also had its implication for "the social" in late Ottoman Beirut. The

emergence of the middle class in the second half of the nineteenth century came about as a result of political and economic changes that had their roots both at home and abroad. These changes were increased access to education through state and missionary institutions; new career paths and professions brought about by the reform of state bureaucracy; shifts in the relationships between the different sections of the population and the state; and a shift in the economic relationship between the industrialized countries of Europe and the Ottoman Empire.

Late Ottoman reforms opened up politics to wider participation and introduced new notions of citizenship that cut across ethnicity and religion. Although these changes did not translate into a form of participatory politics on the level of the state before the Young Turk Revolution of 1908, they introduced ideas about the wider participation of an emerging middle class in shaping the political order. The growing role of the press meant that these ideas could spread to the private sphere, regardless of how effective they actually were in transforming the public sphere. Although the intertwining of private and public in domesticity was not entirely new, the relationship between the two now took a form specific to the emergence of the middle class.[8] Lacking a direct outlet in politics, domesticity became a vehicle for articulating the political and social ambitions of this class, and in turn, the home became a model for the emerging middle class as it created a cultural niche for itself in a changing society.

The age of the *nahda* can in many ways be said to have set the agenda for twentieth-century Arab modernity. Thus, understanding the juncture between the attempts at appropriating modernity, the coagulation of an *ifranji* culture, the designation of a role for women in safeguarding an inner sphere of authenticity, and the centrality of domesticity to these discourses can elucidate the history of Lebanon and the Levant during the later periods of Mandate and independence.

As Elizabeth Thompson shows, the republican paternalism of French Mandate rule in Syria and Lebanon nurtured attempts to re-masculinize public space through a specific form of mass politics that recast women in the image of a nation to be protected by its sons from foreign influence.[9] Also under the French Mandate, as part of the institutionalization of sectarianism, religious law was recast as native custom and, for a growing number of religious confessions, personal matters such as marriage, divorce, inheritance, and custody were then to be dealt with by their religious authorities.[10] These examples indicate how, beyond the issue of domesticity in Beirut, the public and the private can be imbued with gendered politics, and how a sense of authenticity takes form in relation to a putative "other."

That these differences often expressed themselves in outward appearances hints at how a history of modernity can relate to more current debates on issues such as the wearing of the hijab or the celebration of Christmas at schools. Such symbolic acts come to bear the onerousness of conviction and become emblematic of a distinguishing sense of identity—a difference. Particularly in a European or North American context, the use of the hijab as an outward emulation of an authentic Muslim past cannot be understood as a remnant of a nonmodern world or even as a reaction to the spread of Western modernity. It is rather mutually constituted in the encounter between an imagined West and an imagined East, where the difference between the two needs to be projected onto a visual and aesthetic plane. Far from being parochial, the hijab is the by-product of expanding horizons. Just as the removal of the head cover became a symbol of being modern for the women of the interwar Arab world, the hijab is an expression of belonging to our contemporary world.[11]

Sometimes the aesthetics of authenticity take on violent forms, particularly given the role the Internet and social media play in visually mediating violent events to a larger audience. Beheadings using scimitars are an extreme manifestation, but in the more daily enforcements of black *abayas* and *niqabs* covering the entire body for women or the ban on skinny jeans in stringently orthodox Islamic states or by extremist organizations such as the Islamic State of Iraq and the Levant, authenticity is often reduced to its formalistic and performative aspects. That these enforcements persist side by side with cool sunglasses, snoods, and other more commonly fashionable items and weaponry, indicates that localizing difference is not about destabilizing the forces of globalism and capitalism. While perhaps regarded as a forging of a distinct modernity that preserves an authentic identity, attempts at using objects to locate or signal authenticity are fully informed by the conditions of imperialism, nationalism, and capitalism. Though seemingly private, they are publicly constituted at the intersection of four aspects of modernity: increased mobility and homogeneity and the perceived threat to identities that these changes pose; mass-consumerist trends and the circulation of globalized aesthetics; the commodification that constantly shifts the boundary that separates the inside from the outside of each culture; and the accompanying search for a home ground that is both visible and visceral.

APPENDIX

This study is indebted to several published and unpublished surveys of late Ottoman Beiruti houses. The catalogues of the Association for Protecting Natural Sites and Old Buildings in Lebanon (Association pour la protection des sites et anciennes demeures au Liban) include lists of buildings in and around the center of Beirut, giving their function or type, their estimated age, and their locations. There are also more thorough surveys of residential structures, such as the survey conducted under the direction of May Davie, "Maisons traditionnelles de Beyrouth," covering the area of Rumayl-Mudawwar in the eastern part of the city. Anne Mollenhauer's "Continuity and Change in the Architectural Development of Zokak el-Blat" and Ralph Bodenstein's *Villen in Beirut* have detailed surveys of a number of upper-class homes, particularly in the neighborhood of Zuqaq al-Balat (i.e., Zokak el-Blat).

From the buildings indicated on this map, I have collected additional information, particularly on wall decoration in middle-class homes. Surviving examples come from surface scrapings of walls in buildings 1 and 2 in 'Ayn al-Muraysa, building 3 in Qantari, and buildings 7 and 13 in Bashura. These structures all belong to the period 1870–1920; some have been demolished since my research in 2006–2007.

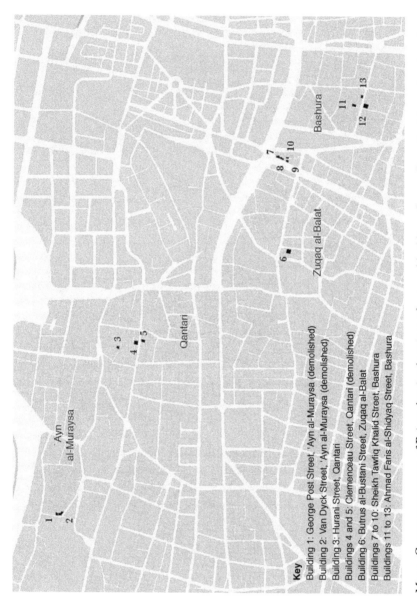

Key

Building 1: George Post Street, 'Ayn al-Muraysa (demolished)
Building 2: Van Dyck Street, 'Ayn al-Muraysa (demolished)
Building 3: Hurani Street, Qantari
Buildings 4 and 5: Clemenceau Street, Qantari (demolished)
Building 6: Butrus al-Bustani Street, Zuqaq al-Balat
Buildings 7 to 10: Sheikh Tawfiq Khalid Street, Bashura
Buildings 11 to 13: Ahmad Faris al-Shidyaq Street, Bashura

Map 3. Contemporary map of Beirut showing locations of surveyed buildings. Source: Børre Ludvigsen, based on data from Jamal Hisham Abed and from Davie, "Maps and the Historical Topography of Beirut."

NOTES

Frequently cited archival and governmental sources are identified by the following abbreviations.

A.MKT.MHM.	Sadaret Mektubi Mühimme Kalemi (Grand Vezirate Office for Important Matters)
BEO	Bab-ı Ali Evrak Odası (Records Office of the Sublime Porte)
BNA	British National Archives, Kew, London
BOA	Başbakanlık Osmanlı Arşivi, Istanbul (Ottoman Archives of the Prime Minister's Office)
CB	Consulat Beyrouth, Série A
CCCB	Correspondance consulaire et commerciale, Beyrouth
CPCT	Correspondance politique et commerciale, Turquié
DH.MKT.	Dahiliye Mektubi Kalemi (Ministry of the Interior, Office of Correspondence)
FO	Foreign Office
İ.MMS.	İrade, Meclis-i Mahsus (Decree, Privy Council)
İ.MSM.	İrade, Mesail-i Mühimme (Decree, Important Matters)
MAE, Nantes	Ministère des Affaires étrangères à Nantes
MAE, Paris	Ministère des Affaires étrangères à Paris
MBB	Qararat al-Majlis al-Baladi li-Madinat Bayrut (Beirut Municipal Council Meeting Minutes)
MSB	al-Mahkama al-Shar'iyya fi Bayrut (Beirut *Shari'a* Court Records)

Ş.D.   Şura-yı Devlet (Council of State)

Y.MTV.   Yıldız Mütenevvi Maruzat (Miscellaneous Reports from the Yıldız
                  Palace Collection)

Also see the Primary Sources section of the Bibliography.

Chapter 1. Beirut, City of the Levant

1. Tu'ma's speech was published as "al-Sama' al-Ula," pts. 1 and 2, in *al-Hasna'*, June and July 1910. 'Aysha al-'Aris's story is discussed in Chapter 3 of this book, and the case concerning the phonograph is discussed in the last section of Chapter 4.

2. The most attractive of these parks lay in the direction of Dubayyah and Antilyas, about an hour's carriage ride northeast of Beirut. Within a shorter distance, southeast of the city, stood the Dawra and the Furn al-Shubbak parks; the latter had a privately owned cafe that played "Lebanese music" on Fridays and Sundays (Khuri, *Dalil Bayrut*, 48).

3. "Al-Iqtisad fi al-Manzil," *al-Mahabba*, 25 May 1901.

4. See the section "Authenticity and *Ifranji* Excesses" in Chapter 4.

5. On salons, see Zeidan, *Arab Women Novelists*, 50–55.

6. Khalidi, *Jawla fi al-Dhikrayat*, 32.

7. For example, Badran, *Feminists, Islam, and the Nation*, 52, 62–65; Kashani-Sabet, "Patriotic Womanhood," 33, 34, 39; and Khater, *Inventing Home*, 4, 16, 71.

8. For Najmabadi, on the one hand, the use of either *discourse* or *cult* to describe this literature prevents an understanding of how adopting the notion of the woman as "manager" formed an empowering basis for entry into public life (Najmabadi, "Crafting an Educated Housewife," 109). Pollard, on the other hand, is concerned with carrying an understanding of the home beyond the niche topic of women, arguing that home life "shaped modern, bourgeois debates about nationalism" for both sexes (Pollard, *Nurturing the Nation*, 8).

9. Ibid. Similarly, Alan Duben and Cem Behar show how state-centered reform with its ideals of modernity and nationalism found an echo in bourgeois domesticity and its ideas of marriage and family (Duben and Behar, *Istanbul Households*).

10. The genealogy of this form and its rootedness in regional architecture as well as other currents specific to the nineteenth century is in and of itself an interesting story, tackled in many of its aspects in *Maison Beyrouthine*, a volume of essays edited by Michael Davie. See also Bodenstein, *Villen in Beirut*; Khater, *Inventing Home*; Mollenhauer, "Continuity and Change"; Saliba, *Domestic Architecture*; and Sehnaoui, *L'occidentalisation de la vie*, 83–112. In his 1923 article, "Notes sur la maison libanaise," Michel Feghali also places the origins of the central-hall house in the nineteenth century, positing a kind of authenticity centered on what he considers a truly indigenous form, "the Lebanese house." In addition, there are also surveys of domestic architecture such as Kalayan and Liger-Belair, *L'habitation au Liban*, vol. 2; Davie, "Maisons tradi-

NOTES TO CHAPTER 1

tionelles de Beyrouth"; Ragette, *Architecture in Lebanon*; and the work done by the Association pour la protection des sites et des ancienne demeures in Beirut.

11. Bodenstein, *Villen in Beirut*, 159–166, 188–192, 223–224, and the drawings on 259–260, 265–266.

12. Ayalon, *Press in the Arab Middle East*, chaps. 2 and 3.

13. Zachs and Halevi, "From *Difā' al-Nisā'*."

14. Foucault, "Governmentality," 98–102.

15. Anderson, *Imagined Communities*, 86.

16. What James Gelvin calls "defensive developmentalism" took the population as its object. As Gelvin explains, beginning in the early nineteenth century, Ottoman sultans, Persian shahs, and Egyptian dynasts undertook policies that aimed at "[strengthening] their states in the face of internal and external threat and [making] their governments more proficient in managing their populations and their resources" (Gelvin, *Modern Middle East*, 73–74). Not coincidentally, it was during that same period, under the leadership of Ottoman Grand Vezier Midhat Pasha, that the census was envisioned as useful in relation to broader educational, economic, and social reforms, rather than being strictly for military and cadastral purposes (Shaw, "Ottoman Census System," 328). Significantly, the Census Department was placed under the Ministry of Interior in 1874, rather than under the Cadastral Section of the Ministry of Finance where it had been languishing since 1858.

17. On the importance of bureaucratic centralization to nineteenth-century Ottoman reform, see, for example, Shaw and Shaw, *History of the Ottoman Empire*, vol. 2, chaps. 2 and 3; Akarlı, "'Abdülhamīd II's Attempts"; and Kayalı, *Arabs and Young Turks*, 75–80.

18. Shaw and Shaw, *History of the Ottoman Empire*, vol. 2, 92–94; see also Çelik, *Remaking of Istanbul*; and Denel, *Batılılaşma Sürecinde*, 15–16, 52–54.

19. See Zandi-Sayek, *Ottoman Izmir*; Lafi, *Municipalités méditerranéennes*; idem, "Municipality of Salonica"; Findley, "System of Provincial Administration"; Kark, "Development of Jerusalem and Jaffa"; Mazza, *Jerusalem*, chap. 1; and Weber, "Reshaping Damascus." On the limits of urban governance, see also Freitag and Lafi, *Urban Governance under the Ottomans*.

20. Although the Provincial Code was promulgated in 1864, lack of funds restricted its initial application to four model provinces: Tuna (Danube), Erzurum (northeastern Anatolia), Aleppo (northern Syria), and Bosnia. These initial efforts formed the basis for the extension of provincial organization to the entire empire by 1876, with the exception of the autonomous provinces of Egypt and the Arabian peninsula (Shaw and Shaw, *History of the Ottoman Empire*, vol. 2, 88–91).

21. Ibid., 88, 243; Abu-Manneh, "Province of Syria," 7–8.

22. Wedeen, *Peripheral Visions*, 24. Wedeen makes this point regarding Ottoman rule in northern Yemen. On education under Abdülhamid II, see Fortna, *Imperial Classroom*. For a study of the ways that imperial notions of citizenship were reflected on the local level, in what the author calls "civic Ottomanism," see Campos, *Ottoman Brothers*.

23. Secessionist movements and the ensuing migration of Muslim populations from newly formed nation-states such as Greece, Malta, and Bulgaria to the remaining Ottoman lands, underlay a shift of emphasis from a multireligious identity to a decidedly Muslim version of Ottomanism. For more on the focus on Hanafi orthodoxy as the official ideology of the state under Abdülhamid II, see Deringil, *Well-Protected Domains*, esp. chaps. 2 and 3.

24. Deringil, "Invention of Tradition."

25. See Hanssen, *Fin de Siècle Beirut*, esp. 55–73.

26. On Beirut becoming a capital city, see ibid., 41–42.

27. Buisson, "Les anciennes défenses."

28. By comparison, landlocked Jerusalem's population grew from eight to eighty thousand during the same period (Issawi, *Economic History*, 101).

29. Hanssen, *Fin de Siècle Beirut*, 27–29.

30. Philipp, *Acre*, 134. For a general discussion on the relation between the rise of Beirut and the decline of Acre, see ibid., 128–135.

31. Özveren, "Making and Unmaking of an Ottoman Port-City," 77–85; Fawaz, *Merchants and Migrants*, 26.

32. David Harvey calls this a "spatial fix," to elucidate the dual aspect of this expansion. On the one hand, by "fixing" space through investments such as infrastructure, capital enables its own further geographical expansion. On the other hand, this investment in spatial ordering "fixes" the problem of overaccumulation by recirculating surplus capital as productive capital (see, Harvey, "Globalization and the 'Spatial Fix,'" 23–30; and idem, *Limits to Capital*, chap. 12).

33. For more on the process of capital investments becoming natural conditions, or "second nature," see Lefebvre, *Production of Space*, 109–110, 345, 409. For a development of this argument in the case of the quarantine and its role in reordering spaces of capital around Beirut, see Abou-Hodeib, "Quarantine and Trade."

34. For more on the super-province of Syria, see Abu-Manneh, "Province of Syria."

35. BOA, A.MKT.MHM. 283/47, Istanbul, A.H. 28 Cemaziyelahır 1280 (28 December 1863).

36. BOA, Y.MTV. 167/200, Beirut, A.H. 23 Rebiyülahir 1315 (24 August 1897). Jens Hanssen discusses the government complex in more detail (Hanssen, *Fin de Siècle Beirut*, 241–247). What is meant by "Islamic" time is not clear from the archival document, but according to other sources, it is a system for counting hours starting with sunset, rather than midnight. On "Islamic" or "Arabic" time, see Antar, "Dinner at When?"; and Midhat, *Avrupa'da bir Cevelan*, 473. Jurji Zaydan also points out that "the third or fourth hour of the Arabic evening" corresponded to ten or eleven o'clock at night in European time (Philipp, *Gurgi Zaydan*, 142).

37. Fakhuri, *Manzul Bayrut*, 239–240.

38. Fortna, "Islamic Morality."

39. Most of the schools in the province of Beirut were missionary schools teaching Arabic, English, and/or French as part of their curriculum. Despite the attempts of Abdülhamid II and of Islamic benevolent societies to counter these schools' effects with an Islamic-Ottoman curriculum that emphasized Ottoman Turkish, the official language of the state, according to the most conservative estimates, at the turn of the century the ratio of students enrolled in confessional (*millet*), foreign, and missionary schools to those enrolled in state schools still stood at a staggering three to one (Fortna, *Imperial Classroom*, 53).

40. Hanssen, "Effect of Ottoman Rule," 9.

41. The dominance of intellectuals and merchants in the history of Beirut can be seen in works such as Fawaz, *Merchants and Migrants*; Zachs, *Making of a Syrian Identity*; Gates, *Merchant Republic of Lebanon*, chap. 2; and Kassir, *Histoire de Beyrouth*, chaps. 6–10. Recent works nuance this image, bringing in, to some degree, other actors (see, e.g., Hanssen, *Fin de Siècle Beirut*; and Khuri-Makdisi, *Eastern Mediterranean*).

42. Works on Syria and Lebanon under the French Mandate highlight the new actors brought into the scene by party politics (e.g., Thompson, *Colonial Citizens*; idem, "Sex and Cinema"; Khoury, "Syrian Urban Politics"; and Watenpaugh, "Middle-Class Modernity").

43. Khuri, *Dalil Bayrut*. The 1889 issue mentions a first volume published in the previous year, but I have been unable to locate a copy.

44. Major *nahda* figure Butrus al-Bustani is one example of such overlapping identities (Abu-Manneh, "Ottomanism and Syrian Nationalism").

45. Jessup, *Women of the Arabs*, 47–52. For more on missionary female education, see Fleischmann, "American Protestant Missions." On the history of missionary work in Syria, see Makdisi, *Artillery of Heaven*.

46. For more on the 1860 civil conflict, see Fawaz, *Occasion for War*.

47. Bayhum, *al-Mar'a fi al-Tarikh*, 230.

48. Ibid., 232–233; Shbaru, *Jam'iyyat al-Maqasid*, 32, 35–37.

49. Levi, *Jews of Beirut*, 84–90.

50. Khuri, *Dalil Bayrut*, 28, 31. Often, boys and girls attended school for only a few years, just long enough to learn how to read and write and to acquire some other basics. The Maqasid Islamic Benevolent Society had to stipulate that girls who entered their schools had to attend for a minimum of four years (Shbaru, *Jam'iyyat al-Maqasid*, 35).

51. Khalidi, *Jawla fi al-Dhikrayat*, 69.

52. Philipp, *Gurgi Zaydan*, 133–134.

53. Davie, *Beyrouth et ses faubourgs*, 46. For a description of one of the wealthy neighborhoods in Beirut, see also Kamel, *Un quartier de Beyrouth*.

54. For an account of the expansion of Beirut and its suburbs before 1880, see Davie, *Beyrouth et ses faubourgs*, 35–46.

55. *Lisan al-Hal*, 1 November 1877, 28 October 1878; *Thamarat al-Funun*, 7 October 1878, 5 May 1879.

56. *Lisan al-Hal*, 12 June 1882.

57. *Lisan al-Hal*, 4 December 1878; *Thamarat al-Funun*, 8 August 1878.

58. Fakhuri, *Manzul Bayrut*, 66–67.

59. On the sectarian distribution of Beirut neighborhoods, see Davie, *Beyrouth et ses faubourgs*, 46. The notion that Ottoman Beirut was an urban center isolated from, even immune to, the civil strife of the countryside was first proposed by Albert Hourani, at the beginning of the Lebanese civil war (Hourani, "Mountain and the City"). Other scholars have echoed this point of view. Samir Kassir, for example, explains the "communitarian cold civil war" as the city "absorbing" the communitarianism of the mountain following the 1860 migrations (Kassir, *Histoire de Beyrouth*, 278–280). But this immunity is a myth; Beirut was subject to the sectarian tensions that characterized much of the region in the late Ottoman period. Clashes erupted primarily between Greek Orthodox Christians and Sunni Muslims, both urban communities, not migrants from the mountains. That these clashes erupted in the less well-off areas of the city points to the presence of other disadvantaged groups and highlights the element of class, which is suppressed by the narrative of Beirut the merchant city where inhabitants want only to conduct business in peace. On the 1903 neighborhood riots, see Hanssen, *Fin de Siècle Beirut*, 204–207.

60. MSB, *Hujaj*, A.H. Dhu al-Qa'da 1333–Rajab 1334, 28 Rabi' al-Thani 1334 (3 March 1916), no. 267/180.

61. See Makdisi, *Culture of Sectarianism*.

62. See Bodenstein, "Making and Remaking," 35–67; Hanssen, "Birth of an Education Quarter"; and Mollenhauer, "Continuity and Change," 109–130. Hanssen argues specifically for a high degree of interconnectedness between Muslim and Christian intellectual circles.

63. On the entanglement of Christian and Muslim residences and the development of the urban fabric in Zuqaq al-Balat during the nineteenth and early twentieth centuries, see Bodenstein, "Making and Remaking," 50–67. Bodenstein points out that different parts of the quarter also had different socioeconomic compositions. The western and southwestern segments, for example, where the hill of Zuqaq al-Balat was most elevated, maintained an upper-class character until the Mandate period.

64. For example, in the period 1910–1915, residents of Zuqaq al-Balat who appeared in court as litigants and witnesses either worked as or were married to carpenters, seamen, customs employees, a city employee, a coachman, a cobbler, a poulterer, and sellers of sweets, radishes, milk, and sesame cakes (*ka'k*); see MSB, *Hujaj*, A.H. Rabi' al-Awwal 1328–Jumada al-Thani 1329, 25 Rajab 1328 (2 August 1910), no. 282; 4 Sha'ban 1328 (11 August 1910), no. 268; 22 Ramadan 1328 (27 September 1910), no. 333; 2 Dhu al-Qa'da 1328 (5 November 1910), no. 371; 26 Dhu al-Hijja 1328 (29 December 1910), no. 422; 15 Muharram 1329 (16 January 1911), no. 474; 2 Safar 1329 (2 February 1911), no. 506; 3 Jumada al-Awwal 1329 (2 May 1911), no. 644; 9 Jumada al-Awwal 1329 (8 May 1911), no. 619; 10 Jumada al-Awwal 1329 (9 May 1911), no. 621; and *Hujaj*, A.H. Dhu al-Qa'da 1333–

Rajab 1334, 9 Dhu al-Hijja 1333 (18 September 1915), no. 407/85; 19 Dhu al-Qa'da 1333 (28 September 1915), no. 364/42; 14 Jumada al-Awwal 1334 (19 March 1916), no. 286/196. Bodenstein ("Making and Remaking," 59) also notes the presence of people of a lower economic status, including Druze peasant families who owned small estates or who rented residences on the western fringes of the quarter.

    65. Dahir, *Bayrut wa-Jabal Lubnan*, 75.

    66. Jiha, *Julia Tu'ma Dimashqiyya*, 23.

    67. Khuri-Makdisi, *Eastern Mediterranean*, 199n44; Sharif, *Imperial Norms*, 11.

    68. Scholars have pointed out the various traps awaiting researchers using court records and have warned against treating court cases as unadulterated reflections of reality. To begin with, there is the danger of attempting to collect quantitative data or to extrapolate generalizations from court processes aimed more at restoring balance than meting out justice. In marital or inheritance conflicts, for instance, there is no way of knowing whether objects listed in court constitute complete lists of possessions (Agmon, "Muslim Women in Court"; Ze'evi, "Ottoman Shari'a Court Records"). In addition, Zouheir Ghazzal convincingly argues that some court cases were "fictitious cases," in that they served a purpose different from the one openly stated. Possessions could be brought into a murder case, for example, in order to fix the identity of the inheritor or to establish a written record of a dowry in an unregistered marriage. Cases could also serve to bypass Islamic inheritance laws by initiating false sales contracts, as in the case of a man selling his possessions to his wife (Ghazzal, *Grammars of Adjudication*, chap. 11). For examples of similar fictitious cases, see MSB, *Hujaj*, A.H. Jumada al-Awwal 1302–Shawwal 1303, 18 Safar 1303 (26 November 1885), no. 443; and *Hujaj*, A.H. Dhu al-Qa'da 1333–Rajab 1334, 4 Safar 1334 (12 December 1915), no. 50. In each of these cases, the court sessions were, uncharacteristically, held at the plaintiff's home due to his ill health, an indication that each case was more about arranging an inheritance than a sales contract.

    69. Similar court records for people of other confessions living in Beirut remain either unavailable or restricted to select researchers.

    70. Given the limited statistical use to be derived from these records, I have opted to focus on regular intervals in order to trace long-term changes and to concentrate on the accelerated changes of the two decades before World War I. There are a total of eighty registers on microform at the National Archives in Beirut (Mu'assasat al-Mahfuzat al-Wataniyya), covering the period from 1843 to 1918, and almost all those registers are present among the 103 registers at the *shari'a* court in Tariq al-Jadida, Beirut. I have chosen thirty samples from among the *Hujaj* and *Da'awa* registers—sixty-five at the National Archives and eighty-six at the *shari'a* court. These samples cover the years 1843–1846, 1865–1868, and 1886–1887 and then regular five-year intervals from 1895 to 1920. The registers at the National Archives are uncatalogued. I cite court cases using the first and last month of the register and the case number. Where there are no case numbers, I use the page numbers instead.

71. Possessions and prices indicated in fictitious cases, for example, do not necessarily reflect a true list of possessions or actual value on the market.

Chapter 2. The Global Intimacies of Taste

1. "Al-Dhawq," *al-Muqtataf,* November 1892, 87.
2. Bustani, *Da'irat al-Ma'arif,* vol. 8, 429–430.
3. Habermas, *Structural Transformation,* 43–51.
4. "To the autonomy of property owners in the market corresponded a self-presentation of human beings in the family. The latter's intimacy, apparently set free from the constraint of society, was the seal on the truth of a private autonomy exercised in competition. Thus it was a private autonomy denying its economic origins . . . that provided the bourgeois family with its consciousness of itself" (ibid., 46).
5. See Fraser, "Rethinking the Public Sphere." As Joan Landes's feminist historical criticism in *Women and the Public Sphere* shows, the seeming neutrality of Habermas's "public sphere" is disturbed by the realities of that sphere's gendered aspect. In a similar vein, Habermas's notion of equal access to the public sphere through dispassionate speech styles has been criticized for glossing over the differences that "private" social privileges or disadvantages, such as race or "proper" education, bring to the public debate (see Young, *Justice and the Politics of Difference*).
6. Davidoff, "Gender and the 'Great Divide.'"
7. For discussions that look beyond the home as a gendered domain and link it to changing conceptions of work, labor, and class, see, for example, on Sweden, Frykman and Löfgren, *Culture Builders*; on India, Chatterjee, *Nation and Its Fragments*; on France, Auslander, *Taste and Power,* esp. chap. 5; on the United States, Motz and Browne, *Making the American Home*; and on England, Davidoff and Hall, *Family Fortunes.*
8. Poovey maintains that separating domestic life from civil society is central to the separation liberal ideology maintained among different forms of social production (Poovey, *Uneven Developments*). See also Davidoff, *Worlds Between*; Davidoff and Hall, *Family Fortunes*; Landes, "Public/Private Distinction"; and Pateman, *Disorder of Women.*
9. Political theorist Uday Singh Mehta points to a "denied link" between imperialism and liberalism in the case of British liberal thought in the nineteenth century, arguing that although liberalism need not be imperialistic, "the urge is *internal* to it" (Mehta, *Liberalism and Empire,* 20, emphasis in the original).
10. Chakrabarty, *Habitations of Modernity,* 62.
11. Chakrabarty, *Provincializing Europe,* esp. pt. 2.
12. Duben and Behar, *Istanbul Households*; Khater, *Inventing Home*; idem, " 'House' to 'Goddess of the House'"; Fay, "Warrior-Grandees to Domesticated Bourgeoisie"; Grehan, *Everyday Life and Consumer Culture.*
13. Bairoch and Kozul-Wright, "Globalization Myths."

14. See on Izmir, Zandi-Sayek, *Ottoman Izmir*; and Exertzoglou, "Cultural Uses of Consumption"; on Istanbul, Çelik, *Remaking of Istanbul*; and Kırlı, "Coffeehouses"; on Beirut, Fawaz, *Merchants and Migrants*; and Sehnaoui, *L'occidentalisation de la vie*; and on Alexandria, Cairo, and Beirut, Khuri-Makdisi, *Eastern Mediterranean*, esp. chap. 3.

15. Bayly, *Birth of the Modern World*, 481–482.

16. Troelenberg, *Eine Ausstellung wird besichtigt*, chap. 4. Troelenberg discusses this aspect specifically in relation to the 1910 Munich Exhibition of Muhammedan Art, remarking that "within a very short time, the Oriental motif had established itself as a topos that could make a major event on a popular scale lucrative and attractive" (ibid., 132). See also Çelik, *Displaying the Orient*.

17. Following the large-scale urban planning of Paris by French emperor Louis Napoleon III and Baron Georges-Eugène Haussmann, at the time prefect of the Paris region, many urban planners in cities around the world started looking to Paris as an urban ideal. On Tokyo, see Sorensen, *Making of Urban Japan*, chap. 2. One of the sections (Convolute E) in Walter Benjamin's unfinished Arcades Project deals precisely with how Haussmann's plans for renovating Paris reduced "for all times" the ability of protestors to resort to barricade fighting in the streets of that city, highlighting a direct—if also crude in this instance—relationship between urban planning and managing the population (Benjamin, *Arcades Project*, 11–13, 120–149).

18. Çelik, *Remaking of Istanbul*, 49.

19. See Sehnaoui, *L'occidentalisation de la vie*, 85–96.

20. On the typologies of houses in the inner city, see Davie and Nordiguian, "L'habitat de Bayrut al-Qadimat."

21. See Bashkin, "Journeys from Civility to Wilderness."

22. See Frierson, "Gender, Consumption, and Patriotism"; and Çetinkaya, "Muslim Merchants," esp. chap. 2.

23. Bourdieu distinguishes between different kinds of capital: cultural, social, economic, and symbolic. There is a relationship between them, but it is not always a direct one. For more, see Bourdieu, "Forms of Capital."

24. Bourdieu, "Social Space and Symbolic Space," 6 (emphasis in the original).

25. Bourdieu, "Social Space and the Genesis of 'Classes,'" 229, 237.

26. For example, Göçek, *Rise of the Bourgeoisie*; Khater, *Inventing Home*; and Fawaz, *Merchants and Migrants*.

27. Bourdieu, "Social Space and Symbolic Space," 11. Speaking of modern Europe, Terry Eagleton argues that aesthetics is "at the heart of the middle class's struggle for political hegemony" (Eagleton, *Ideology of the Aesthetic*, 4).

28. Bourdieu, *Distinction*, 57.

29. See Cole, *Colonialism and Revolution*.

30. Hall, *White, Male, and Middle Class*. Leonore Davidoff's and Catherine Hall's groundbreaking *Family Fortunes*, published in 1987, established the role of gender in the

construction of middle-class institutions, values, and material culture. These authors' exploration of the middle class in an industrial context argues that class was, at its core, a gendered phenomenon. In making its point, their book brings to the fore domesticity as well as the relationship between public and private.

31. López and Weinstein, *Making of the Middle Class*, 6. See also Chakrabarty, "The Difference."

32. López and Weinstein, *Making of the Middle Class*, 12. See, for example, on Zimbabwe, West, *African Middle Class*; on Chile, Barr-Melej, *Reforming Chile*; on Mexico, French, *Peaceful and Working People*; on Brazil, Owensby, *Intimate Ironies*; and Wolfe, *Autos and Progress*; on India, Joshi, *Fractured Modernity*; and Chatterjee, *Nation and Its Fragments*; and on Japan, Ambaras, "Social Knowledge."

33. Simon Gunn's "Between Modernity and Backwardness," illustrates that the English middle class was far from being regarded unequivocally as a paragon of modernity and was often accused of "backwardness."

34. Watenpaugh, "Middle-Class Modernity."

35. For example, Göçek, *Rise of the Bourgeoisie*; Kechriotis, "Civilisation and Order"; Ryzova, *Age of the Efendiyya*; and Watenpaugh, *Being Modern*.

36. Khater, *Inventing Home*.

37. In *The Culture of Sectarianism*, Ussama Makdisi argues convincingly for the formation of sect as a political identity in Mount Lebanon in the nineteenth century. This also had its parallels in Beirut.

38. For more on Beirut's municipal medical services, see Sharif, *Imperial Norms*, chap. 7.

39. Chakrabarty, "The Difference," 1.

40. Partha Chatterjee, for example, argues that this was the case for women in India (Chatterjee, *Nation and Its Fragments*, 116–134).

41. Shakry, "Schooled Mothers." See also Noorani, *Culture and Hegemony*; and Najmabadi, *Women with Mustaches*, chap. 7.

42. Auslander, *Taste and Power*.

43. For example, Kassir, *Histoire de Beyrouth*, 247–253; Mardin, "Super Westernization"; and Sehnaoui, *L'occidentalisation de la vie*.

44. See, for example, Shechter, *Smoking, Culture and Economy*. Economic historian Donald Quataert's groundbreaking work emphasizes the relevance of production to modern consumption practices and the relationship between capitalist transformations and changing forms of labor. Going beyond the theory of nineteenth-century Ottoman decline, he shows how some areas of small-scale, local manufacture picked up by incorporating industrialized products (Quataert, *Ottoman Manufacturing*).

45. MAE, Paris, CCCB 1868–1888, vol. 9, Beirut, 22 February 1868. Later reports are more moderate in their depiction, pointing out the presence of some local producers.

46. Guha, *Dominance without Hegemony*, 97.

Chapter 3. Home Is Where the Investment Is

1. Quoted in Leary, *Syria, the Land of Lebanon*, 37. Leary attributes the existence of this proverb to the fact that homes in Beirut were built of sandstone, which is porous right after construction. But after two or three winters, the stone dissolved by rain and deposited in the interstices leads to a decrease in the porosity.

2. Farley, *Two Years in Syria*, 27.

3. Twain, *Innocents Abroad*.

4. Abi Halaqa, *Rihla fi Suriyya wa-Filastin*, pt. 1, 8.

5. Warner, *In the Levant*, 158.

6. Lortet, *La Syrie d'aujourd'hui*, 72; Chauvet, *Conférence sur la Palestine*, 30.

7. See, for example, Baer, "Beginnings of Municipal Government"; Cleveland, "Municipal Council of Tunis"; Lafi, *Municipalité méditerranéennes*; Zandi-Sayek, *Ottoman Izmir*; Çelik, *Remaking of Istanbul*; and Rosenthal, "Urban Elites." On Beirut, see Hanssen, *Fin de Siècle Beirut*; and Sharif, *Imperial Norms*.

8. Asad, "Anthropology of Islam"; see also Graham, "Traditionalism in Islam." Even though late nineteenth-century reformers reached back to acknowledged sources of Islamic jurisprudence to grant historical and religious legitimacy to the categories they were forging, it does not suffice to think of this process as an invention of tradition. Continuity with the past cannot be described simply as "fictitious," this being what defines a tradition as invented (Hobsbawm, "Inventing Traditions," 2). Asad points out that when reformers such as Muhammad 'Abduh or Rashid Rida disagreed or differed with other Muslims, past and contemporary, that difference still constituted part of a tradition of Islamic jurisprudence whose reasoning relied on "a theological vocabulary and a set of problems derived from the Qur'an (the divine revelation), the *sunna* (the Prophet's tradition), and the major jurists (that is, those cited as authoritative)" (Asad, "Reconfigurations of Law and Ethics," 220).

9. For an insightful article on the terms and their uses as categories of practice by modernist reformers, see Hamzah, "La pensée de 'Abduh."

10. Kerr, *Islamic Reform*, 22.

11. Zaman, "'Ulama of Contemporary Islam," 131–132; see also Calhoun, "Public Good."

12. Opwis, "Maslaha," 188–189.

13. Ghazali, *al-Mustasfa min 'Ilm al-Usul*, vol. 1, 286–287; see also Binder, "al-Ghazali's Theory of Islamic Government," 234–235. *Maslaha*'s potential for separating governance from *shari'a* law turned it into a necessary tool for reform in the hands of the Salafiyya school of thought, of which Muhammad 'Abduh was a major figure. Appropriating medieval theorists, 'Abduh gave *maslaha* precedence over sources of the law and, even further, over *hadith* and religious practices. In *Risalat al-Tawhid*, he argues that one of the main reasons behind the stagnation of Islam and the corruption of its political culture was the neglect of the common good and the privileging of obedience

over justice (Eickelman and Piscatori, *Muslim Politics*, 34; Hourani, *Arabic Thought*, 130–160). The term *salafiyya* refers to the Islamic reform movement of the late nineteenth century. The term derives from *al-salaf al-salih* (the righteous predecessors).

14. Opwis, "Maslaha," 195.

15. Ibid., 196.

16. Hamzah, "La pensée de 'Abduh." Notably, it was during his stay in Beirut in 1883-1885 that 'Abduh first delivered the lectures later published as his most famous work, *Risalat al-Tawhid*, where he argues against seeing essential enmity between Islam and critical reason (Euben, "Premodern, Antimodern or Postmodern?" 438).

17. Powell, *Different Shade of Colonialism*, 52.

18. Mitchell, *Colonising Egypt*, 107. Given his diagnosis that there is an Egyptian malaise and that it can be defined as the absence of the spirit of industriousness, Tahtawi focuses on the importance of education for boys and girls alike in inculcating patriotism and the virtues of hard work. He does not go into the relationship between divine and human law except to indicate that the *shari'a* circumscribes the limits of human law. For more on *Manahij*, see Hourani, *Arabic Thought*, 72–83.

19. Kara, *Leitbilder und Handlungsgrundlagen*, 62, 68–69.

20. The term for "public benefit" in the Ottoman text (*menafi-i umumiye*) is based on the Arabic equivalent (*Düstur*, 338–339). The continued relevance of the category in the twentieth century is evidenced by the adoption of the term *al-maslaha al-'amma* in the context of urban management (see, e.g., Thabit, *al-I'mar wa-l-Maslaha al-'Amma*).

21. Abdel Nour, *Introduction à l'histoire urbaine*, 158.

22. The court records of Beirut do not go further back than 1840, but they still show the role of waqf in urban management. For examples of how urban management was carried out in other cities in the region, see, on Istanbul, Çelik, *Remaking of Istanbul*, 43; on Aleppo, Marcus, *Middle East on the Eve of Modernity*, 293–313; and on Damascus, Grehan, *Everyday Life and Consumer Culture*, 168–169. See also Abdel Nour, *Introduction à l'histoire urbaine*, 183–211.

23. Marcus, *Middle East on the Eve of Modernity*, 293.

24. Abdel Nour, *Introduction à l'histoire urbaine*, 138–141. The position of *mi'mar bashi* (head architect of a town) was created by Sultan Muhammad II (r. 1444–1446, 1451–1481) to supervise the construction of public and religious buildings in the large cities of the empire.

25. Hanssen, *Fin de Siècle Beirut*, 116–127.

26. See Sharif, *Imperial Norms*, chap. 1.

27. On Chadwick, see Hamlin, *Public Health*; on Haussmann's Paris, see Saalman, *Haussmann: Paris Transformed*; and on urban planning during the Meiji period (1868–1912), see Sorensen, *Making of Urban Japan*, 45–84.

28. Faroqhi, *Subjects of the Sultan*, 255. For an idea of the anti-fire measures taken in Istanbul, see BOA, İ.MSM. 9/185, Istanbul, A.H. 5 Zilhicce 1264 (2 November 1848).

29. In addition to the Street and Building Regulation, there were the 1858 Regulation on Streets (Sokaklara dair Nizamname), the 1875 Regulation on Construction Methods in Istanbul (Istanbul ve Belade-i Selasede Yapılacak Ebniyenin Suret-i İnşaiyesine dair Nizamname), and the 1877 Istanbul Municipal Law (Dersaadet Belediye Kanunu) (Çelik, *Remaking of Istanbul*, 51; Denel, *Batılılaşma Sürecinde*, xxxiv–xxx).

30. "Wajibat al-Baladiyyat," *al-Mahabba*, 10 March 1906.

31. 'Abd al-Nur, *Sharh Qanun al-Abniya*, 85.

32. See "Qanun al-Abniya wa-Qarar al-Istimlak," in Khuri, *Jami'at al-Qawanin*; and 'Abd al-Nur, *Sharh Qanun al-Abniya*, 2. The latter publication also included the expropriation decree, translated by Niqula Naqqash. Beirut was not the only province that had to deal with conflicting interpretations of the law. A letter was also sent from Damascus asking for clarification; see BOA, Ş.D. 2277/22, Damascus, A.M. 4 Nisan 1305 (16 April 1889).

33. Article 42 of the Municipal Code states that in cases where the municipal council needs permission for making decisions about matters not within its scope of duties, the president of the council should refer to the local government (Young, *Corps de droit*, vol. 1, 77). Malek Sharif also argues that the municipal council had a weak position vis-à-vis the governor (Sharif, *Imperial Norms*, chap. 6).

34. BOA, A.MKT.MHM. 283/47, Istanbul, A.H. 28 Cemaziyelahır 1280 (28 December 1863).

35. Article 3 in Young, *Corps de droit*, vol. 1, 70–71.

36. As part of the Young Turks' reforms for increasing the authority of provincial governors, the new Provincial Administration Law of 1913 reorganized the police force and placed it entirely under civilian authority (Shaw and Shaw, *History of the Ottoman Empire*, vol. 2, 71–72, 306).

37. BOA, Ş.D. 2277/9, Beirut, A.H. 27 Rebiyülahir 1306 (31 December 1888).

38. See, for example, MBB, A.M. 9 Haziran 1320 (22 June 1904), no. 1; A.M. 8 Mayis 1329 (21 May 1913), no. 4; and A.M. 8 Aylul 1330 (17 September 1914), no. 1/113.

39. BOA, Ş.D. 2282/28, A.H. 29 Cemaziyelahır 1312 (28 December 1894). For more on fire regulations for the provinces, see BOA Ş.D. 2758/6, A.H. 10 Recep 1327 (28 July 1909).

40. Articles 1 and 2 in Young, *Corps de droit*, vol. 6, 137.

41. Article 8 in ibid., 138.

42. Article 3 in ibid., 137.

43. Articles 6 and 7 in ibid., 128.

44. Articles 5, 8, and 10 in ibid.

45. MBB, A.M. 11 Kanun Thani 1318 (24 January 1903), no. 4.

46. MBB, A.M. 13 Aylul 1316 (26 September 1900), no. 4; A.H. 11 Rabi'al-Thani 1319 (28 July 1901), no. 1.

47. This can be clearly observed in the neighborhood of Zuqaq al-Balat (Bodenstein, "Making and Remaking," 47).

48. Laporte, *History of Shit*, 14.

49. Ibid., 48.

50. The legal code listed several instances where expropriation could be used for public benefit: "paving and widening streets, squares, souks, harbors, and city gardens; repairing sewers and water canals; fixing rivers and streams; laying roads for harbors, train tracks, and carriages; digging water cisterns for extinguishing fires; building hospitals and army barracks; and necessary cleaning and purification meant to preserve sanitary conditions" (Article 1 in Young, *Corps de droit*, vol. 6, 127).

51. Article 3 in Young, *Corps de droit*, vol. 1, 70–71.

52. MBB, A.M. 8 Mayis 1329 (21 May 1913). Similarly, also on the occasion of the arrival of summer, the municipal council decided to install additional urinals in public places in order to try to prevent urination in streets and alleys; see MBB, A.M. 24 Haziran 1329 (7 July 1913); and also MBB, A.M. 5 Nisan 1331 (18 April 1915), no. 28/147. According to Benoît Boyer, only the large and most frequented arteries of the city were watered, and the public urinals did not take into account the exigencies of modern hygiene, thus actually contributing to infections (Boyer, *Conditions hygiéniques actuelles*, 8, 11).

53. Article 62 in Young, *Corps de droit*, vol. 1, 81.

54. MBB, A.M. 11 Tammuz 1316 (24 July 1900), no. 2.

55. MBB, A.M. 4 Aylul 1330 (17 September 1914), no. 1/113.

56. Quoted in Jenner, "Follow Your Nose," 338–339. Although the early nineteenth century witnessed a scientific skepticism towards contagion theory, policy acting upon these beliefs persisted to the end of the nineteenth century. Even after the development of germ theory in the 1880s and 1890s, which discredited ideas about the lethal effects of noxious smells, "there was no epistemic shift in general attitudes towards foul odors" (ibid., 346; see also McNeill, *Plagues and Peoples*, 244–246).

57. Boyer, *Conditions hygiéniques actuelles*, 10.

58. Ibid., 11. For a critique of Boyer's discourse as reflective of the intersection at that time of medicinal and colonial knowledge, see Hanssen, *Fin de Siècle Beirut*, 128–132.

59. MBB, A.M. 18 Mayis 1316 (31 May 1900), no. 6.

60. MBB, A.M. 13 Mayis 1325 (26 May 1909), no. 13.

61. MBB, A.M. 9 Haziran 1320 (22 June 1904), no. 1.

62. MBB, A.M. 3 Mayis 1320 (16 May 1904), no. 3.

63. MBB, A.M. 13 Nisan 1320 (26 April 1904), no. 6.

64. MBB, A.M. 30 Mart 1329 (12 April 1913).

65. Young, *Corps de droit*, vol. 6, 142.

66. The allowed overhang was 1.3 meters for squares and the two widest categories of streets, and 1.1 meters, 0.9 meters, and 0.75 meters for the remaining three categories of street widths. Protrusions on two adjacent houses also had to be at least 4 meters apart (see chap. 4 in Young, *Corps de droit*, vol. 6, 140–141).

67. Chap. 9 in ibid., 144–145.

68. MBB, A.M. 31 Kanun Awwal 1319 (13 January 1904), no. 3.

69. Chap. 12 in Young, *Corps de droit*, vol. 6, 147–148.

70. Article 67 in Young, *Corps de droit*, vol. 1, 84

71. MBB, A.M. 11 Tammuz 1316 (24 July 1900), no. 3; A.M. 3 Tishrin Thani 1326 (16 November 1910), no. 3.

72. MBB, A.M. 4 Mayis 1331 (17 May 1915), no. 39/263.

73. MBB, A.M. 27 Mayis 1331 (9 June 1915), no. 4/313.

74. MBB, A.M. 8 Haziran 1332 (21 June 1916), no. 1/156.

75. MBB, A.M. 13 Haziran 1321 (26 June 1905), no. 45; see also MBB, A.M. 15 Shubat 1320 (28 February 1905), no. 16; and A.M. 14 Nisan 1321 (27 April 1905), no. 25. A plateau overlooking Rumayl and the quarantine area, the al-Ghaba agglomeration took shape in the three decades before World War I (Davie, *Beyrouth et ses faubourgs*, 46, 61).

76. MBB, A.M. 18 Haziran 1319 (1 July 1903), no. 3.

77. MBB, A.M. 25 Aylul 1318 (8 October 1902), no. 6.

78. On Suq al-Fashkha and the involvement of successive provincial governors in the project, see Hanssen, *Fin de Siècle Beirut*, 216–221. For more on the three governors and their relationship with the municipal council, see Sharif, *Imperial Norms*, 170–177.

79. The first of the two petitions is missing, but is referred to in the two draft communications to Beirut's provincial council as well as in 'Aysha's second petition; see BOA, BEO 46724, Istanbul, A.H. 21 Zilkade 1312 (17 May 1895); BEO 47447, Istanbul, A.H. 6 Zilhicce 1312 (31 May 1895), A.M. 15 Mayis 1311 (27 May 1895). The latter document, 'Aysha's petition, contains no indication of where she was petitioning from. Although the year on the document seems to be 1310 *mali* (1894), the subsequent petition places her first two petitions in April and May of 1895.

80. BOA, DH.MKT. 384/11, Istanbul, A.M. 19 Haziran 1311 (1 July 1895); BEO 50202, Istanbul A.H. 1313 (1895).

81. BOA, Ş.D. 2285/22, Beirut, A.H. 29 Safer 1313 (21 August 1895).

82. BOA, Ş.D. 2285/22, A.M. 3 Kanun Awwal 1311 (15 December 1895).

83. BOA, Ş.D. 2285/22, Beirut, A.H. 21 Zilkade 1313 (4 May 1896).

84. BOA, DH.MKT. 552/48, Istanbul, A.H. 24 Rebiyülahir 1320 (30 July 1902). This is a draft communication to the Beirut provincial council that provides a summary of the petition. I was not able to locate the original petition, only references to it in the bureaucratic trail, so it is not clear where 'Aysha was petitioning from. See also DH.MKT. 618/3, Istanbul, A.H. 25 Şaban 1320 (27 November 1902).

85. BOA, DH.MKT. 552/48, Beirut, A.H. 16 Recep 1320 (18 October 1902).

86. The first Arabic petition was followed in the ensuing month by another petition in Ottoman Turkish; see BOA, Ş.D. 2277/4, A.H. 9 Şevval 1321 (29 December 1903). Only references to the Arabic petition can be found in DH.MKT. 720/49, Istanbul, A.H. 5 Rebiyülevvel 1321 (1 June 1903).

87. For the first time in the string of petitions, we get a clear idea of the extent of

the damage involved and its effects on the inhabitants. It turns out that 'Aysha had two affected properties. The smaller one, which together with her family she had inhabited and which she had mentioned previously in her petitions, consisted of two stories, each with three rooms and a kitchen. Of those, only the staircase and one of the two kitchens were left intact. The larger property, not mentioned previously by 'Aysha, also had two stories and consisted of five rooms and a kitchen on the upper floor and five rooms on the lower floor, the latter of which she presumably rented out as stores. Of those, only the staircase and one room had been demolished.

88. To back up his claim that the municipal council acted illegally, the legal representative cites Article 1216 of the *Mecelle*, which states that property can be expropriated, but it cannot be removed from the owner's possession before she receives compensation (Hawawini, *al-Majalla*, 310).

89. BOA, Ş.D. 2277/4, Beirut, A.H. 26 Şaban 1321 (15 November 1903); DH.MKT. 720/49, Beirut, A.H. 11 Ramazan 1321 (30 November 1903). These two replies coming from the provincial council were addressed to the Council of State and the Ministry of Interior, respectively, and summarized the municipal council's reply to 'Aysha's petition.

90. MBB, A.M. 5 Aghustus 1320 (18 August 1904), no. 2. The reason for the silence surrounding the monthly payment could be that the dispute concerned another property, which she rented out but did not inhabit. Another possibility is that Fatima was a hesitant partner in the petition, brought on board by 'Aysha to broaden the latter's claims against the municipal council. Either way, the fact that Fatima was being compensated by the municipal council in terms of rent underlines the centrality of the home in the conflicts between the municipal council and the affected inhabitants of Beirut.

91. MBB, A.M. 11 Tishrin Awwal 1321 (24 October 1905), no. 33. Available records of municipal minutes go only as far back as 1902. It is possible that 'Aysha had resorted to the council before she began petitioning in Istanbul, but this is the earliest available record of her having a direct interaction with the municipal council.

92. MBB, A.M. 26 Tishrin Thani 1325 (9 December 1909), no. 5; A.M. 15 Nisan 1326 (28 April 1910), no. 4. Another reduction was approved on the same day for another woman owning property on New Street. Both reductions were made in accordance with a decision by the provincial council that affected properties demolished around the same time.

93. MSB, *Hujaj*, A.H. Rabi' al-Awwal 1328–Jumada al-Thani 1329, 10 Rabi' al-Awwal 1328 (22 March 1910), no. 323. Although she is described as a resident of Bab Idris, it is not entirely clear whether this case concerned the same property she owed tax for or even whether she still owned that property.

94. BOA, BEO 50202, Istanbul, A.H. 1313 (1895).

95. MBB, A.H. 11 Rabi' al-Thani 1319 (28 July 1901), no. 1; A.M. 29 Tammuz 1318 (11 August 1902), no. 7.

96. Islamoglu, "Towards a Political Economy," in her *Constituting Modernity*, 9. Distinguishing this from an approach that would follow Michel Foucault, where the emphasis is on the objectified control exercised by the centralized state regardless of the context, Islamoglu emphasizes instead resistance and contestation as fundamental parts of the constitutive fabric of private property (ibid., 10).

97. Young, *Corps de droit*, vol. 6, 138; see also 'Abd al-Nur, *Sharh Qanun al-Abniya*, 13–20.

98. Young, *Corps de droit*, vol. 1, 76.

99. 'Abd al-Nur, *Sharh Qanun al-Abniya*, 88–90.

100. BOA, İ.MMS. 6/13, Istanbul, A.H. 5 Rebiyülahir 1332 (2 March 1914).

101. MBB, A.M. 25 Shubat 1319 (9 March 1904), no. 6.

102. MBB, A.M. 3 Mart 1320 (16 March 1904), no. 6; A.M. 18 Mart 1320 (31 March 1904), no. 1.

103. MBB, A.M. 31 Mart 1320 (13 April 1904), no. 6; see also MBB, A.M. 13 Aylul 1316 (26 September 1900), no. 2. In the latter case, the inhabitants of an area petitioned the municipal council because the maps showed expropriation on one side of the street only. The council dismissed the objection, explaining that the buildings on the other side of the street were strong and of great value in contrast to the buildings on the side being expropriated.

104. For more on the major concession projects in Beirut, see Hanssen, *Fin de Siècle Beirut*, 84–104.

105. Rafeq, "Ownership of Real Property."

106. Ibid., 224. This exemption applied specifically to the *vergu* tax (*wirku* in Arabic), which was estimated with reference to rent.

107. On Aleppo, see Marcus, *Middle East on the Eve of Modernity*, 188–190; and on Damascus, see Grehan, *Everyday Life and Consumer Culture*, 157.

108. Davie, *Beyrouth 1825–1975*, 21–22.

109. Philipp, *Gurgi Zaydan*, 133.

110. Ibid., 133–134. Zaydan's family was typical of the emerging middle class. His father, an illiterate Greek Orthodox migrant from 'Ayn 'Anub in Mount Lebanon, worked his way up from the baking trade to owning his own restaurant on Burj Square. Zaydan himself went on to become an eminent member of the Syrian intelligentsia, attending the Syrian Protestant College for a few years before moving to Cairo in 1882, where he went on to found the influential journal *al-Hilal*. But the ethic of hard work and self-reliance that motivated Zaydan was regarded by many as key to social mobility in Beirut, and by the time of Zaydan's writing, it was a valued quality among members of the emerging middle class. As Zaydan explains it: "[My father] did not have any skills and his will to work was his only capital" (ibid., 129).

111. See BOA, Ş.D., 2285/4, Beirut, A.H. 7 Rebiyülahir 1313 (27 September 1895); and Ş.D., 2289/9, Beirut, A.H. 29 Şevval 1315 (23 March 1898). For a sample rental contract,

see BNA, FO, 195, Beirut, annex to 1 June 1908. See also the Beirut municipal council announcements in the newspaper *Lisan al-Hal*, 6 February 1879 and 12 November 1888.

112. See, for example, *Lisan al-Hal*, 10 April 1880, 17 July 1882, 21 June 1888, 7 May 1890; and *Bayrut*, 23 May 1887. That some of these advertisements offered four- to five-room furnished apartments for a period of three months also indicates the existence of temporary residents passing through the city.

113. See, for example, *Bayrut*, 30 August 1886; and MSB, *Da'awa*, A.H. Muharram 1328–Jumada al-Thani 1332, 7 Jumada al-Thani 1328 (16 June 1910), no. 49.

114. MSB, *Hujaj*, A.H. Jumada al-Thani 1290–Rabi' al-Awwal 1291, 10 Sha'ban 1290 (3 October 1873), no. 94; *Hujaj*, A.H. Jumada al-Awwal 1302–Shawwal 1303, 11 Ramadan 1302 (24 June 1885), no. 171; 19 Rajab 1303 (23 April 1886), no. 905; *Hujaj*, A.H. Rabi' al-Awwal 1328–Jumada al-Thani 1329, 24 Rajab 1328 (1 August 1910), no. 287.

115. By way of example, this was the amount paid in rent by the divorced wife of a baker; see MSB, *Hujaj*, A.H. Rabi' al-Awwal 1328–Jumada al-Thani 1329, 24 Rajab 1328 (1 August 1910), no. 287. The rent for a home in the better-off suburb of Qantari was around 55 piasters a month; see MSB, *Hujaj*, A.H. Jumada al-Awwal 1302–Shawwal 1303, 5 Jumada al-Thani 1302 (22 March 1885), no. 66. The size of this home is not speci-fied, but it seems the tenant in question was a male living by himself. Around the same time, according to the Ukrainian Orientalist Ahatanhel Krymsky, some families would also provide room and board for students for 110–150 piasters a month (Dahir, *Bayrut wa-Jabal Lubnan*, 120, 142).

116. MSB, *Hujaj wa-Da'awa*, A.H. Shawwal 1323–Shawwal 1326, 30 Rabi' al-Thani 1323 (4 July 1905), 9–10. In this case, the home in question was the lower floor of a two-story structure. The number of rooms is not specified, but based on rents for other homes in the same neighborhood and appearing in the same court case, it seems the home was meant for more than two people.

117. To put these numbers in context, in 1904 an unskilled laborer earned 200–400 piasters a month, while a skilled laborer, such as welder, mason, or plumber, earned 550–700 piasters (MAE, Nantes, CB 1895–1914, carton 348, Beirut, 2 January 1904). Fur-ther estimates on wages and living costs come from Issawi, *Fertile Crescent*, 90–91, 428.

118. Promulgated between 1869 and 1876, the *Mecelle* represented a codification of principles and precepts derived from the *shari'a*.

119. Hawawini, *al-Majalla*, 303–314. Other articles in Book 10 also refer to the home but either treat it like any other property—in the sections on ownership and partition—or use it as an example to illustrate general principles of joint ownership.

120. Article 1199 in Hawawini, *al-Majalla*, 305.

121. MSB, *Hujaj*, A.H. Sha'ban 1289–Dhu al-Qa'da 1289, 17 Dhu al-Qa'da 1289 (16 January 1873), no. 293; see also MSB, *Hujaj*, A.H. Muharram 1285–Jumada al-Awwal 1285, 24 Rabi' al-Awwal 1285 (15 July 1868), no. 239; and *Hujaj*, A.H. Jumada al-Awwal 1302–Shawwal 1303, 19 Sha'ban 1302 (3 June 1885), no. 138.

122. Thomson, *Land and the Book*, 49–51.

123. Articles 1202–1206 and 1209. In addition, article 1207 uses women's quarters as an illustrative example (Hawawini, *al-Majalla*, 306–309).

124. Marcus, *Middle East on the Eve of Modernity*, 293–294.

125. MSB, *Hujaj*, A.H. Muharram 1285–Jumada al-Awwal 1285, 24 Rabi' al-Awwal 1285 (15 July 1868), no. 239; *Hujaj*, A.H. Jumada al-Thani 1290–Rabi' al-Awwal 1291, 1 Dhu al-Qa'da 1291 (10 December 1874), no. 305; 12 Muharram 1291 (29 February 1874), no. 323; *Hujaj*, A.H. Jumada al-Awwal 1302–Shawwal 1303, 20 Rabi' al-Awwal 1303 (27 December 1885), no. 500.

126. Article 1201 in Hawawini, *al-Majalla*, 306.

127. MSB, *Hujaj*, A.H. Jumada al-Thani 1290–Rabi' al-Awwal 1291, 1 Dhu al-Qa'da 1291 (10 December 1874), no. 305. This case specifies the size of a *shar'i* opening as 0.75m high and 0.5m wide; see also MSB, *Hujaj*, A.H. Jumada al-Awwal 1302–Shawwal 1303, 19 Jumada al-Thani 1303 (25 March 1886), no. 863; 26 Jumada al-Thani 1303 (1 April 1886), no. 865. In the cases brought to court, tenants had the same rights to visual protection and daylight as owners and were permitted to modify the property they were renting accordingly.

128. *Khalwa*, which is privacy between a man and a woman, was equated with sexual intercourse in the fatwas, and *khalwa* between husband and wife was legally sufficient to consider that the marriage had been consummated. Conversely, a marriage was not considered consummated if the married couple had not been able to enjoy a certain degree of privacy, such as that provided by a *legal abode* (as discussed in Chapter 4). A nonsupervised meeting between a man and a woman in private, therefore, was a legally loaded act as well as a moral issue (Tucker, *House of Law*, 148–156).

129. MSB, *Hujaj*, A.H. Jumada al-Thani 1290–Rabi' al-Awwal 1291, 2 Sha'ban 1290 (25 August 1873), no. 85; 23 Rajab 1290 (16 September 1873), no. 80; *Hujaj*, A.H. Jumada al-Awwal 1302– Shawwal 1303, 19 Sha'ban 1302 (3 June 1885), no. 138. Rubin argues that the *Mecelle* functioned as a single legal standard for both the civil and Hanafi courts, "whereas previously, the judge addressing civil and criminal matters at the local Hanafi court had considerable leeway in choosing the sources relevant to a particular case" (Rubin, "Legal Borrowing," 283). The fact that the ruling in the final court case cited in the previous note was based on a fatwa shows that, in practice, this was not always the case. The discrepancy can be explained by the relatively early date of the case and the fact that personnel at local Hanafi courts tended to be selective in their implementation of instructions from Istanbul (on this latter point, see Agmon, "Recording Procedures").

130. For example, Fortna, *Imperial Classroom*; and Rubin, "Legal Borrowing."

Chapter 4. Things at Home

1. "Al-Sama' al-Ula," pt. 2, *al-Hasna'*, July 1910.

2. Ottoman Sultan Abdülmecid I (r. 1839–1861) opened his reign by accepting the

Treaty of Balta Liman, the price he had to pay for British assistance in driving Egyptian forces out of Syria. Once the Ottoman government ceded these privileges to Britain, it was only a matter of time before it signed similar treaties with other European states. By abolishing monopolies within the Ottoman Empire and reducing tariffs on foreign goods, the Balta Liman treaty effectively opened the empire (including Egypt) to a flood of industrially manufactured goods. For more on this treaty, see Kütükoğlu, "Ottoman-British Commercial Treaty."

3. For approaches that deal with objects as means for generating rather than merely conveying meaning, see Appadurai, *Social Life of Things*; Brown, "Secret Life of Things"; Lubar and Kingery, *History from Things*; Meyer, "'There Is a Spirit'"; Miller, *Home Possessions*; and Roche, *History of Everyday Things*.

4. Because of the nature of the *jawish*'s job, the law drew a line between the *jawish* as a municipal employee and the *jawish* as a person, specifying the behavior appropriate to his position and forbidding him from socializing while on duty. Article 61 of the Municipal Code states that

> police sergeants are not allowed to smoke in alleys, carry umbrellas or sticks, or mix and socialize with anyone in the streets outside the bounds of their duties. They are also forbidden from sitting in neighborhoods, coffeehouses, and gazinos [café-concerts], but are allowed to sit in the coffeehouses for the purposes of rest only. (Young, *Corps de droit*, vol. 1, 81)

5. "Nur al-Shams wa-l-Hawa' al-Naqi," *al-Muqtataf*, December 1881, 435.

6. MAE, Nantes, CB 1895–1914, carton 348, Beirut, 2 January 1904.

7. There was an increase in demand for well water after Beirut Waterworks hiked the prices in 1887 (*Thamarat al-Funun*, 5 January 1888).

8. A habitation unit within the *hara* was called *bayt*, the contemporary word for "home." For more on the different residential typologies of the early nineteenth century, see Davie, *Beyrouth 1825–1975*, 21–22; and idem, "Maisons traditionnelles de Beyrouth."

9. Twain, *Innocents Abroad*.

10. MAE, Paris, CCCB 1897–1901, vol. 12, Beirut, 15 March 1898.

11. Khater, *Inventing Home*, 121–127. The adoption of this new style to signal a break into modernity is also discussed in Davie, *Maison beyrouthine*.

12. For a recent study of such houses, see Bodenstein, *Villen in Beirut*.

13. Thomson, *Land and the Book*, 53–55.

14. Boyer, *Conditions hygiéniques actuelles*, 26–28.

15. See Bodenstein, *Villen in Beirut*, 71–76.

16. On the importation of various popular construction materials, see MAE, Paris, CCCB 1888–1894, vol. 10, Beirut, 30 May 1889, June 1890; CCCB 1895–1896, vol. 11, Beirut, 4 June 1895; and CCCB 1897–1901, vol. 12, Beirut, 15 March 1898. Although a portion of the imports to Beirut were reexported regionally, only Tripoli is mentioned as having imported a considerable quantity of tiles.

17. MAE, Paris, CCCB 1895–1896, vol. 11, Beirut, 15 December 1896; CPCT 1900–1914, vol. 476, Beirut, 15 December 1906.

18. For example, the speech by Rujina Shukri—delivered in Beirut at a literary society, Jam'iyyat Bakurat Suriyya—"Farsh al-Buyut wa-Tartibuha" (Furnishing and Ordering Homes), *al-Muqtataf*, September 1885, 743–745.

19. For example, an advertisement for the upscale Sioufi's Qasr al-Mafrushat lists furniture by main hall, living, dining, bed and bath, and kitchen (*Lisan al-Hal*, 12 April 1911).

20. See, for example, "Dakhiliyyat al-Manzil," *al-Hasna'*, October 1911. Today the word *bayt* signifies both "house" and "home." *Ghurfa* and the Turkish word *oda* refer to a "room," but in the late nineteenth and early twentieth centuries, these were still fluid concepts and *bayt* was frequently used to mean "room." This word is also used to refer to a family, for example: *bayt al-'Aris* (al-'Aris family).

21. Although the Turkish word *oda* was sometimes used for "room," in the context of the court it continued to refer to the kind of abode outlined by the concept of *maskan shar'i*; see, e.g., MSB, *Hujaj*, A.H. Dhu al-Qa'da 1333–Rajab 1334, 28 Rabi' al-Thani 1334 (3 March 1916), no. 267/180; 14 Jumada al-Awwal 1334 (18 March 1916), no. 283/196. The phrase *manzil shar'i* was used in the Palestinian context to refer to the same legal rights. For more on the concept, see Tucker, *House of Law*, 61–63.

22. "Al-Maskan," *al-Mahabba*, 24 January 1899. See the case of a Jewish woman from Beirut demanding a *maskan shar'i* in MSB, *Hujaj*, A.H. Dhu al-Qa'da 1314–Rabi' al-Thani 1316, 24 Safar 1315 (25 July 1897), no. 105. The phrase was also used in the press (see, e.g., the announcement in *Lisan al-Hal*, 24 September 1888).

23. MAE, Paris, CCCB 1888–1894, vol. 10, Beirut, June 1890. For example, rather than reduce the popularity of certain consumer items to purely economic and utilitarian terms, Bayly shows how compatibility with cultural preferences was behind the success of Lancashire cloth in certain parts of nineteenth-century India (Bayly, "Origins of Swadeshi," 308–309).

24. *Lisan al-Hal*, 3 October 1887.

25. Douglas and Isherwood, *World of Goods*, 59–60. This approach critiques the overemphasis on the role of objects in communicating positions in the social world in classic works such as those of Thorstein Veblen and Pierre Bourdieu.

26. Bodenstein, *Villen in Beirut*, 76.

27. Ibid., 312–349.

28. Bodenstein's innovative analysis deals primarily with the spatial and material transformations of the central-hall house. The section on furniture derives mainly from *al-Muqtataf* and posed photographs from upper-class homes. The exception to this is his discussion of the use of elevated divans for seating (see ibid., 279–303).

29. Noueiry, *Ra's Bayrut*, 24–25.

30. For more on the place of the guest in the central-hall house, see Bodenstein, *Villen in Beirut*, 317–332. The *manzul* was a reception room usually occupying a corner of

the house and directly accessible from the outside. The *liwan* was located at the rear end of the central hall and often partially open onto it. It was usually used as a family living room and for the reception of less formal guests.

31. On bentwood in France, see Auslander, *Taste and Power*, 261. Bentwood furniture was the result of years of experimentation with shaping wood with steam by German-born Michel Thonet. After acquiring a patent in Austria, he formed Thonet Gebrüder with his sons and started producing bentwood furniture in mass quantities. When the company relinquished its patent in 1869, following a lawsuit, the adoption of the bentwood method became open to replication and was subject to various attempts at competition both in Austria and abroad. The only real competition to Thonet Gebrüder, however, was Kohn, which meant that the production of bentwood furniture remained mostly in Austrian hands. Austrian bentwood furniture represented the first successful industrial production of furniture. The success of this method was reflected in the scale of production at the time, which was comparable only to that for Singer sewing machines, another popular import in the Levant. For more on bentwood furniture, see Kyriazidou and Pesendorfer, "Viennese Chairs," 143–166; and Rieder, "Bentwood Furniture," 106–111.

32. Becker, "Thonet."

33. In 1875, Chair No. 14 constituted two thirds, and the various bentwood chair models together three quarters, of Thonet's total production (Kyriazidou and Pesendorfer, "Viennese Chairs," 148).

34. MAE, Paris, CCCB 1888–1894, vol. 10, Beirut, June 1890.

35. For example, see the advertisement for Sioufi in *Lisan al-Hal*, 12 April 1911. For more on this point, see also Bodenstein, who points out that this was a regional phenomenon, also found in Damascus (Bodenstein, *Villen in Beirut*, 282–284, 288–289).

36. *Lisan al-Hal*, 3 and 20 May 1899, 28 December 1911.

37. MAE, Paris, CCCB 1897–1901, vol. 12, Beirut, 5 September 1901.

38. For example, French companies specializing in such products were asking for representation in Beirut; see MAE, Nantes, CB 1893, vol. 158, 28 January 1893, 6 March 1893; CB 1894, vol. 160, 18 January 1894, 15 May 1894; CB 1899, vol. 173, Paris, 26 September 1899; and CB 1908, vol. 210, Paris, 12 May 1908, Paris, 6 August 1908.

39. For a sampling of serving items available in homes in the period 1910–1915, see MSB, *Da'awa*, A.H. Shawwal 1323–Safar 1326, 20 Rabi' al-Thani 1324 (13 May 1906), 40–42; *Hujaj*, A.H. Rabi' al-Awwal 1328–Jumada al-Thani 1329, 21 Shawwal 1328 (26 October 1910), no. 363; 2 Dhu al-Qa'da 1328 (5 November 1910), no. 371; 7 Dhu al-Qa'da 1328 (10 November 1910), no. 380; 3 Jumada al-Awwal 1329 (2 May 1911), no. 644; and *Hujaj*, A.H. Dhu al-Qa'da 1333–Rajab 1334, 6 Shawwal 1333 (17 August 1915), no. 302/215; 18 Dhu al-Qa'da 1333 (27 September 1915), no. 365/43; 18 Dhu al-Qa'da 1333 (27 September 1915), no. 369/47. These include both Christian and Muslim cases.

40. "Farsh al-Buyut wa-Tartibuha," *al-Muqtataf*, September 1885, 745.

41. Philipp, *Gurgi Zaydan*, 133.

42. The price depended on the size and quality, but remained constant throughout that period, with the more ordinary and in demand models costing 24–28 francs (130–150 piasters) (MAE, Paris, CCCB 1888–1894, vol. 10, Beirut, 30 May 1889, June 1890; CPCT 1900–1914, vol. 476, Beirut, 15 December 1906).

43. Duffy, *Competitive Cities*, 69; Briggs, *Victorian Cities*, 63.

44. MAE, Paris, CPCT 1908–1914, vol. 429, Beirut, 12 March 1914. Based on turn-of-the-century wage estimates, the cheapest model would have been difficult to afford for a nonskilled laborer with a family, earning 200–400 piasters a month. It was affordable for a skilled laborer, earning up to 800 piasters a month. Wage estimates come from MAE, Nantes, CB 1895–1914, carton 348, Beirut, 2 January 1904.

45. In a detailed letter on bedsteads, the French consulate in Beirut informed the Ministry of Foreign Affairs that French merchants and manufacturers wishing to export beds to Beirut could deal directly with Nasr Allah Jirjis 'Araman, Orosdi-Back, Bérangé and Co., Au Gant Rouge, and Sioufi, otherwise they should contact other retailers through local agents (MAE, Paris, CPCT 1908–1914, vol. 429, Beirut, 12 March 1914).

46. Lists of possessions surveyed for the period 1865–1867 reveal only three bed owners. Only one of these beds was a metal bedstead, belonging to a clerk for land registration (*katib tabu*) and estimated at 372 piasters. The others were wooden beds, ranging in price from 20 to 50 piasters; see MSB, *Hujaj*, A.H. Jumada al-Thani 1282-Rajab 1282, 10 Jumada al-Awwal 1282 (1 August 1865), no. 25; *Hujaj*, A.H. Rajab 1282–Muharram 1283, 22 Ramadan 1282 (8 January 1866), no. 399; and *Hujaj*, A.H. Safar 1283–Muharram 1284, 9 Muharram 1284 (13 May 1867), no. 189. Later lists show a marked increase in beds among possessions: MSB, *Hujaj*, A.H. Dhu al-Qa'da 1314–Rabi' al-Thani 1316, 9 Safar 1316 (29 June 1898), no. 293; *Da'awa*, A.H. Sha'ban 1317–Jumada al-Thani 1320, 3 Jumada al-Thani 1318 (28 September 1900), 44; *Hujaj wa-Da'awa*, A.H. Dhu al-Qa'da 1312–Jumada al-Awwal 1315, 22 Rabi' al-Thani 1314 (30 September 1896), no. 33–42; *Da'awa*, A.H. Rabi' al-Thani 1323–Rabi' al-Awwal 1325, 10 Jumada al-Thani 1323 (12 August 1905), 21–22, 30 Muharram 1324 (15 March 1906), 64–66; *Hujaj wa-Da'awa*, A.H. Shawwal 1323–Shawwal 1326, 30 Rabi' al-Thani 1323 (3 July 1905), 9–10, 2 Ramadan 1323 (31 October 1905), 50–52; *Da'awa*, A.H. Muharram 1328–Jumada al-Thani 1332, 10 Muharram 1329 (11 January 1911), 105–107, 1 Sha'ban 1329 (28 July 1911), 117.

47. MAE, Nantes, CB 1893, vol. 158, Beirut, 19 April 1893.

48. Advertisement for Willer Tiller paints, *Lisan al-Hal*, 9 July 1898.

49. Consumption of ceruse and minium (white lead and red lead), which were used in mural painting, was increasing at the turn of the century (MAE, Nantes, CB 1910, vol. 221, Beirut, 20 March 1910).

50. Prices per kilo were zinc white (3–6 francs), yellow ocher (4.50 francs), green ocher (7.50–12 francs), and red ocher (22.50–37.50 francs). For the less well-off, lime constituted a cheap replacement for interiors painted with oil colors (MAE, Paris, CCCB 1897–1901, vol. 12, Beirut, 15 March 1898, 20 January 1900). Of the imports to Beirut,

less than a quarter were reexported to the region. While indigo imports, used in dyeing cloth, steadily declined around the turn of the century, oil colors, by contrast, increased (MAE, Paris, CCCB 1897–1901, vol. 12, Beirut, 15 March 1898; CPCT 1900–1914, vol. 476, Beirut, 20 January 1909, 31 March 1911).

51. Weber, "Images of Imagined Worlds," 145–171.

52. In addition to Bodenstein, *Villen in Beirut*, a plan and a brief description of the villa are provided in Mollenhauer, "Continuity and Change," 115–117.

53. These observations come from surface scrapings of walls in buildings that survived into the twenty-first century (see the Appendix in this volume).

54. MAE, Paris, CCCB 1897–1901, vol. 12, Beirut, 15 March 1898.

55. Khuri, *Dalil Bayrut*, 98; see also MAE, Paris, CCCB 1895–1896, vol. 11, Beirut, 4 June 1895, December 1896.

56. "Zinat al-Bayt," *al-Muqtataf*, November 1881, 368.

57. "Alwan al-Sitarat (al-Bardayat)," *al-Muqtataf*, November 1881, 242. It is not clear whether *suwar* here refers to paintings, prints, or photographs.

58. See the advertisements for the Rahma bookstore and the Sarafyan photography studio in *Lisan al-Hal*, 7 March 1899, 30 November 1905, 8 December 1905. On Spiridyun Shu'ayb, see Debbas, *Des photographes à Beyrouth*, 52.

59. MAE, Nantes, CB 1910, vol. 221, Beirut 24 January 1910.

60. Sheehi, "Early Arab Photography."

61. In addition to the seven studios listed in *Dalil Bayrut* of 1888, Fouad Debbas mentions eight other professional photographers. A majority of those studios were run by Ottoman subjects (Debbas, *Des photographes à Beyrouth*, 42–52).

62. Dahir, *Bayrut wa-Jabal Lubnan*, 291.

63. See on consumption, Micklewright, "Personal, Public, and Political"; on bourgeois portraiture, Sheehi, "Early Arab Photography"; on Ottoman rule and symbols of modernity, Lemke, "Ottoman Photography"; and on Ottoman community, Woodward, "Between Orientalist Clichés"; see also Çizgen, *Photography in the Ottoman Empire*. In contrast to the other studies, Sheehi reads late Ottoman bourgeois portraiture as a prolegomenon to a national, Lebanese "imago," focusing thereby on categories of European rather than Ottoman modernity (Sheehi, "Early Arab Photography," 179–186).

64. For a sampling of advertisements directed specifically at homes, see *Lisan al-Hal*, 5 January 1882, 4 January 1899, 4 May 1901, 22 August 1905, 8 December 1905.

65. "Tarbiyatuna al-Baytiyya," *al-Mawrid al-Safi*, vol. 1 (1910): 105.

66. "Tartib al-Qa'a," *al-Muqtataf*, February 1889, 331.

67. See, for example, "Zinat al-Bayt," *al-Muqtataf*, November 1881, 368; and "Farsh al-Buyut wa-Tartibuha," *al-Muqtataf*, September 1885, 743.

68. *Lisan al-Hal*, 4 January 1899.

69. "Al-Ziyara wa-l-Diyafa," *al-Muqtataf*, December 1883, 244–245; see also Sarkis, *al-'Adat fi al-Ziyarat*.

70. See "al-Tasliya Awqat al-Faragh," *al-Muqtataf*, February 1899, 133. Chapter 5 goes into more detail on both *al-Muqtataf* and *al-Mahabba*, specifically their influence on developing an ideal of domesticity.

71. See in *al-Mahabba*, "Kayfa Yamduna Saharatihim," 26 May 1900; "'Adatuna wa-Afatuha," pt. 2, 18 June 1904; "Waraq al-La'ib," 6 January 1906; and "al-Mar'a wa-l-Qimar," 10 March 1906.

72. "Kayfa Yamduna Saharatihim," *al-Mahabba*, 26 May 1900.

73. "Waraq al-La'ib," *al-Mahabba*, 6 January 1906.

74. "Al-Funughraf," *al-Mahabba*, 23 November 1907.

75. "Kayfa Yamduna Saharatihim," *al-Mahabba*, 26 May 1900.

76. Dahir, *Bayrut wa-Jabal Lubnan*, 113.

77. For an overview covering 1904 to 1932, see Racy, "Record Industry."

78. Ibid., 39–43. According to a Baidaphon Company catalogue from 1926, the company also sought out and recorded popular *adwar* and *taqatiq* from Egypt, Syria, Palestine, and Iraq.

79. Educated at the Conservatoire de Paris, Sabra describes the publication as "Oriental songs in *ifranji* musical notation" (*Lisan al-Hal*, 6 September 1906). The songs listed were "Ahwa al-Ghazal al-Rabrabi," "wa-Asqini al-Rah," "Qadduka al-Mayyas," "Rayih fayn ya Msallini," "Anta al-Mumna' wa-l-Bakhtu Sa'adani," and "Marsh Sharqi."

80. *Lisan al-Hal*, 30 May 1900, 21 February 1905.

81. As in these cases, for example: MSB, *Hujaj*, A.H. Jumada al-Awwal 1302-Shawwal 1303, 11 Safar 1303 (19 November 1885), no. 419; *Hujaj*, A.H. Dhu al-Qa'da 1314–Rabi' al-Thani 1316, 22 Rabi' al-Awwal 1316 (10 August 1898), no. 1347; *Hujaj*, A.H. Sha'ban 1317-Jumada al-Thani 1320, 16 Jumada al-Awwal 1319 (31 August 1901), 74; *Da'awa*, A.H. Jumada al-Thani 1320–Rajab 1325, 10 Dhu al-Qa'da 1320 (8 February 1903), 8; *Hujaj wa-Da'awa*, A.H. Rajab 1321–Dhu al-Hijja 1322, 15 Jumada al-Thani 1322 (27 August 1904), 64–65; and *Da'awa*, A.H. Shawwal 1323–Safar 1326, 20 Rabi' al-Thani 1324 (13 June 1906), 40–42.

82. In the examined records, most women laying claim to bedsteads do so in inheritance cases. I found only two exceptions in which a woman laid claim to a bed in a marriage dispute: MSB, *Hujaj wa-Da'awa*, A.H. Shawwal 1323–Shawwal 1326, 2 Ramadan 1323 (31 October 1905), 50–52; and *Da'awa*, A.H. Muharram 1328–Jumada al-Thani 1332, 1 Sha'ban 1329 (28 July 1911), 117. The disposition of metal bedsteads in cases in Beirut presents an interesting study when contrasted with the gendered division of spaces that developed in France with the introduction of furniture into bourgeois homes during the eighteenth century. There, the bedroom constituted the most feminine of spaces, the space of reproduction, and it was the wife who brought bedroom furnishings, including the bed, into the marriage as part of the dower (Auslander, *Taste and Power*, 279–281).

83. MSB, *Hujaj*, A.H. Rabi' al-Awwal 1328–Jumada al-Thani 1329, 10 Jumada al-Awwal 1328 (20 May 1910), no. 227.

84. MSB, *Daʿawa*, A.H. Muharram 1328–Jumada al-Thani 1332, 10 Muharram 1329 (11 January 1911), 105–107.

85. MSB, *Hujaj wa-Daʿawa*, A.H. Dhu al-Qaʿda 1312–Jumada al-Awwal 1315, 22 Rabiʿ al-Awwal 1314 (31 August 1896), 33–42.

86. MAE, Paris, CCCB 1897-1901, vol. 12, Beirut, 5 September 1901.

87. Leary, *Syria, the Land of Lebanon*, 37.

88. On alimony scales in Jaffa and Haifa, see also Agmon, *Family and Court*, 112–113. The amount to be paid in alimony was decided based on testimonies on the economic condition of the person paying the alimony as well as the standard of living the grantee was expected to maintain.

89. *Lisan al-Hal*, 17 February 1905.

90. See phonograph advertisements in *Lisan al-Hal* for Au Gant Rouge, 30 December 1900; Edison, 1 May 1901; and ʿAbd al-Karim Fadil's store, 17 February 1905. For advertisements for Singer sewing machines, see *al-Mahabba*, 10 June 1905. See also Kupferschmidt, "Social History of the Sewing Machine."

91. Barghuti, *al-Marahil*, 126. For another example from Jerusalem, Café Jawhariyya, see Tamari, "Jerusalem's Ottoman Modernity," 20–23.

92. In another marital court case, testimonies were rejected because the mode of socialization they referenced was that of two married couples spending evenings together in mixed company; see MSB, *Hujaj*, A.H. Rabiʿ al-Awwal 1328–Jumada al-Thani 1329, 6 Muharram 1328 (18 January 1910), no. 435.

Chapter 5. A Matter of Taste

Portions of this chapter are adapted from Abou-Hodeib, "Taste and Class in Late Ottoman Beirut," *International Journal of Middle East Studies* 43 (2011): 475–492.

1. "Mamlakat al-Marʾa," *al-Hasnaʾ*, July 1909. Esther Moyal (1873–1948), née Azhari, was a Beirut-born, Jewish journalist and feminist, who studied at the Syrian Protestant College before living and working in Cairo, Istanbul, Jaffa, and Marseilles. In Cairo, she issued the bimonthly *al-ʿAʾila* (The Family) between 1899 and 1904. She was involved in the literary society Bakurat Suriyya and wrote in *al-Hasnaʾ*, *al-Ahram*, and *al-Hilal* (Yarid, *al-Katibat al-Lubnaniyyat*, 142; Behar and Benite, *Middle Eastern Jewish Thought*, 30).

2. For more on the ideal home in the American, English, and French contexts, see, respectively, Hareven, "Home and the Family," 253–285; Davidoff, *Worlds Between*; and Auslander, *Taste and Power*, esp. chap. 7.

3. See, for example, Booth, "'May Her Likes'"; Baron, *Women's Awakening in Egypt*, chap. 7; Chatterjee, "Women's Question"; Radhakrishnan, "Nationalism, Gender, and the Narrative of Identity"; Sand, *House and Home*; and Frykman and Löfgren, *Culture Builders*.

4. On the relations of the home with the public sphere, see Habermas, *Structural Transformation*, 43–51.

5. Ferry, *Homo Aestheticus*, 25.

6. Bourdieu, "Symbolic Power," 81.

7. "Al-Sama' al-Ula," pt. 1, *al-Hasna'*, June 1910.

8. Ibid.

9. Tu'ma received her education first in her home village, then at the American School for Girls in Sidon and the Shuwayfat School. For more on Tu'ma, see Dimechkie, "Julia Tu'mi Dimashqiyi"; and Jiha, *Julia Tu'ma Dimashqiyya*.

10. Jiha, *Julia Tu'ma Dimashqiyya*, 23.

11. Dimechkie, "Julia Tu'mi Dimashqiyi," 61.

12. Najmabadi, "Crafting an Educated Housewife," 114.

13. Khater, " 'House' to 'Goddess of the House.'"

14. Works on Egypt also bring forth this aspect of the home (see, e.g., Russell, *New Egyptian Woman*). On the recasting of *tarbiya* along scientific lines and its relationship to modern conceptions of motherhood in turn-of-the-century Egypt, see Shakry, "Schooled Mothers."

15. Bustani, "Khitab fi Ta'lim al-Nisa'," 37–38.

16. "Ramyatun min Ghayri Ramin," *al-Jinan*, December 1870. See also in *al-Jinan*, "Umm al-Dunya," June 1870; "Fi Tarbiyat al-Nisa'," November 1872; and "al-Zawj wa-l-Zawja," June 1875. Not all women were presented as ideally in *nahda* fictions that were preoccupied with modern, middle-class female subjects. In her study of "sensation stories" of the same period, Ghenwa Hayek argues for the presence of a different kind of female character, one that was "more flawed, more multidimensional, and, consequently, more troubling" (Hayek, "Experimental Female Fictions," 252).

17. This section was a regular feature in the magazine from its introduction in 1881 until 1928, when it was transformed into "women's issues," before disappearing completely in 1936.

18. Some of these debates are discussed in Zachs and Halevi, "From *Difā' al-Nisā'*," 8–12.

19. In addition to having agents in the main cities and towns of the Levant, letters to the editor show that *al-Muqtataf* drew reader participation from the region as well as from Australia and the Americas. The incident that precipitated Sarruf and Nimr's departure to Egypt, also referred to as "the Lewis Affair," involved a conflict with the more conservative faculty of the Syrian Protestant College over Darwinism and the use of Arabic language at the college (for more, see Farag, "Lewis Affair"; and Meier, *Al Muqtataf*).

20. "Muqaddima," *al-Muqtataf*, June 1876, 1.

21. "Tabdhir al-Sharq wa-Tadbir al-Gharb," pt. 1, *al-Muqtataf*, October 1876, 110–111; see also "La Tahtaqir al-Sagaha'ir," *al-Muqtataf*, September 1879, 242.

22. For information on the societies, see Zaydan, *Tarikh Adab al-Lugha al-'Arabiyya*, vol. 4, 65–74; see also Kallas, *al-Haraka al-Fikriyya al-Nasawiyya*, 200, 212–215. According to Ibrahim (in *al-Haraka al-Nisa'iyya al-Lubnaniyya*, 21), Yadd al-Musa'da was founded

in 1919. But the society had been in existence at least since 1911, when a speech delivered at the society was published as "al-Mamlaka al-Sughra," in *al-Hasna'*, May 1911.

23. In *al-Haraka al-Fikriyya al-Nasawiyya*, 212, Kallas claims the society was founded in 1873, but in an obituary for Maryam Makariyus, Yaqut Sarruf mentions that she founded a literary society with her friends in the beginning of 1880. *Al-Muqtataf*, October 1888, 435–439.

24. See in *al-Muqtataf*, "al-Akhlaq wa-l-ʻAwa'id," March 1883, 367–369; "Al-Hay'a al-Ijtimaʻiyya ʻind Baʻd al-Mutawahhishin," July 1883, 585–587; "Adab al-Ma'ida," March 1885, 370–373; and "Farsh al-Buyut wa-Tartibuha," September 1885, 743–745.

25. Sami, *Qawl al-Haqq*, 14.

26. Syrian Christian intellectuals were also instrumental in shaping ideas about the home in Egypt; see Baron, *Women's Awakening in Egypt*. On the intellectual dissemination networks linking Beirut, Cairo, and Alexandria, see Khuri-Makdisi, *Eastern Mediterranean*, esp. chap. 2.

27. Khalidi, *Jawla fi al-Dhikrayat*, 68. Under Sultan Abdülhamid II's strict control over the press, some Egyptian publications, such as *al-Ahram*, were forbidden in the Levant.

28. Pollard, "Learning Gendered Modernity," 258. For more on the content of these textbooks, see Russell, *New Egyptian Woman*, chap. 8.

29. Fleischmann, " 'Under an American Roof,' " 69.

30. On other subjects taught at the British Syrian Training College, see Makdisi, *Teta, Mother and Me*, 179, 182–185. Although it is not clear what "object lessons" included at the college, we know that in the curriculum of the Egyptian Ministry of Culture, it included topics such as proper dress and hygiene, the house and its rooms, and how best to build a house (Pollard, "Family Politics," 56).

31. "Taqdir Nafaqat al-Bayt," *al-Muqtataf*, May 1890, 557–558.

32. On press regulations under Abdülhamid II, see Cioeta, "Ottoman Censorship."

33. Khuri-Makdisi, *Eastern Mediterranean*, 113. Baz was married to one of the earliest practicing female doctors in Syria, Anistas Barakat. See Kallas, *al-Haraka al-Fikriyya al-Nasawiyya*, 96; and Daghir, *Masadir al-Dirasa al-Adabiyya*, vol. 3, 160–164.

34. "Bint al-Madrasa," *al-Hasna'*, June 1910.

35. "Al-Mamlaka al-Sughra," *al-Hasna'*, May 1911. Jurji Niqula Baz's *al-Hasna'* (begun in 1909, in Beirut), Mary ʻAjami's *al-ʻArus* (begun in 1910, in Damascus), and Sulayma Abu Rashid's *Fatat Lubnan* (begun in 1914, in Beirut) were all journals that constituted a new phase in politically engaged female writing that was to pick up with greater zeal after World War I.

36. See, for example, "Ma Hiya al-Mar'a," *Thamarat al-Funun*, 1 July 1901; "Al-Ibna fi al-Bayt," *al-Mawrid al-Safi*, 1 (1910): 39–43; and "al-Fatat wa-Tadbir al-Manzil," *al-Hasna'*, April 1912. Emblematic of these differences in opinion is the debate between Hana Kasbani Kurani and Zaynab Fawwaz in the Egyptian newspaper *al-Nil* in 1893, republished in Salim, *al-Rasa'il al-Zaynabiyya*, 54–61, 68–84.

37. See, for example, "Tartib al-Ma'ida," *al-Muqtataf*, November 1884, 112; "Athath al-Bayt wa-Tartibuhu," *al-Muqtataf*, February 1897, 137–138; and "Tadbir al-Manzil," *al-Hasna'*, June 1909.

38. For explicit references to "those of middling means," see, for example, in *al-Muqtataf*, "al-Tartib," May 1882, 751; "Al-Ziyara wa-l-Diyafa," December 1883, 244; "Zinat al-Ma'ida," June 1885, 554; and "Farsh al-Buyut wa-Tartibuha," September 1885, 742; see also "al-Muda Aydan," *al-Mahabba*, 29 April 1905; "Al-Muda," *al-Mahabba*, 13 May 1905; and "al-Ibna fi al-Bayt," *al-Mawrid al-Safi*, 1 (1910): 40. Sometimes the expression *al-'amma al-mutawassitu al-hal* was used. The word *'amma* (commoners) did not always have negative connotations. In earlier times, it referred to nonranking orders, including peasants and rich merchants alike, to distinguish them from the ranking orders (Traboulsi, *History of Modern Lebanon*, 4). In the present context, it refers simply to the average person.

39. "Athath al-Bayt wa-Tartibuhu," *al-Muqtataf*, February 1897, 137; see also "Tadbir al-Manzil," *al-Hasna'*, June 1909.

40. "Al-Tartib," *al-Hasna'*, August 1909.

41. "Athath al-Bayt wa-Tartibuhu," *al-Muqtataf*, February 1897, 137. The distinction between essential and contingent is also brought up in relation to differences in taste in "al-Dhawq wa-Qiyasuhu," *al-Muqtataf*, March 1890, 372–379.

42. "Al-Fatat wa-Tadbir al-Manzil," *al-Hasna'*, April 1912; also published in Hashim, *Kitab fi al-Tarbiya*, 87–95. Labiba Hashim (1882–1952) was born in Beirut where she received her education at the hands of missionaries. After moving to Egypt with her family in 1900, she founded the women's magazine *Fatat al-Sharq* (1906) and lectured at the women's college of the Egyptian University, later Cairo University.

43. In industrialized societies, the idea of the efficient home "arose out of an unlikely marriage between women's efforts to rationalize and organize housework and theories that had been developed to improve industrial production in factories" (Rybczynski, *Home*, 167).

44. Kafawi, *al-Kuliyyat*, 462. Al-Kafawi's lexicon was printed in Cairo in 1838 and 1864 by the Bulaq Press, established by Muhammad 'Ali in 1821–1922 (on the Bulaq Press, see Crabbs, *Writing of History*, 201).

45. Metcalf, introduction to *Moral Conduct and Authority*, 2–3. Shakry points out how a modern discourse on *tarbiya* was also related to an "indigenous" concept of *adab* (Shakry, "Schooled Mothers," 127–128).

46. Metcalf, introduction to *Moral Conduct and Authority*, 18–19.

47. This distinction is elaborated in Musbah Tabbara's "al-Dhawq," pts. 1 & 2, *Thamarat al-Funun*, 8 and 15 June 1908. The history of the word *dhawq* is complex in its own right. The modern interpretations also brought to the fore an element most prominent in mystic, particularly sufi, adaptations of taste as an attempt to revive ethics through practices of the self (Moosa, "Muslim Ethics?").

48. "Al-Zayy (al-Muda)," *al-Muqtataf*, February 1886, 305–308; "Dhawq al-Nas fi al-Jamal," *al-Muqtataf*, July 1890, 702–703; "Al-Dhawq," *Thamarat al-Funun*, 15 June 1908.

49. "Al-Dhawq wa-Qiyasuhu," *al-Muqtataf*, March 1890, 372–79; "Al-Dhawq," *al-Muqtataf*, November 1892, 81–87. On acquiring taste, see "al-Dhawq," *Thamarat al-Funun*, 8 June 1908; "Al-Ibna fi al-Bayt," *al-Mawrid al-Safi*, 1 (1910): 39–43; and "Tarbiyat al-Dhawq," in Hashim, *Kitab fi al-Tarbiya*, 113–121, also published in *al-Hasna'*, November 1911 and December 1911. The phrase "correct taste" was also used in connection with educating women ("Mas'alat al-Nisa'," *Thamarat al-Funun*, 4 December 1899); with socialization ("Kayfa Yamduna Saharatihim," *al-Mahabba*, 26 May 1900); and with dress ("Al-Muda," *al-Mahabba*, 13 May 1905; "Al-Zahir al-Ma'luf min al-Mafrush wa-l-Malbus," *Thamarat al-Funun*, 28 May 1900).

50. Shalhut also finds this sufficient evidence that "the Arabic language is in need of edification and reform in accordance with the dictates of taste" ("Al-Dhawq," *al-Muqtataf*, November 1892, 87). *Ifranja*, the term Shalhut uses, is the noun form of *ifranji* and means "Europeans" or, more generally, "Westerners."

51. Ibid., 85.

52. Ibid.

53. Bourdieu, *Distinction*, 2.

54. Ibid., 57–60, 170–173.

55. Ibid., 56–57, 60.

56. "Ghuraf al-Nawm," *al-Muqtataf*, November 1889, 410–411.

57. Hashim, *Kitab fi al-Tarbiya*, 116–117. For others tackling the same theme, see "Intiqa' al-Zawja," *al-Mahabba*, 23 March 1901; "Al-Mar'a wa-l-Rajul," pt. 1, *Thamarat al-Funun*, 8 July 1901; and "al-Sama' al-Ula," pt. 1, *al-Hasna'*, June 1910. It was not uncommon for writers to lump the poor and the middle class together as a group with common characteristics (see, e.g., "Zinat al-Mar'a wa-l-Iqtisad," *al-Mahabba*, 10 March 1901).

58. "Al-Sama' al-Ula," pt. 2, *al-Hasna'*, July 1910.

59. For additional articles on privileging taste over riches, see, for example, "al-Ibna fi al-Bayt," *al-Mawrid al-Safi* 1 (1910): 39–43; "Al-Mar'a wa-l-Rajul," *Thamarat al-Funun*, pt. 1, 8 July 1901; and "Tarbiyat al-Dhawq," *al-Hasna'*, November 1911. Criticism of the placement of chairs also appears in "Farsh al-Buyut wa-Tartibuha," *al-Muqtataf*, September 1885, 744; and "Zinat al-Bayt," *al-Muqtataf*, May 1892, 564.

60. "Zinat al-Ma'ida," *al-Muqtataf*, June 1885, 555; "Tartib al-Suwar," *al-Muqtataf*, April 1890, 484–485.

61. Bourdieu, *Distinction*, 56.

62. This reaction was especially true of *al-Muqtataf* articles (see, for example, "Zinat al-Bayt," November 1881, 368; "Alwan al-Athath," September 1881, 242; "Al-Tartib," May 1882, 751–752; and "Ikhtiyar al-Zawja," October 1887, 709–714).

63. "Zinat al-Bayt," *al-Muqtataf*, November 1881, 368.

64. Bodenstein, "Housing the Foreign," 123–127. See also idem, "Qasr Heneiné." On World Fairs, see Çelik, *Displaying the Orient*, esp. chap. 2.

65. "Zinat al-Bayt," *al-Muqtataf*, May 1892, 565.

66. See in *al-Muqtataf*, "Adab al-Ziyara," November 1881, 606–608; "Al-Ziyara wa-l-Diyafa," October 1883, 243-244; and "Tartib al-Qaʿa," February 1889, 329–331.

67. "Banat Suriyya," *al-Muqtataf*, September 1881, 304.

68. Initially, Christians, Muslims, and Jews in the region used *al-rum* to refer to both the Byzantines and the Crusaders in medieval times. With changing military realities and the weakening of the Byzantine Empire the term *ifranj* was adopted to refer specifically to the Crusaders (El-Cheikh, "Byzantium through the Islamic Prism"). The current Arabic word for Crusaders, *salibiyyun*, from *salib* (cross), came into use in the nineteenth century (Hillenbrand, *Crusades*, 31).

69. Philipp claims that *al-Muqtataf* "was the most enthusiastic in accepting modern Europe as a model for Arab society" (Philipp, "Perceptions of the First World War," 211–221). For a more thorough refutation of this claim, see Glaß, *Der Muqtataf und seine Öffentlichkeit*, vol. 1.

70. "Al-Tamaddun wa-l-Tawahhush," *al-Muqtataf*, April 1885, 393.

71. This view was most famously expressed by Jamal al-Din al-Afghani who argued for acquiring technical developments by a return to Muslim reason rather than through imitation, because behind the European arts "lay an entire way of thought and—more important still—a system of social morality" (Hourani, *Arabic Thought*, 114).

72. For more on this point and on *al-Muqtataf*'s attitude towards the "objects" of progress, see Bou Ali, "Performing the Nahda," 89–93.

73. See, for example, "Mutalaʿat al-Muqtataf" (*al-Muqtataf*, February 1877, 205), a didactic article on how to read *al-Muqtataf* and put the information it provides into practice, directed explicitly at an audience "with little experience in reading, particularly those in the industry branch."

74. "Al-Tamaddun wa-l-Tawahhush," *al-Muqtataf*, April 1885, 393.

75. For example, "ʿAlaqat al-Mashriq bi-l-Maghrib," *al-Muqtataf*, June 1891, 572–576; and "Atfal al-Yabaniyyin," *al-Muqtataf*, July 1899, 542–543. For more on this point, see Worringer, *Ottomans Imagining Japan*.

76. "Al-Muda wa-Asbabuha," *al-Mahabba*, 3 March 1906.

77. "Al-Sinaʿa," *al-Jinan*, January 1870.

78. Ibid.

79. See, for example, "al-ʿIlm Muftah al-Sinaʿa," *al-Muqtataf*, April 1877, 241-242; "Al-Sanaʾiʿ al-Dakhiliyya, Ayy al-Wataniyya," *Thamarat al-Funun*, 29 April 1889; and "Inhad al-Ghayra al-Wataniyya li-Tarqiyat al-Badaʾiʿ al-Sharqiyya," *al-Fatat*, April and May 1893.

80. MAE, Nantes, CB 1886–1914, carton 339, Beirut, 22 February 1909. Sasson Farhi, a manufacturer based in Egypt, complained that his merchandise was suspected of being Austrian and had been seized by the dockworkers (see also Kayalı, *Arabs and Young Turks*, 63, 120).

81. Kupferschmidt, *European Department Stores*, 33.

82. Ma'luf (1869–1956) was born in Kfar 'Aqab and educated at the missionary school in Shuwayr. He taught in schools in Kfar 'Aqab, Tripoli, Zahla, and Damascus, and was active in several scientific and literary societies, such as al-Majma' al-'Ilmi al-'Arabi (The Arabic Academy of Sciences) and Majma' al-Lugha al-'Arabiyya in Cairo (Academy of the Arabic Language). He regularly published articles in Syria, Egypt, and the Americas and also several books as well as putting out his own periodicals: *Al-Athar*, *al-Sharqiyya*, and *al-Muhadhdhab* (Ma'luf, *Dawani al-Qutuf*, vol. 1, 5; Tarrazi, *Tarikh al-Sahafa al-'Arabiyya*, vol. 2, 234–238).

83. Bustani, *Khitab fi al-Hay'a al-Ijtima'iyya*.

84. Ma'luf, *al-Akhlaq Majmu' Adat*, 16.

85. Ibid., 45. Ma'luf's criticism of Europeanization and Westernization is less about the actual realities of Europe or the West and more of a repository of concepts against which a particular and moral self could be defined. Nowhere in his speech does he define in detail what it is about *ifranji* culture that should be avoided.

86. Khuri, *Dalil Bayrut*, 87–98.

87. For example, *al-Mahabba*, 29 November 1902, 10 January 1903; and *Lisan al-Hal*, 23 August 1906, 29 January 1910, 22 February 1910, 11 August 1910.

88. *Lisan al-Hal*, 22 February 1910.

89. On what women wore to town, see Noueiry, *Ra's Bayrut*, 34–35. According to Thoumin, "[Towards 1880] Christians already formed the majority [in Beirut], but they still lived in fear of Muslims and their women went out veiled. This custom was soon to disappear, and in 1890, they had abandoned the veil" (Thoumin, *Géographie humaine de la Syrie centrale*, 320). Citing Thoumin, Gabriel Baer repeats the claim that Christian women in Beirut "ceased wearing veils in 1890" (Baer, *Population and Society*, 42). However, the assertion that Christian women "unveiled" in Beirut in the 1890s is not only hard to maintain but also does not take into consideration the different groups that co-existed and shared public spaces well beyond that point. Even in 1906, years after Christian women in Beirut supposedly stopped wearing the veil, when the Greek Orthodox periodical *al-Mahabba* took up the issue of women's fashion, it was by no means taken for granted that Christian women would appear uncovered in the souks.

90. This view was unique neither to Beirut nor to the region. For example, in *A Vindication of the Rights of Woman* (41–44), Mary Wollstonecraft argues, in contrast to Rousseau, that women's pursuit of fashion is not a "natural" inclination, but a result of the lack of proper education. Thorstein Veblen, in *Theory of the Leisure Class* (111–124), analyzes women's fashion as a manifestation of abstinence from productive employment. On the relation between reforming women and reforming fashion in other contexts, see Kelly, *New England Fashion*; and Cunningham, *Reforming Women's Fashion*.

91. For more on al-Qabbani and his tenure as mayor, see Sharif, *Imperial Norms*, 134–139.

92. For more, see Sayyah, "Sahifat *Thamarat al-Funun*"; and Cioeta, "Islamic Benevolent Societies."

93. See, for example, "al-Ma'isha fi Bayrut," *Thamarat al-Funun*, 4 June 1906, originally published in the Jesuit weekly *al-Bashir*. It was not unusual for *Thamarat al-Funun* to find itself in the same trench with *al-Bashir* on issues of morality and science, particularly in context of the latter's attacks on *al-Muqtataf* (e.g., "al-Muqtataf wa-l-Mar'a," *Thamarat al-Funun*, 30 March 1896).

94. "Madha Nurid bi-Ta'lim al-Mar'a," *Thamarat al-Funun*, 10 February 1908.

95. "Mas'alat al-Nisa'," *Thamarat al-Funun*, 4 December 1899.

96. This saying (*hadith*) is attributed to the prophet Muhammad (see, in *Thamarat al-Funun*, "al-Adab," 5 June 1884; "Mas'alat al-Nisa'," 4 December 1899; and "al-Zahir al-Ma'luf min al-Mafrush wa-l-Malbus," 28 May 1900). For a similar attempt at understanding a modern phenomenon by grounding it in a familiar Islamic tradition, see Lockman, "Imagining the Working Class" (168), where an author seeks to establish the authenticity of the middle class by citing the same hadith.

97. The phrase *yatabarrajna tabarruj nisa' al-jahiliyya* appeared in "al-Zawaj," pts. 2 and 3, *Thamarat al-Funun*, April 1884. On women working, see "Mas'alat al-Nisa'," *Thamarat al-Funun*, 18 December 1899.

98. "Al-Mar'a wa-l-Rajul," pt. 1, *Thamarat al-Funun*, 8 July 1901; "Madha Nurid bi-Ta'lim al-Mar'a," *Thamarat al-Funun*, 10 February 1908.

99. According to the daily Hebrew newspaper *Ha-Hirut*, "[*al-Mahabba*'s] closure is regrettable, for it contended with our enemies and defended our settlements" (cited in Yahusha', *Tarikh al-Sahafa al-'Arabiyya*, 134).

100. "Al-Nisa' fi al-Aswaq," *al-Mahabba*, 31 March 1906.

101. For more on speculation on the Istanbul Stock Exchange, see Toprak, "Financial Structure"; and Hanssen, "'Malhamé–Malfamé,'" 40. On the 1895 collapse, see Helten, "Mining, Share Manias, and Speculation," 170–173.

102. MAE, Paris, CCCB 1895–1896, vol. 11, Beirut, 4 June 1895, 15 December 1896.

103. "Al-Nahda al-Nisa'iyya wa-l-'Muda.'" *al-Mahabba*, 10 May 1901.

104. The editorials were unsigned, and it is not clear whether Abi Halaqa wrote them. But judging by the content, they were clearly written by a man who was well-known in the Greek Orthodox community of Beirut.

105. Implicit, and sometimes explicit, in this attack was a critique of the educational system for having taught women the alphabet "only to read fashion magazines" ("Nisa'una wa-l-Muda," *al-Mahabba*, 22 April 1905; "Al-Muda Aydan," *al-Mahabba*, 29 April 1905).

106. "'Aqibat al-Israf," *al-Mahabba*, 3 June 1905. See also in *al-Mahabba*, "Dhayl lil-Muda," 6 May 1905; "Al-Muda," 13 May 1905; and "al-Mar'a, wa-Tahamul al-Kuttab 'Alayha," 2 June 1906. Only the last of these was signed, by a woman residing in Belgium, which points to some hesitancy on the part of *al-Mahabba*'s regional female readership to publicly participate in this kind of debate.

107. "Al-Muda wa-Asbabuha," *al-Mahabba*, 3 March 1906; "Al-Rajul wa-l-Muda," *al-Mahabba*, 26 May 1906.

108. *Al-Mahabba* continued to pursue the theme of fashion, linking it to various ills in society such as gambling and marriage customs. Though women remained central to the critique, the editorials seemed to be more careful to include men also, suggesting that the criticism did have an influence on the debate (see, in *al-Mahabba*, "Waraq al-La'ib," 6 January 1906; "Al-Wilada wa-l-Zija ('ala al-Muda)," 24 February 1906; and "Wajibat al-Ab fi Tarbiyat al-Awlad," 9 June 1906).

109. Haris Exertzoglou shows how such an ambiguity in matters of consumption was also prevalent among the Hellenized Greek Orthodox urban communities of the late Ottoman Empire (Exertzoglou, "Cultural Uses of Consumption"). See also "Junun Ahl al-Zayy (Ayy al-Muda)," *al-Nashra al-Usbu'iyya*, December 1882, an article criticizing fashion from a scientific point of view.

110. "Al-Dhawq," *al-Muqtataf*, November 1892, 86.

111. "Fi al-Fatat al-Haqiqiyya," *al-Mahabba*, 14 July 1900.

112. Elsewhere, the dichotomy between the appearance of wealth and the inner value of morals is even expressed in verse: "Be not enamored by someone's dress / Forget dress and look for the morals" ("Al-Ibna fi al-bayt," *al-Mawrid al-Safi*, vol. 1 (1910): 40).

113. Chatterjee, *Nation and Its Fragments*, 116–134.

114. Goswami, *Producing India*, 24.

Chapter 6. Local Forms and *Ifranji* Pleasures

1. Khuri, *Dalil Bayrut*, 94–95.

2. This argument is succinctly put forth in Auslander, *Taste and Power*, 141–146.

3. Ibid., 185.

4. Following Meyer, "'There Is a Spirit,'" I am emphasizing Meyer's point that different settings create—even structure—the possibility for excess in things.

5. The limitations of using Hanafi court records for statistical purposes are discussed in Chapter 1. When it comes to consular trade reports, although they do provide statistics, the units of measurement as well as the categories of imports change from report to report, making it impossible to draw any long-term analysis of import trends. In addition, not all imports to Beirut were destined for that city, as many were channeled further, into the hinterlands.

6. Saisselin, *Bourgeois and the Bibelot*; Auslander, "Regeneration Through the Everyday?" 244.

7. Exactly what the advertisement is referring to is not clear, but it mentions "the famous old *tuhfa* known as the lamp of the deceased Ilyas Musa al-Humsi. It is made in a strange Oriental way that amazes the sight and confuses the minds" (Khuri, *Dalil Bayrut*, 93).

8. MAE, Paris, CCCB 1897–1901, vol. 12, Beirut, 15 March 1898, 20 January 1900.

9. MAE, Paris, CCCB 1888–1894, vol. 10, Beirut, June 1890; CPCT 1900–1914, vol. 476, Beirut, 15 December 1906.

10. MAE, Paris, CCCB 1888-1894, vol. 10, Beirut, June 1890; CCCB 1897–1901, vol. 12, Beirut, 27 December 1900; CPCT 1900–1914, vol. 476, Beirut, 12 March 1903, 16 June 1905, 31 March 1911.

11. MAE, Paris, CCCB 1888–1894, vol. 10, Beirut, June 1890; see also Archives Nationales, Paris, Commerce et Industrie, carton F/12/9849, 1919.

12. "Kassab Ikhwan," *Lisan al-Hal*, 10 November 1910.

13. See the advertisements for Grands Magasins Bérangé, *Lisan al-Hal*, 18 January 1912; and Sioufi, *Lisan al-Hal*, 9 January 1906.

14. See the advertisements for Grand Magasin, *Lisan al-Hal*, 11 December 1894; and Magasin Cristal, *Lisan al-Hal*, 12 November 1904, 30 December 1905.

15. On emphasizing abundance in turn-of-the-century department stores, see Miller, *Bon Marché*, 165–178; and Outka, "Crossing the Great Divides."

16. Information on local carpenters, stores, and their merchandise comes from Khuri, *Dalil Bayrut*, and from advertisements in the back sections of *Thamarat al-Funun*, *Lisan al-Hal*, and *al-Mahabba*. For more on Orosdi-Back, see Kupferschmidt, "Who Needed Department Stores in Egypt?"; and idem, *European Department Stores*.

17. See advertisements for Bishara 'Awda in Khuri, *Dalil Bayrut*, 93; Adami, Khuri, and Co., *Lisan al-Hal*, 18 November 1886; Makhzan Suriyya, *Lisan al-Hal*, 3 October 1887; Au Petit Bon Marché, *Lisan al-Hal*, 20 October 1904; and Magasin Cristal, *Lisan al-Hal*, 12 November 1904.

18. Darwaza, *Mudhakkirat*, 169.

19. See, for example, advertisements in *Lisan al-Hal* by Amin Bhamduni, 8 November 1877; Mahmud al-Hajja al-Shami & Co., 20 July 1878; 'Adami and Khuri, 18 November 1886; 'Abd al-Karim Fadil & Co., 3 May 1899, 19 October 1900; Shukri 'Awda & Bros., 17 November 1900; Au Gant Rouge, 30 December 1900; Ilyas Abi 'Akar, 22 October 1904; and Shukri Abi Rashid, 13 January 1910.

20. For example, advertisements in *Lisan al-Hal* for Au Gant Rouge, 4 March 1878; 'Aradati and Da'uq, 3 October 1887; and Nasr Allah and Jirjis 'Araman, 20 May 1899.

21. See advertisements for Grand Dépot, *Lisan al-Hal*, 15 November 1886; and Magasin du Printemps, *Thamarat al-Funun*, 4 June 1888.

22. Advertisement for Nasri Malik, *Lisan al-Hal*, 11 August 1910.

23. See advertisements for Sioufi in *al-Mahabba*, 20 April 1901, 10 May 1901.

24. See advertisements for Bishara 'Awda in Khuri, *Dalil Bayrut*, 93; Makhzan Jirjis Sayqali and Yusuf and Mikha'il Ghibril, *Lisan al-Hal*, 23 November 1898; Mikha'il Rahma, *Lisan al-Hal*, 4 January 1899; Grand Magasin, *Lisan al-Hal*, 11 December 1894; Khalil Qurm, *Lisan al-Hal*, 4 May 1901; Harraj Mubilya, *Lisan al-Hal*, 17 May 1901; Ka'di Ikhwan and Ibrahim Mikhbat, *al-Mahabba*, 29 November 1902; and Muhyi al-Din Nusuli, *Thamarat al-Funun*, 13 July 1908.

25. See the advertisement for Mahmud al-Hajja Shami & Co., *Lisan al-Hal*, 20 July 1878.

26. See advertisements for 'Adami and Khuri, *Lisan al-Hal*, 17 October 1887; 'Aradati and Da'uq, *Lisan al-Hal*, 21 October 1887; and Makhzan al-Bada'i' al-Inkliziyya and Makhzan al-Khawajat Bishara 'Awda in Khuri, *Dalil Bayrut*, 92, 93.

27. See in *Lisan al-Hal*, advertisements for Khalil Hashim, 29 August 1878; Williams Depot, 22 July 1881; Dawud al-Qurm, 24 January 1882; and Mikha'il Rahma, 4 January 1899.

28. "Al-Tabbakh al-Ghazi," *Lisan al-Hal*, 20 May 1899.

29. Kupferschmidt, "Social History of the Sewing Machine."

30. See the advertisement for Singer in *al-Mahabba*, 10 June 1905. Various brands of sewing machines were imported to Beirut, but Singer remained by far the most successful. While only 300 Singer machines were imported to Beirut in 1892 (with probably around half of those reexported to the region), in 1908, 2,000 machines were imported to Beirut, with 500 to 600 ending up in the city itself. In 1908, importation of all other brands of sewing machines together added up to about 1,000 machines (MAE, Nantes, CB 1892, vol. 156, carton 16, 1892; CB 1908, vol. 210, Beirut, 16 September 1908).

31. See the advertisement for Naumann sewing machines in *Lisan al-Hal*, 12 November 1904.

32. "Ma'mal al-Siyufi," *al-Mahabba*, 29 November 1902.

33. Unsi, *Dalil Bayrut*, 128, 132.

34. For example, advertisements for the Haddad and Nasri Malik stores in *Lisan al-Hal*, 23 August 1906, 11 August 1910.

35. Hanssen, *Fin de Siècle Beirut*, 217.

36. MBB, A.M. 25 Shubat 1319 (9 March 1904), no. 6; A.M. 3 Mart 1320 (16 March 1904), no. 6; A.M. 18 Mart 1320 (31 March 1904), no. 1; and A.M. 31 Mart 1320 (13 April 1904), no. 6.

37. In this case, Khan Bayhum extended considerably into Suq al-Tawila and Suq Siyur (Fakhuri, *Manzul Bayrut*, 191–192).

38. MAE, Paris, CCCB 1897–1901, vol. 12, Beirut, 15 March 1898.

39. Davie, *Beyrouth et ses faubourgs*, 59–60.

40. An advertisement for Suq Ra'd wa-Hani shows that the owners were pushing towards making textiles a specialty in their souk (*Lisan al-Hal*, 7 October 1886).

41. The advertisement for Makhzan Suriyya in *Lisan al-Hal*, 3 October 1887, is an example. Makhzan Suriyya was owned by 'Aradati and Da'uq. For more on Makhzan Suriyya, see MAE, Nantes, CB 1897, vol. 168, Beirut, 10 December 1897. Information on the souks is from *Dalil Bayrut*.

42. Advertisement for Sioufi, *Lisan al-Hal*, 23 October 1900.

43. An example is the advertisement for Qasr al-Mafrushat in *Lisan al-Hal*, 3 June 1910, 12 April 1911.

44. MAE, Paris, CCCB 1895–1896, vol. 11, Beirut, 15 December 1896. The lack of an agreement between the Ottoman Empire and France on protecting trademarks meant that the French could fight out these battles only in local commercial courts. For more on forgery of French products, see MAE, Nantes, CB 1894, vol. 160, Beirut, 12 March 1894. On at least one occasion, the police found and confiscated equipment used for forgeries from a home in Beirut (MAE, Nantes, CB 1891, vol. 153, Beirut, 24 October 1891).

45. See, for example, advertisements for Milhim al-Hunud Sa'igh and for Yusuf al-Gharib Najjar in Khuri, *Dalil Bayrut*, 94–95; for Ma'mal al-Balat al-Istina'i in idem, 98; for the Sioufi furniture factory in *al-Mahabba*, 29 November 1902; for Butrus and Rizq Allah al-Dibs's tile factory in *Lisan al-Hal*, 10 December 1900; and for As'ad and Shihada's silk factory in *Lisan al-Hal*, 28 December 1905.

46. Shipping costs added to the price of imported furniture, which occupied more space than textiles. As an indication of the small amount of furniture imported, a list of importers from 1895 shows only four houses of commerce—August Duplan, Weber, Wener, and Luciano—none of which belonged to Ottoman subjects. Tellingly, none of these specialized solely in furniture, and their imports also included textiles and construction materials. Duplan was most concerned with cloth imports and was the representative of the Tuilerie réunie de Marseilles, but also dealt with *nouveauté* (novelties), food, metal, and pharmaceutical imports. Duplan was often recommended by the French consul to various businesses looking for representation in Beirut. Weber and Wener also dealt mainly in cloth and *nouveauté*, with other specialized imports on the side. Luciano imported construction material in addition to alimentary products and spirits (MAE, Nantes, CB 1895, vol. 162, 9 September 1895).

47. MAE, Paris, CCCB 1897–1901, vol. 12, Beirut, 15 March 1898, 19 December 1898. A list of cabinetmakers in Beirut in 1889 appeared in Khuri, *Dalil Bayrut*. One of them went by the name of "Johan the Prussian." It is unclear whether this was the cabinetmaker's real name and whether he was, indeed, Prussian.

48. MAE, Paris, CCCB 1895–1896, vol. 11, "Annexe no. 1 à la dépêche commerciale no. 20," 15 December 1896, 161; Khuri, *Dalil Bayrut*, 93–95.

49. Ibid., 94–95.

50. The buffet cost 50 French livres, the equivalent of about 5,500 Ottoman piasters, or more than half a year's wages for a skilled laborer.

51. MAE, Paris, CCCB 1895–1896, vol. 11, Beirut, 15 December 1896.

52. MAE, Nantes, CB 1910, vol. 221, folder 41/3, 1910. See also MAE, Nantes, CB 1908, vol. 210, Beirut, 23 August 1908; and MAE, Paris, CPCT 1900–1914, vol. 476, Beirut, 1 July 1909.

53. Advertisement for Karl Altans, *Lisan al-Hal*, 7 July 1899, 28 September 1899.

54. For example, *Lisan al-Hal*, 18 March 1880.

55. For the use of *min al-tarz al-jadid* (of the latest fashion) and *akhir tarz* (the

latest fashion), see advertisements for Bishara 'Awda in Khuri, *Dalil Bayrut*, 93; and "Makhzan Jirjis Sayqali," *Lisan al-Hal*, 25 November 1898.

56. "Zinat al-bayt," *al-Muqtataf*, November 1881, 368.

57. Qurm employed workers who did gilding and carpentry jobs for average prices (Khuri, *Dalil Bayrut*, 92). Another of the Qurm family, Dawud Efendi, marketed himself as a high-class painter of prominent persons and church pieces, but an 1880 advertisement reveals that his earlier work for churches also involved gilding frames, mirrors, and furniture in general (*Lisan al-Hal*, 22 March 1880).

58. For example, advertisements for Salim Dakkash, Bishara 'Awda, and Milhim al-Hunud Sa'igh in Khuri, *Dalil Bayrut*, 93–94. In court records, domestic items such as mirrors, picture frames, cups, vases, pitchers, and plates are often described as decorated in the ubiquitous golden hue: see, for example, MSB, *Hujaj wa-Da'awa*, A.H. Dhu al-Qa'da 1312–Jumada al-Awwal 1315, 22 Rabi' al-Thani 1314 (30 September 1896), 33–42; *Hujaj*, A.H. Dhu al-Qa'da 1314–Rabi' al-Thani 1316, 9 Safar 1316 (29 June 1898), no. 293; *Da'awa*, A.H. Rabi' al-Thani 1323–Rabi' al-Awwal 1326, 30 Muharram 1324 (26 March 1906), 64–66; *Da'awa*, A.H. Shawwal 1323–Safar 1326, 21 Shawwal 1323 (19 December 1905), 4; 4 Rajab 1325 (13 August 1907), 123–126; and *Hujaj*, A.H. Rabi' al-Awwal 1328–Jumada al-Thani 1329, 4 Dhu al-Qa'da 1328 (7 November 1910), no. 370; 18 Dhu al-Qa'da 1328 (21 November 1910), no. 385. These include marriage and inheritance cases, the latter including cases involving Christians.

59. Khuri, *Dalil Bayrut*, 94.

60. Advertisement for Qasr al-Mafrushat, *Lisan al-Hal*, 12 April 1911. Another example is the advertisement for Karam 'Awn, *Thamarat al-Funun*, 6 July 1908. Earlier advertisements for this same manufacturer do not mention sofas (e.g., *al-Mahabba*, 10 January 1903).

61. Imported wood consisted mostly of wooden planks and beams for construction, and even those imports were diminishing with the introduction of steel (MAE, Paris, CPCT 1900–1914, vol. 476, Beirut, 15 December 1906).

62. Levi, *Jews of Beirut*, 51.

63. Issawi, "British Trade."

64. MAE, Paris, CCCB 1888–1894, vol. 10, Beirut, 20 May 1889.

65. According to figures from 1894, out of a total of 2 million francs' worth of linen imports, 600,000 francs' worth were English imports, 500,000 francs' worth were Austrian, 250,000 francs' worth were Belgian, and 150,000 francs' worth were French (MAE, Paris, CCCB 1895–1896, vol. 11, Beirut, 4 June 1895). Similarly, England's share of cotton imports for 1898 was 45% to 50%, with almost complete monopoly over the calico and the Indian textiles, followed by Germany (13%) and Austria (11%).

66. MAE, Paris, CPCT 1900–1914, vol. 476, Beirut, 12 March 1903.

67. Capital equipment is equipment used for the production of other commodities. Ottoman production also witnessed some revival in this period. The textile sector

remained vigorous enough to continue producing for local consumption into the years of the First World War (Quataert, *Ottoman Manufacturing*, 15–16).

68. MAE, Paris, CCCB 1888–1894, vol. 10, Beirut, June 1890.

69. MAE, Paris, CPCT 1900–1914, vol. 476, Beirut, annex to 31 March 1911.

70. MAE, Paris, CPCT 1900–1914, vol. 476, Beirut, 12 March 1903, 15 December 1906, 31 March 1911; MAE, Paris, CCCB 1897–1901, vol. 12, Beirut, 15 March 1898; Archives Nationales, Paris, Commerce et Industrie, carton F/12/9849, Oyonnax, 16 May 1919, Beirut, 24 May 1919.

71. MAE, Paris, CCCB 1897–1901, vol. 12, Beirut, 27 December 1900; CPCT 1900–1914, vol. 476, Beirut 12 March 1903, 31 March 1911. The visual example provided in figure 11 cannot be definitively linked to Beirut, but in the absence of traceable catalogues, it gives some idea of what was meant by "fantaisie."

72. This proved to be cheaper because undyed yarn cost one fifth to one third less than dyed yarn. In Aleppo, for example, the local dyehouses survived the onslaught of industrially dyed yarn, probably even increasing in number over the nineteenth century (Quataert, *Ottoman Manufacturing*, 30; MAE, Paris, CCCB 1895–1896, vol. 11, Beirut, 15 December 1896). Local dying using imported indigo blue continued to be important even after local dying in other colors lost out to other sources around 1900 (MAE, Paris, CCCB 1897–1901, vol. 12, Beirut, 27 December 1900).

73. Quataert, *Ottoman Manufacturing*, 30–32. See also MAE, Paris, CCCB 1895-1896, vol. 11, Beirut, 15 December 1896; and CCCB 1897–1901, vol. 12, Beirut, 27 December 1900.

74. Aleppo and Damascus cottons and colored half-silks were known for being both inexpensive and strong (Quataert, *Ottoman Manufacturing*, 72–73).

75. MAE, Paris, CCCB 1888–1894, vol. 10, Beirut, June 1890.

76. On *dima* and *alaca*, see ibid. On *manusa*, see Quataert, *Ottoman Manufacturing*, 101. Spinning and weaving in small workshops and inside homes also continued well into the twentieth century. Production methods not only adapted and incorporated new imports but also undercut the role of ready-mades brought in by the department stores of the pre–World War I period. Quataert shows this to be true in the case of Aleppo, for example (Quataert, *Ottoman Manufacturing*, 39–40).

77. Ibid., 78.

78. Unsi, *Dalil Bayrut*, 128, 132–133, 161–162. Al-Unsi mentions only the factories of the city and its suburbs, but it is clear that the term "national textiles" refers to Ottoman production, since no other category appears for silks, cottons, and wools.

79. MAE, Paris, CPCT 1908–1914, vol. 429, Beirut, 30 March 1914. Cement was imported mainly from France, Belgium, and Germany.

80. Hanssen, *Fin de Siècle Beirut*, 97–98, 200–201.

81. MAE, Nantes, CB 1895–1914, carton 348, Beirut, 2 January 1904. See also CB 1893, vol. 158, Beirut, 28 January 1893.

82. Christensen, *Den norske byggeskikken*, 177–178.

83. Advertisement for Makhzan [sic] al-Kahraba'i al-Watani, *Lisan al-Hal*, 15 December 1909. On the various types of lamps available, see advertisements for Hans Henny, *al-Bashir*, 30 December 1891; for Muhyi al-Din Nusuli, *Thamarat al-Funun*, 13 July 1908; and for Trad and Juraydini, *Lisan al-Hal*, 28 June 1911. In addition to wick lamps and gas mantle lamps, there were also kerosene pressure lamps, which used kerosene vaporized under pressure as opposed to ordinary kerosene oil. It is not clear how popular these were in Beirut at the time.

84. Ministry of Interior, Germany, "Berichte über Handel," 43.

85. This kind of labor continues today on some of the same production sites that developed in the second half of the nineteenth century: namely, al-Basta al-Tahta and Damascus Road, where, for example, imitation Louis XIV furniture can still be ordered and customized on demand.

86. Cohen, "Oriental by Design."

87. Gloag, *Victorian Comfort*, 37–38, 42.

Conclusion

1. Ma'luf, *al-Akhlaq Majmu'Adat*, 16–17.

2. Here, I follow Talal Asad's understanding of weak states as those with an absence of administrative and judicial manipulative power over citizens. Paradoxically, it is weak states that find themselves having to resort to violence or brute force—or nonpersuasive power—in order to transform people into modern citizens (Asad, "Conscripts of Western Civilization," 336).

3. Said, *Orientalism*, 321–325.

4. 'Azm, "Orientalism and Orientalism in Reverse," 19–25. See also Abu-Lughod, "Writing against Culture." For more on related notions such as "self Orientalism" and "Oriental Orientalism," see Chu, "Importance of Being Chinese;" Mazzarella, *Shoveling Smoke*, 138–142; Kikuchi, "Oriental Orientalism;" and Chun, "Oriental Orientalism."

5. Fox, "East of Said," 146.

6. Auslander, *Taste and Power*, 142.

7. Ibid., 145.

8. For example, on the relation between public and private in eighteenth-century Egypt, see Fay, "Warrior-Grandees to Domesticated Bourgeoisie," 83–88.

9. Thompson, *Colonial Citizens*.

10. Robson, *Colonialism and Christianity*; Weiss, *Shadow of Sectarianism*.

11. On veiling and unveiling in the nineteenth and early twentieth centuries, see Baron, "Unveiling"; and Najmabadi, *Women with Mustaches*, esp. chap. 5. On how women's identities become central to the consolidation of state power, see Sedghi, *Women and Politics*.

BIBLIOGRAPHY

Primary Sources

Archives and Collections

Arab Image Foundation, Beirut

Archives Nationales, Paris

Association pour la protection des sites et anciennes demeures, Beirut

Başbakanlık Osmanlı Arşivi, Istanbul

British Library, Asia, Pacific, and Africa Collections, London

British National Archives, Kew, London

Jafet Library, American University of Beirut

Ministère des Affaires étrangères à Nantes

Ministère des Affaires étrangères à Paris

Mu'assasat al-Mahfuzat al-Wataniyya, Beirut

National Art Library, Victoria and Albert Museum, London

Official Publications

Düstur (The Constitution), 1st ed., vol. 1. Istanbul: Matbaa-i Amire, 1299 [1882].

Salname-i Vilayet-i Bayrut (Yearbook for the Province of Beirut), A.H. 1311–1312 (1893–1894)

Salname-i Vilayet-i Bayrut, A.H. 1319 (1901)

Salname-i Vilayet-i Bayrut, A.H. 1324 (1906)

Salname-i Vilayet-i Bayrut, A.H. 1326 (1908)

Journals and Newspapers

Al-Bashir (The Herald), Beirut

Bayrut, Beirut

Al-Fatat (The Young Woman), Alexandria

Al-Hasna' (The Fair Lady), Beirut

Al-Jinan (The Gardens), Beirut

Lisan al-Hal (Voice of the Present), Beirut

Al-Mahabba ([God is] Love), Beirut

Al-Mawrid al-Safi (The Pure Spring), Beirut

Al-Muqtataf (The Digest), Beirut and Cairo

Al-Nashra al-Usbu'iyya (The Weekly Bulletin), Beirut

Thamarat al-Funun (Fruits of the Arts), Beirut

Other Published and Unpublished Sources

'Abd al-Nur, Amin. *Tarjamat wa-Sharh Qanun al-Abniya wa-Qarar al-Istimlak*. Beirut: Al-Matba'a al-Adabiyya, 1896.

Abdel Nour, Antoine. *Introduction à l'histoire urbaine de la Syrie ottomane (XVIe–XVIIIe siècle)*. Beirut: Lebanese University, 1982.

Abi Halaqa, Faris. "Rihla fi Suriyya wa-Filastin, 1891 wa-1892." Jafet Library, American University of Beirut, 15 October 1892.

Abou-Hodeib, Toufoul. "The Material Life of the Ottoman Middle Class." *History Compass* 10 (2012): 584–595.

———. "Quarantine and Trade: The Case of Beirut, 1831–1840." *International Journal of Maritime History* 19 (2007): 223–243.

———. "Taste and Class in Late Ottoman Beirut." *International Journal of Middle East Studies* 43 (2011): 475–492.

Abu-Lughod, Lila. "Writing against Culture." In *Recapturing Anthropology: Working in the Present*, edited by Richard G. Fox, 137–162. Santa Fe, NM: School of American Research Press, 1991.

Abu-Manneh, Butrus. "The Christians between Ottomanism and Syrian Nationalism: The Ideas of Butrus al-Bustani." *International Journal of Middle East Studies* 11 (1980): 287–304.

———. "The Establishment and Dismantling of the Province of Syria, 1865–1888." In *Problems of the Modern Middle East in Perspective: Essays in Honour of Albert Hourani*, edited by John P. Spagnolo, 7–26. Ithaca, NY: Ithaca Press, 1992.

Agmon, Iris. *Family and Court: Legal Culture and Modernity in Late Ottoman Palestine*. Syracuse, NY: Syracuse University Press, 2006.

———. "Muslim Women in Court According to the *Sijill* of Late Ottoman Jaffa and Haifa: Some Methodological Notes." In *Women, the Family, and Divorce Laws in*

Islamic History, edited by Amira El Azhary Sonbol, 126–140. Syracuse, NY: Syracuse University Press, 1996.

———. "Recording Procedures and Legal Culture in the Late Ottoman Shari'a Court of Jaffa, 1865–1890." *Islamic Law and Society* 11 (2004): 333–377.

Akarlı, Engin Deniz. " 'Abdülḥamīd II's Attempts to Integrate Arabs into the Ottoman System." In *Palestine in the Late Ottoman Period: Political, Social and Economic Transformations*, edited by David Kushner, 74–89. Jerusalem: Yad Izhak Ben-Zvi, 1986.

Ambaras, David R. "Social Knowledge, Cultural Capital, and the New Middle Class in Japan, 1895–1912." *Journal of Japanese Studies* 24 (1998): 1–33.

Anderson, Benedict. *Imagined Communities: Reflections on the Origin and Spread of Nationalism*. Rev. ed. London: Verso, 1991.

Antar, Elias. "Dinner at When?" *Aramco World* 20 (1969): 2–3.

Appadurai, Arjun, ed. *The Social Life of Things: Commodities in Cultural Perspective*. Cambridge: Cambridge University Press, 1986.

Asad, Talal. "Conscripts of Western Civilization." In *Civilization in Crisis*, vol. 1, edited by Christine W. Gailey, 333–351. Gainesville: Florida University Press, 1992.

———. "The Idea of an Anthropology of Islam." Center for Contemporary Arab Studies Occasional Papers, Georgetown University, 1986.

———. "Reconfigurations of Law and Ethics in Colonial Egypt." In *Formations of the Secular: Christianity, Islam, Modernity*, 205–256. Stanford, CA: Stanford University Press, 2003.

Auslander, Leora. "Regeneration through the Everyday? Clothing, Architecture and Furniture in Revolutionary Paris." *Art History* 28 (2005): 227–247.

———. *Taste and Power: Furnishing Modern France*. Berkeley: University of California Press, 1996.

Ayalon, Ami. *The Press in the Arab Middle East: A History*. New York: Oxford University Press, 1995.

'Azm, Sadik Jalal al-. "Orientalism and Orientalism in Reverse." *Khamsin* 8 (1981): 5–26.

Badran, Margot. *Feminists, Islam, and Nation: Gender and the Making of Modern Egypt*. Princeton, NJ: Princeton University Press, 1995.

Baer, Gabriel. "The Beginnings of Municipal Government in Egypt." *Middle Eastern Studies* 4 (1968): 118–140.

———. *Population and Society in the Arab East*. London: Routledge & Kegan Paul, 1964.

Bairoch, Paul and Richard Kozul-Wright. "Globalization Myths: Some Historical Reflections on Integration, Industrialization and Growth in the World Economy." United Nations Conference on Trade and Development, 1996. http://unctad.org/en/docs/dp_113.en.pdf.

Barghuti, 'Umar Salih al-. *Al-Marahil*. Beirut: Al-Mu'assasa al-'Arabiyya lil-Dirasat wa-l-Nashr, 2001.

Baron, Beth. "Unveiling in Early Twentieth Century Egypt: Practical and Symbolic Considerations." *Middle Eastern Studies* 25 (1989): 370–386.

———. *The Women's Awakening in Egypt: Culture, Society, and the Press.* New Haven, CT: Yale University Press, 1994.

Barr-Melej, Patrick. *Reforming Chile: Cultural Politics, Nationalism, and the Rise of the Middle Class.* Chapel Hill: University of North Carolina Press, 2001.

Bashkin, Orit. "Journeys between Civility and Wilderness: Debates on Civilization and Emotions in the Arab Middle East, 1861–1939." In *Civilizing Emotions: Concepts in Nineteenth-Century Asia and Europe*, Margrit Pernau, Helge Jordheim, Orit Bashkin, Christian Bailey, Oleg Benesch, Jan Ifversen, Mana Kia, Rochona Majumdar, Angelika C. Messner, Myoungkyu Park, Emmanuelle Saada, Mohinder Singh, and Einar Wigen, 126–145. Oxford: Oxford University Press, 2015.

Bayhum, Muhammad Jamil. *Al-Mar'a fi al-Tarikh wa-l-Shara'i'.* Beirut: [n.p.], 1921.

Bayly, C. A. *The Birth of the Modern World, 1780–1914: Global Connections and Comparisons.* Malden, MA: Blackwell, 2004.

———. "The Origins of Swadeshi (Home Industry): Cloth and Indian Society, 1700–1930." In *The Social Life of Things: Commodities in Cultural Perspective*, edited by Arjun Appadurai, 285–321. Cambridge: Cambridge University Press, 1986.

Baz, Jurji Niqula. *Iklil Ghar li-Ra's al-Mar'a.* Beirut: Matba'at al-Qiddis Jawirjiyus, n.d.

———. *Nazik 'Abid.* Beirut: Matba'at al-Salam, 1927.

———. *Al-Nisa'iyyat: Kitab Adabi Akhlaqi Ijtima'i.* Beirut: Al-Matba'a Al-'Abbasiyya, 1920

Becker, Bettina. "Thonet—A Modern Design Institution." Goethe Institute, 2009. http://www.goethe.de/kue/des/prj/des/dth/en4514582.htm.

Behar, Moshe and Zvi Ben-Dor Benite. *Modern Middle Eastern Jewish Thought: Writings on Identity, Politics, and Culture, 1893–1958.* Waltham, MA: Brandeis University Press, 2013.

Benjamin, Walter. *The Arcades Project.* Cambridge, MA: Belknap Press of Harvard University Press, 1999.

Binder, Leonard. "Al-Ghazali's Theory of Islamic Government." *The Muslim World* 45 (1955): 229–241.

Bodenstein, Ralph. "Housing the Foreign: A European's Exotic Home in Late Nineteenth-Century Beirut." In *The Empire in the City: Arab Provincial Capitals in the Late Ottoman Empire*, edited by Jens Hanssen, Thomas Philipp, and Stefan Weber, 105–127. Beirut: Orient Institute, 2002.

———. "The Making and Remaking of Zokak el-Blat: The History of an Urban Fabric." In *History, Space and Social Conflict in Beirut: The Quarter of Zokak el-Blat*, edited by Hans Gebhardt, Dorothée Sack, Ralph Bodenstein, Andreas Fritz, Jens Hanssen, Bernhard Hillenkamp, Oliver Kögler, Anne Mollenhauer, and Friederike Stolleis, 35–107. Beirut: Orient Institute, 2005.

————. "Qasr Heneiné: Memories and History of a Late Ottoman Mansion in Beirut." Master's thesis, Universität Bonn, 1999.

————. *Villen in Beirut: Wohnkultur und sozialer Wandel, 1860–1930.* Petersberg, Hesse: Michael Imhof Verlag, 2012.

Booth, Marilyn. " 'May Her Likes Be Multiplied': 'Famous Women' Biography and Gendered Prescription in Egypt, 1892–1935." *Signs* 22 (1997): 827–890.

Bou Ali, Nadia Walid. "Performing the *Nahda*: Science and Progress in the Nineteenth Century *Muqtataf*." Master's thesis, American University of Beirut, 2008.

Bourdieu, Pierre. *Distinction: A Social Critique of the Judgment of Taste.* Cambridge, MA: Harvard University Press, 1984.

————. "The Forms of Capital." In *Handbook of Theory and Research for the Sociology of Education*, edited by John G. Richardson, 241–258. New York: Greenwood, 1986.

————. "Social Space and the Genesis of 'Classes.'" In *Language and Symbolic Power*, edited by John B. Thompson, 229–251. Cambridge: Polity Press, 1991.

————. "Social Space and Symbolic Space." In *Practical Reason: On the Theory of Action*, 1–13. Stanford, CA: Stanford University Press, 1998.

————. "Symbolic Power." *Critique of Anthropology* 4 (1979): 77–85.

Boyer, Benoît. *Conditions hygiéniques actuelles de Beyrouth et de ses environs immédiats.* Lyon: Imprimerie Alexandre Rey, 1897.

Briggs, Asa. *Victorian Cities.* New York: Harper & Row, 1965.

Brown, Bill. "The Secret Life of Things (Virginia Woolf and the Matter of Modernism)." *Modernism/Modernity* 6 (1999): 1–28.

————. "Thing Theory." *Critical Inquiry* 28 (2001): 1–22.

Buisson, Du Mesnil du. "Les anciennes défenses de Beyrouth." *Syria* 2 (1921): 235–257, 317–327.

Bustani, Butrus al-. *Da'irat al-Ma'arif*, 7 vols. Beirut: Matba'at al-Ma'arif, 1876–1900.

————. *Khitab fi al-Hay'a al-Ijtima'iyya wa-l-Muqabala bayna al-'Awa'id al-'Arabiyya wa-l-Ifranjiyya.* Beirut: Matba'at al-Ma'arif, 1869.

————. "Khitab fi Ta'lim al-Nisa'." In *A'mal al-Jam'iyya al-Suriyya*, 27–40. Beirut: Matba'at al-Amirkan, 1852.

Calhoun, Craig, ed. *Habermas and the Public Sphere.* Cambridge, MA: MIT Press, 1992.

————. "The Public Good as a Social and Cultural Project." In *Private Action and the Public Good*, edited by Walter W. Powell and Elisabeth S. Clemens, 20–35. New Haven, CT: Yale University Press, 1998.

Campos, Michelle U. *Ottoman Brothers: Muslims, Christians, and Jews in Early Twentieth-Century Palestine.* Stanford, CA: Stanford University Press, 2011.

Çelik, Zeynep. *Displaying the Orient: Architecture of Islam at Nineteenth-Century World's Fairs.* Berkeley: University of California Press, 1992.

————. *The Remaking of Istanbul: Portrait of an Ottoman City in the Nineteenth Century.* Seattle: University of Washington Press, 1986.

Çetinkaya, Y. Doğan. "Muslim Merchants and Working-Class in Action: Nationalism, Social Mobilization and Boycott Movement in the Ottoman Empire 1908–1914." Ph.D. thesis, Leiden University, 2010.

Chakrabarty, Dipesh. "The Difference—Deferral of (A) Colonial Modernity: Public Debates on Domesticity in British Bengal." *History Workshop* 36 (1993): 1–34.

———. *Habitations of Modernity: Essays in the Wake of Subaltern Studies.* Chicago: University of Chicago Press, 2002.

———. *Provincializing Europe: Postcolonial Thought and Historical Difference.* Princeton, NJ: Princeton University Press, 2000.

Chatterjee, Partha. *The Nation and Its Fragments: Colonial and Postcolonial Histories.* Princeton, NJ: Princeton University Press, 1993.

———. "The Nationalist Resolution of the Women's Question." In *Recasting Women: Essays in Indian Colonial History*, edited by Kumkum Sangari and Sudesh Vaid, 233–253. New Brunswick, NJ: Rutgers University Press, 1990.

Chauvet, Adolphe. *Conférence sur la Palestine et la Syrie.* Rouen: Cagniard, 1891.

Christensen, Arne Lie. *Den norske byggeskikken: Hus og bolig på landsbygda fra middelalder til vår egen tid.* Oslo: Pax Forlag, 1995.

Chu, Yiu-Wai. "The Importance of Being Chinese: Orientalism Reconfigured in the Age of Global Modernity." *boundary 2* 35 (2008): 183–206.

Chun, Allen. "An Oriental Orientalism: The Paradox of Tradition and Modernity in Nationalist Taiwan." *History and Anthropology* 9 (1995): 27–56.

Cioeta, Donald. "Islamic Benevolent Societies and Public Education in Ottoman Syria, 1875–1882." *Islamic Quarterly* 26 (1982): 40–55.

———. "Ottoman Censorship in Lebanon and Syria, 1876–1908." *International Journal of Middle East Studies* 10 (1979): 167–186.

Çizgen, Engin. *Photography in the Ottoman Empire, 1839–1919.* Istanbul: Haşet Kitabevi, 1987.

Cleveland, William L. "The Municipal Council of Tunis, 1858–1870: A Study in Urban Institutional Change." *International Journal of Middle East Studies* 9 (1978): 33–61.

Cohen, Julia Phillips. "Oriental by Design: Ottoman Jews, Imperial Style, and the Performance of Heritage." *The American Historical Review* 119 (2014): 364–398.

Cole, Juan Ricardo. *Colonialism and Revolution in the Middle East: Social and Cultural Origins of Egypt's 'Urabi Movement.* Princeton, NJ: Princeton University Press, 1993.

Crabbs, Jack A. *The Writing of History in Nineteenth-Century Egypt: A Study in National Transformation.* Cairo: American University in Cairo Press; Detroit, MI: Wayne State University Press, 1984.

Cunningham, Patricia A. *Reforming Women's Fashion, 1850–1920: Politics, Health, and Art.* Kent, OH: Kent State University Press, 2003.

Daghir, Yusuf As'ad. *Masadir al-Dirasat al-Adabiyya.* Beirut: Maktabat Lubnan, 2000.

Dahir, Mas'ud, ed. *Bayrut wa-Jabal Lubnan 'ala Masharif al-Qarn al-'Ishrin: Dirasa fi al-Tarikh al-Ijtima'i min khilal Mudhakkirat al-'Alim al-Rusi al-Kabir A. Kremski.* Beirut: Dar al-Mada, 1985.

Darwaza, Muhammad 'Azzah. *Mudhakkirat Muhammad 'Azzah Darwaza (1887–1984).* Beirut: Dar al-Gharb al-Islami, 1993.

Davidoff, Leonore. "Gender and the 'Great Divide': Public and Private in British Gender History." *Journal of Women's History* 15 (2003): 11–27.

———. *Worlds between: Historical Perspectives on Gender and Class.* Cambridge: Polity Press, 1995.

Davidoff, Leonore and Catherine Hall. *Family Fortunes: Men and Women of the English Middle Class, 1780–1850.* Chicago: University of Chicago Press, 1987.

Davie, May. *Beyrouth 1825–1975, un siècle et demi d'urbanisme.* Beirut: Order of Engineers and Architects, 2001.

———. *Beyrouth et ses faubourgs (1840–1940): Une intégration inachevée.* Beirut: CERMOC, 1996.

———. "Maisons traditionnelles de Beyrouth: Typologie, culture domestique, valeur patrimoniale." Beirut: Association pour la protection et la sauvegarde des anciennes demeures; Tours: Centre d'Histoire de la Ville Moderne et Contemporaine, Université François-Rabelais, 2004. http://almashriq.hiof.no/lebanon/900/902/MAY-Davie/maisons-I/html.

Davie, May and Levon Nordiguian. "L'habitat de Bayrut al-qadimat." *Berytus* 35 (1987): 165–197.

Davie, Michael F. "Maps and the Historical Topography of Beirut." *Berytus* 35 (1987): 141–164.

Davie, Michael F., ed. *La maison beyrouthine aux trois arcs: Une architecture bourgeoise du Levant.* Beirut: Académie Libanaise des Beaux-Arts; Tours: Centre de Recherche et d'Études sur l'Urbanisation du Monde Arabe, 2003.

Debbas, Fouad C. *Des photographes à Beyrouth, 1840–1918.* Paris: Marval, 2001.

Denel, Serim. *Batılılaşma Sürecinde Istanbul'da Tasarım ve Dış Mekanlarda Değişim ve Nedenleri.* Ankara: Orta Doğu Teknik Üniversitesi, 1982.

Deringil, Selim. "The Invention of Tradition as Public Image in the Late Ottoman Empire, 1808 to 1908." *Comparative Studies in Society and History* 35 (1993): 3–29.

———. *The Well-Protected Domains: Ideology and Legitimation of Power in the Ottoman Empire, 1876–1909.* London: I. B. Tauris, 1998.

Dimechkie, Hala Ramez. "Julia Tu'mi Dimashqiyi and *al-Mar'a al-Jadida*, 1883–1954." Master's thesis, American University of Beirut, 1998.

Douglas, Mary and Baron Isherwood. *The World of Goods: Towards an Anthropology of Consumption.* Rev. ed. New York: Routledge, 1996.

Doumani, Beshara, ed. *Family History in the Middle East: Household, Property, and Gender.* Albany: State University of New York Press, 2003.

Duben, Alan and Cem Behar. *Istanbul Households: Marriage, Family, and Fertility, 1880–1940*. Cambridge: Cambridge University Press, 1991.

Duffy, Hazel. *Competitive Cities: Succeeding in the Global Economy*. London: E. & F. N. Spon, 1995.

Eagleton, Terry. *The Ideology of the Aesthetic*. Oxford: Blackwell, 1990.

Eickelman, Dale F. and James Piscatori. *Muslim Politics*. 2nd ed. Princeton, NJ: Princeton University Press, 2004.

El-Cheikh, Nadia Maria. "Byzantium through the Islamic Prism from the Twelfth to the Thirteenth Century." In *Crusades from the Perspective of Byzantium and the Muslim World*, edited by Angeliki E. Laiou and Roy Parviz Mottahedeh, 53–69. Washington, DC: Dumbarton Oaks Research Library and Collection, 2001.

Elias, Norbert. *The Civilizing Process: Sociogenetic and Psychogenetic Investigations*. Rev. ed. Oxford: Blackwell, 2000.

Euben, Roxanne L. "Premodern, Antimodern or Postmodern? Islamic and Western Critiques of Modernity." *The Review of Politics* 59 (1997): 429–460.

Exertzoglou, Haris. "The Cultural Uses of Consumption: Negotiating Class, Gender, and Nation in the Ottoman Urban Centers during the 19th Century." *International Journal of Middle East Studies* 35 (2003): 77–101.

Fakhuri, 'Abd al-Latif Mustafa. *Manzul Bayrut*. Beirut: n.p., 2003.

Farag, Nadia. "The Lewis Affair and the Fortunes of *al-Muqtataf*." *Middle Eastern Studies* 8 (1972): 73–83.

———. "Al-Muqtataf, 1876–1900: A Study of the Influence of Victorian Thought on Modern Arabic Thought." Ph.D. thesis, University of Oxford, 1969.

Farley, James Lewis. *Two Years in Syria*. 2nd ed. London: Saunders & Otley, 1859.

Faroqhi, Suraiya. *Subjects of the Sultan: Culture and Daily Life in the Ottoman Empire*. London: B. Tauris, 2000.

Fawaz, Leila Tarazi. *Merchants and Migrants in Nineteenth-Century Beirut*. Cambridge, MA: Harvard University Press, 1983.

———. *An Occasion for War: Civil Conflict in Lebanon and Damascus in 1860*. London: I. B. Tauris, 1994.

Fay, Mary Ann. "From Warrior-Grandees to Domesticated Bourgeoisie: The Transformation of the Elite Egyptian Household into a Western-Style Nuclear Family." In *Family History in the Middle East: Household, Property, and Gender*, edited by Beshara Doumani, 77–97. Albany: State University of New York Press, 2003.

Feghali, Michel. "Notes sur la maison libanaise." In *Mélanges René Basset: Études nordafricaines et orientales*, vol. 1, 163–186. Paris: Leroux, 1923.

Ferry, Luc. *Homo Aestheticus: The Invention of Taste in the Democratic Age*. Chicago: University of Chicago Press, 1993.

Findley, Carter V. "The Evolution of the System of Provincial Administration as Viewed from the Center." In *Palestine in the Late Ottoman Period: Political, Social and Economic Transformations,* edited by David Kushner, 3–29. Jerusalem: Yad Izhak Ben-Zvi, 1986.

Fleischmann, Ellen L. "The Impact of American Protestant Missions in Lebanon on the Construction of Female Identity, c. 1860–1950." *Islam and Christian-Muslim Relations* 13 (2002): 411–426.

———. " 'Under an American Roof': The Beginnings of the American Junior College for Women in Beirut." *The Arab Studies Journal* 17 (2009): 62–84.

Fortna, Benjamin C. *Imperial Classroom: Islam, the State, and Education in the Late Ottoman Empire.* New York: Oxford University Press, 2002.

———. "Islamic Morality in Late Ottoman 'Secular' Schools." *International Journal of Middle East Studies* 32 (2000): 369–393.

Foucault, Michel. "Governmentality." In *The Foucault Effect: Studies in Governmentality,* edited by Graham Burchel, Colin Gordon, and Peter Miller, 87–104. Chicago: University of Chicago Press, 1991.

Fox, Richard G. "East of Said." In *Edward Said: A Critical Reader,* edited by Michael Sprinker, 144–156. Oxford: Blackwell, 1992.

Fraser, Nancy. "Rethinking the Public Sphere: A Contribution to the Critique of Actually Existing Democracy." In *Habermas and the Public Sphere,* edited by Craig Calhoun, 109–142. Cambridge, MA: MIT Press, 1992.

Freitag, Ulrike and Nora Lafi, eds. *Urban Governance under the Ottomans: Between Cosmopolitanism and Conflict.* Abingdon, UK: Routledge, 2014.

French, William E. *A Peaceful and Working People: Manners, Morals, and Class Formation in Northern Mexico.* Albuquerque: University of New Mexico Press, 1996.

Frierson, Elizabeth B. "Gender, Consumption, and Patriotism: The Emergence of an Ottoman Public Sphere." In *Public Islam and the Common Good,* edited by Armando Salvatore and Dale F. Eickelman, 99–125. Leiden: Brill, 2004.

Frykman, Jonas and Orvar Löfgren. *Culture Builders: A Historical Anthropology of Middle-Class Life.* New Brunswick, NJ: Rutgers University Press, 1987.

Gates, Carolyn L. *The Merchant Republic of Lebanon: Rise of an Open Economy.* London: I. B. Tauris, 1998.

Gebhardt, Hans, Dorothée Sack, Ralph Bodenstein, Andreas Fritz, Jens Hanssen, Bernhard Hillenkamp, Oliver Kögler, Anne Mollenhauer, and Friederike Stolleis, eds. *History, Space and Social Conflict in Beirut: The Quarter of Zokak el-Blat.* Beirut: Orient Institute, 2005.

Gelvin, James L. *The Modern Middle East: A History.* New York: Oxford University Press, 2005.

Ghazali, Abu Hamid al-. *Al-Mustasfa min 'Ilm al-Usul,* 2 vols. Baghdad: Muthanna, [1970].

Ghazzal, Zouhair. *The Grammars of Adjudication: The Economics of Judicial Decision Making in Fin-de-Siécle Ottoman Beirut and Damascus.* Beirut: Institut Français du Proche-Orient, 2007.

Glaß, Dagmar. *Der Muqtataf und seine Öffentlichkeit: Aufklärung, Räsonnement und Mei-nungsstreit in der frühen arabischen Zeitschriftenkommunikation*, 2 vols. Würzburg: Ergon Verlag, 2004.

Gloag, John. *Victorian Comfort: A Social History of Design from 1830–1900*. Newton Abbot, UK: David & Charles, 1973.

Goswami, Manu. *Producing India: From Colonial Economy to National Space*. Chicago: University of Chicago Press, 2004.

Graham, William A. "Traditionalism in Islam: An Essay in Interpretation." *Journal of Interdisciplinary History* 23 (1993): 495–522.

Grehan, James. *Everyday Life and Consumer Culture in 18th-Century Damascus*. Seattle: University of Washington Press, 2007.

Guha, Ranajit. *Dominance without Hegemony: History and Power in Colonial India*. Cambridge, MA: Harvard University Press, 1997.

Göçek, Fatma Müge. *Rise of the Bourgeoisie, Demise of Empire: Ottoman Westernization and Social Change*. New York: Oxford University Press, 1996.

Gunn, Simon. "Between Modernity and Backwardness: The Case of the English Middle Class." In *The Making of the Middle Class: Toward a Transnational History*, edited by A. Ricardo López and Barbara Weinstein, 58–74. Durham, NC: Duke University Press, 2012.

Habermas, Jürgen. *The Structural Transformation of the Public Sphere: An Inquiry into a Category of Bourgeois Society*. Cambridge, MA: MIT Press, 1991.

Hall, Catherine. *White, Male, and Middle-Class: Explorations in Feminism and History*. New York: Routledge, 1992.

Hallaq, Hassan. *Al-Tarikh al-Ijtima'i wa-l-Iqtisadi wa-l-Siyasi fi Bayrut wa-l-Wilayat al-'Uthmaniyya fi al-Qarn al-Tasi' 'Ashar: Sijillat al-Mahkama al-Shar'iyya fi Bayrut*. Beirut: Al-Dar al-Jami'iyya, 1987.

Hamlin, Christopher. *Public Health and Social Justice in the Age of Chadwick: Britain, 1800–1854*. Cambridge: Cambridge University Press, 1998.

Hamzah, Dyala. "La pensée de 'Abduh à l'âge utilitaire: L'intérêt général entre *maṣlaḥa* et *manfa'a*." In *Modernités islamiques*, edited by Maher al Charif and Sabrina Mervin, 29–51. Damascus: Institut Français du Proche-Orient, 2006.

Hanssen, Jens. "The Birth of an Education Quarter: Zokak el-Blat as a Cradle of Cultural Revival in the Arab World." In *History, Space and Social Conflict in Beirut: The Quarter of Zokak el-Blat*, edited by Hans Gebhardt, Dorothée Sack, Ralph Bodenstein, Andreas Fritz, Jens Hanssen, Bernhard Hillenkamp, Oliver Kögler, Anne Mollenhauer, and Friederike Stolleis, 143–174. Beirut: Orient Institute, 2005.

———. "The Effect of Ottoman Rule on Fin de Siècle Beirut: The Province of Beirut, 1888–1914." Ph.D. thesis, University of Oxford, 2001.

———. *Fin de Siècle Beirut: The Making of an Ottoman Provincial Capital*. Oxford: Oxford University Press, 2005.

———. " 'Malhamé–Malfamé': Levantine Elites and Transimperial Networks on the Eve of the Young Turk Revolution." *International Journal of Middle East Studies* 43 (2011): 25–48.

———. " 'Your Beirut Is on My Desk': Ottomanizing Beirut under Sultan Abdülhamid II." In *Projecting Beirut: Episodes in the Construction and Reconstruction of a Modern City*, edited by Peter Rowe and Hashim Sarkis, 41–67. Munich: Prestel, 1998.

Hanssen, Jens, Thomas Philipp, and Stefan Weber, eds. *The Empire in the City: Arab Provincial Capitals in the Late Ottoman Empire.* Beirut: Orient Institute, 2002.

Hareven, Tamara K. "The Home and the Family in Historical Perspective." *Social Research* 58 (1991): 253–285.

Harvey, David. *The Limits to Capital.* Chicago: University of Chicago Press, 1982.

———. "Globalization and the 'Spatial Fix.'" *Geographische Revue* 3 (2001): 23–30.

Hashim, Labiba. *Kitab fi al-Tarbiya.* Cairo: Matba'at al-Ma'arif, 1911.

Hawawini, Najib, ed. *Al-Majalla, aw Jami' al-Adilla 'ala Mawad al-Majalla.* Hadath [Lebanon]: Al-Matba'a al-Sharqiyya, 1905.

Hayek, Ghenwa. "Experimental Female Fictions; Or, The Brief Wondrous Life of the *Nahḍa* Sensation Story." *Middle Eastern Literatures* 16 (2013): 249–265.

Helten, Jean-Jacques van. "Mining, Share Manias, and Speculation: British Investment in Overseas Mining, 1880–1913." In *Capitalism in a Mature Economy: Financial Institutions, Capital Exports and British Industry, 1870–1939*, edited by Jean-Jacques van Helten and Youssef Cassis, 159–185. Aldershot, UK: E. Elgar & Gower, 1990.

Hillenbrand, Carole. *The Crusades: Islamic Perspectives.* Edinburgh: Edinburgh University Press, 1999.

Hobsbawm, Eric. "Introduction: Inventing Traditions." In *The Invention of Tradition*, edited by Eric Hobsbawm and Terence Ranger, 1–14. Cambridge: Cambridge University Press, 1992.

Hourani, Albert. *Arabic Thought in the Liberal Age, 1798–1939.* Cambridge: Cambridge University Press, 1983.

———. "Ideologies of the Mountain and the City: Reflections on the Lebanese Civil War." In *Essays on the Crisis in Lebanon*, edited by Roger Owen, 33–41. London: Ithaca Press, 1976.

Ibrahim, Imili Faris. *Al-Haraka al-Nisa'iyya al-Lubnaniyya.* Beirut: Dar al-Thaqafa, 1966.

Islamoglu, Huri. *Constituting Modernity: Private Property in the East and West.* London: I. B. Tauris, 2004.

Issawi, Charles. "British Trade and the Rise of Beirut, 1830–1860." *International Journal of Middle East Studies* 8 (1977): 91–101.

———. *An Economic History of the Middle East and North Africa.* New York: Columbia University Press, 1982.

———. *The Fertile Crescent, 1800–1914: A Documentary Economic History.* New York: Oxford University Press, 1988.

Jenner, Mark S. R. "Follow Your Nose? Smell, Smelling, and Their Histories." *The American Historical Review* 116 (2011): 335–351.

Jessup, Henry Harris. *The Women of the Arabs*. New York: Dodd & Mead, 1873.

Jiha, Michel. *Julia Tu'ma Dimashqiyya*. Beirut: Riad el-Rayyes Books, 2003.

Joshi, Sanjay. *Fractured Modernity: Making of a Middle Class in Colonial North India*. New Delhi: Oxford University Press, 2001.

Kafawi, Ayyub bin Musa al-. *Al-Kuliyyat: Mu'jam fi al-Mustalahat wa-l-Furuq al-Lughawiyya*. 2nd ed. Beirut: Mu'assasat al-Risala, 1998.

Kalayan, Haroutune Y. and Jacques Liger-Belair. *L'habitation au Liban*, 2 vols. Beirut: L'Association pour la protection des sites et anciennes demeures, 1966.

Kallas, Jurj. *Al-Haraka al-Fikriyya al-Nasawiyya fi 'Asr al-Nahda, 1849–1928*. Beirut: Dar al-Jil, 1996.

Kamel, Leila Salameh. *Un quartier de Beyrouth, Saint-Nicolas: Structures familiales et structures foncières*. Beirut: Dar el-Machreq, 1998.

Kara, Şenda. *Leitbilder und Handlungsgrundlagen des modernen Städtebaus in der Türkei von der osmanischen zur türkischen Stadt*. Berlin: LIT Verlag, 2006.

Kark, Ruth. "The Contribution of the Ottoman Regime to the Development of Jerusalem and Jaffa, 1840–1917." In *Palestine in the Late Ottoman Period: Political, Social and Economic Transformations*, edited by David Kushner, 46–58. Jerusalem: Yad Izhak Ben-Zvi, 1986.

Kashani-Sabet, Firoozeh. "Patriotic Womanhood: The Culture of Feminism in Modern Iran, 1900–1941." *British Journal of Middle Eastern Studies* 32 (2005): 29–46.

Kassir, Samir. *Histoire de Beyrouth*. Paris: Librairie Arthème Fayard, 2003.

Kayalı, Hasan. *Arabs and Young Turks: Ottomanism, Arabism, and Islamism in the Ottoman Empire, 1908–1918*. Berkeley: University of California Press, 1997.

Kechriotis, Vangelis. "Civilisation and Order: Middle-Class Morality among the Greek-Orthodox in Smyrna/Izmir at the End of the Ottoman Empire." In *Social Transformation and Mass Mobilization in the Balkan and Eastern Mediterranean Cities, 1900–1923*, edited by Lyberatos Andreas, 137–153. Rethymnon: Crete University Press, 2013.

Kelly, Catherine E. *In the New England Fashion: Reshaping Women's Lives in the Nineteenth Century*. Ithaca, NY: Cornell University Press, 1999.

Kerr, Malcolm H. *Islamic Reform: The Political and Legal Theories of Muḥammad 'Abduh and Rashīd Riḍā*. Berkeley: University of California Press, 1966.

Khalidi, 'Anbarah Salam al-. *Jawla fi al-Dhikrayat bayna Lubnan wa-Filastin*. 2nd ed. Beirut: Dar al-Nahar, 1997.

Khater, Akram Fouad. " 'House' to 'Goddess of the House': Gender, Class, and Silk in 19th-Century Mount Lebanon." *International Journal of Middle East Studies* 28 (1996): 325–348.

———. *Inventing Home: Emigration, Gender, and the Middle Class in Lebanon, 1870–1920.* Berkeley: University of California Press, 2001.

Khoury, Philip S. "Syrian Urban Politics in Transition: The Quarters of Damascus during the French Mandate." *International Journal of Middle East Studies* 16 (1984): 507–540.

Khuri, Amin. *al-Jami'a aw Dalil Bayrut.* Beirut: Al-Matba'a al-Adabiyya, 1889.

Khuri, Khalil, ed. *Jami'at al-Qawanin.* Beirut: Matba'at al-Adab, 1893.

Khuri-Makdisi, Ilham. *The Eastern Mediterranean and the Making of Global Radicalism, 1860–1914.* Berkeley: University of California Press, 2010.

Kikuchi, Yuko. "Hybridity and the Oriental Orientalism of 'Mingei' Theory." *Journal of Design History* 10 (1997): 343–354.

Kırlı, Cengiz. "Coffeehouses: Public Opinion in the Nineteenth-Century Ottoman Empire." In *Public Islam and the Common Good*, edited by Armando Salvatore and Dale F. Eickelman, 75–97. Leiden: Brill, 2004.

Kupferschmidt, Uri M. *European Department Stores and Middle Eastern Consumers: The Orosdi-Back Saga.* Istanbul: Ottoman Bank Archives and Research Centre, 2007.

———. "The Social History of the Sewing Machine in the Middle East." *Die Welt des Islams* 44 (2004): 195–213.

———. "Who Needed Department Stores in Egypt? From Orosdi-Back to Omar Effendi." *Middle Eastern Studies* 43 (2007): 175–192.

Kushner, David, ed. *Palestine in the Late Ottoman Period: Political, Social and Economic Transformations.* Jerusalem: Yad Izhak Ben-Zvi, 1986.

Kütükoğlu, Mühabat. "The Ottoman-British Commercial Treaty of 1838." In *Four Centuries of Turco-British Relations: Studies in Diplomatic, Economic and Cultural Affairs*, edited by William Hale and Ali İhsan Bağış, 53–61. Beverley, UK: Eothen Press, 1984.

Kyriazidou, Ekaterini and Martin Pesendorfer. "Viennese Chairs: A Case Study for Modern Industrialization." *The Journal of Economic History* 59 (1999): 143–166.

Lafi, Nora. "The Municipality of Salonica between Old Regime, the Ottoman Reforms and the Transition from Empire to Nation State: Questions and Research Perspectives." Thessaloniki Municipality, 2014. https://halshs.archives-ouvertes.fr/halshs-00981804.

———, ed. *Municipalités méditerranéennes: Les réformes urbaines ottomanes au miroir d'une histoire comparée (Moyen-Orient, Maghrab, Europe méridionale).* Berlin: Klaus Schwarz, 2005.

Landes, Joan B. "Further Thoughts on the Public/Private Distinction." *Journal of Women's History* 15 (2003): 28–39.

———. *Women and the Public Sphere in the Age of the French Revolution.* Ithaca, NY: Cornell University Press, 1988.

Laporte, Dominique. *History of Shit.* Cambridge, MA: MIT Press, 2000.

Leary, Lewis Gaston. *Syria, the Land of Lebanon*. New York: McBride, Nast, 1913.

Lefebvre, Henri. *The Production of Space*. Oxford: Blackwell, 1991.

Lemke, Wolf-Dieter. "Ottoman Photography: Recording and Contributing to Modernity." In *The Empire in the City: Arab Provincial Capitals in the Late Ottoman Empire*, edited by Jens Hanssen, Thomas Philipp, and Stefan Weber, 237–249. Beirut: Orient Institute, 2002.

Levi, Tomer. *The Jews of Beirut: The Rise of a Levantine Community, 1860s–1930s*. New York: Peter Lang, 2012.

Lockman, Zachary. "Imagining the Working Class: Culture, Nationalism, and Class Formation in Egypt, 1899–1914." *Poetics Today* 15 (1994): 157–190.

López, A. Ricardo and Barbara Weinstein, eds. *The Making of the Middle Class: Toward a Transnational History*. Durham, NC: Duke University Press, 2012.

Lortet, Louis. *La Syrie d'aujourd'hui: Voyages dans la Phénicie, le Liban, et la Judée, 1875–1880*. Paris: Hachette, 1884.

Lubar, Steven D. and W. D. Kingery, eds. *History from Things: Essays on Material Culture*. Washington, DC: Smithsonian Institution Press, 1993.

Makdisi, Jean Said. *Teta, Mother and Me: An Arab Woman's Memoir*. London: Saqi Books, 2005.

Makdisi, Ussama. *Artillery of Heaven: American Missionaries and the Failed Conversion of the Middle East*. Ithaca, NY: Cornell University Press, 2008.

———. *The Culture of Sectarianism: Community, History, and Violence in Nineteenth-Century Ottoman Lebanon*. Berkeley: University of California Press, 2000.

Ma'luf, 'Isa Iskandar. *Al-Akhlaq Majmu' 'Adat*. Beirut: Al-Matba'a al-Adabiyya, 1902.

———. *Dawani al-Qutuf fi Tarikh Bani Ma'luf*, 2 vols. 2nd ed. Damascus: Dar Hawran lil-Tiba'a wa-l-Nashr, 2003.

Marcus, Abraham. *The Middle East on the Eve of Modernity: Aleppo in the Eighteenth Century*. New York: Columbia University Press, 1989.

Mardin, Şerif. "Super Westernization in Urban Life in the Ottoman Empire in the Last Quarter of the Nineteenth Century." In *Turkey: Geographic and Social Perspectives*, edited by Benedict Peter, Erol Tümertekin, and Fatma Mansur, 403–446. Leiden: Brill, 1974.

Mazza, Roberto. *Jerusalem: From the Ottomans to the British*. London: I. B. Tauris, 2009.

Mazzarella, William. *Shoveling Smoke: Advertising and Globalization in Contemporary India*. Durham, NC: Duke University Press, 2003.

McNeill, William Hardy. *Plagues and Peoples*. Oxford: Blackwell, 1977.

Mehta, Uday Singh. *Liberalism and Empire: A Study in Nineteenth-Century British Liberal Thought*. Chicago: University of Chicago Press, 1999.

Meier, Olivier. *Al Muqtataf et le débat sur le Darwinisme, Beyrouth 1876–1885*. Cairo: Les dossiers de CEDEJ, 1996.

Metcalf, Barbara Daly, ed. *Moral Conduct and Authority: The Place of Adab in South Asian Islam*. Berkeley: University of California Press, 1984.

Meyer, Birgit. " 'There Is a Spirit in That Image': Mass-Produced Jesus Pictures and Protestant-Pentecostal Animation in Ghana." *Comparative Studies in Society and History* 52 (2010): 100–130.

Micklewright, Nancy C. "Personal, Public, and Political (Re)Constructions, Photographs and Consumption." In *Consumption Studies and the History of the Ottoman Empire 1550–1922: An Introduction*, edited by Donald Quataert, 261–287. Albany: State University of New York Press, 2000.

Midhat, Ahmed. *Avrupa'da bir Cevelan*. Istanbul: Tercüman-ı Hakikat Matbaası, 1889.

Miller, Daniel, ed. *Home Possessions: Material Culture behind Closed Doors*. Oxford: Berg, 2001.

Miller, Michael B. *The Bon Marché: Bourgeois Culture and the Department Store, 1869–1920*. Princeton, NJ: Princeton University Press, 1981.

Ministry of Interior, Germany. "Berichte über Handel und Industrie: Die wirtschaftlichen Verhältnisse in Anatolien, Kurdistan und Arabistan." History from Below in the Ottoman Empire and the Modern Middle East: An Archive, 20 August 1907. http://harvey .binghamton.edu/ottmiddl/index.php?dir=Ottoman+Empire/Anatolia/ Documents/.

Mitchell, Timothy. *Colonising Egypt*. Berkeley: University of California Press, 1991.

Mollenhauer, Anne. "Continuity and Change in the Architectural Development of Zokak el-Blat." In *History, Space and Social Conflict in Beirut: The Quarter of Zokak el-Blat*, edited by Hans Gebhardt, Dorothée Sack, Ralph Bodenstein, Andreas Fritz, Jens Hanssen, Bernhard Hillenkamp, Oliver Kögler, Anne Mollenhauer, and Friederike Stolleis, 109–142. Beirut: Orient Institute, 2005.

Moosa, Ebrahim. "Muslim Ethics?" In *The Blackwell Companion to Religious Ethics*, edited by William Schweiker, 237–243. Malden, MA: Blackwell, 2005.

Motz, Marilyn Ferris and Pat Browne, eds. *Making the American Home: Middle-Class Women and Domestic Material Culture, 1840–1940*. Bowling Green, OH: Bowling Green State University Popular Press, 1988.

Najmabadi, Afsaneh. "Crafting an Educated Housewife in Iran." In *Remaking Women: Feminism and Modernity in the Middle East*, edited by Lila Abu-Lughod, 91–125. Princeton, NJ: Princeton University Press, 1998.

———. *Women with Mustaches and Men without Beards: Gender and Sexual Anxieties of Iranian Modernity*. Berkeley: University of California Press, 2005.

Noorani, Yaseen. *Culture and Hegemony in the Colonial Middle East*. New York: Palgrave Macmillan, 2010.

Noueiry, Hayat Labban. *Ra's Bayrut Kama 'Ariftahu*. Beirut: Al-Sharika al-'Alamiyya lil-Kitab, 2004.

Opwis, Felicitas. "Maslaha in Contemporary Islamic Legal Theory." *Islamic Law and Society* 12 (2005): 182–223.

Outka, Elizabeth. "Crossing the Great Divides: Selfridges, Modernity, and the Commodified Authentic." *Modernism/Modernity* 12 (2005): 311–328.

Owen, Roger, ed. *New Perspectives on Property and Land in the Middle East*. Cambridge, MA: Harvard University Press, 2000.

Owensby, Brian Philip. *Intimate Ironies: Modernity and the Making of Middle-Class Lives in Brazil*. Stanford, CA: Stanford University Press, 1999.

Özveren, Yaşar Eyüp. "The Making and Unmaking of an Ottoman Port-City: Nineteenth-Century Beirut, Its Hinterland, and the World-Economy." Ph.D. thesis, State University of New York at Binghamton, 1990.

Pateman, Carole. *The Disorder of Women: Democracy, Feminism and Political Theory*. Cambridge: Polity Press, 1989.

Philipp, Thomas. *Acre: The Rise and Fall of a Palestinian City, 1730–1831*. New York: Columbia University Press, 2001.

———, ed. *Gurgi Zaidan: His Life and Thought*. Beirut: Orient Institute, 1979.

———. "Perceptions of the First World War in the Contemporary Arab Press." In *Ottoman Reform and Muslim Regeneration: Studies in Honour of Butrus Abu-Manneh*, edited by Itzchak Weismann and Fruma Zachs, 211–224. London: I. B. Tauris, 2005.

Pollard, Lisa. "The Family Politics of Colonizing and Liberating Egypt, 1882–1919." *Social Politics* 7 (2000): 47–79.

———. "Learning Gendered Modernity: The Home, the Family, and the Schoolroom in the Construction of Egyptian National Identity (1885–1919)." In *Beyond the Exotic: Women's Histories in Islamic Societies*, edited by Amira El-Azhary Sonbol, 249–269. Syracuse, NY: Syracuse University Press, 2005.

———. *Nurturing the Nation: The Family Politics of Modernizing, Colonizing and Liberating Egypt (1805–1923)*. Berkeley: University of California Press, 2005.

Poovey, Mary. *Uneven Developments: The Ideological Work of Gender in Mid-Victorian England*. Chicago: University of Chicago Press, 1988.

Powell, Eve Troutt. *A Different Shade of Colonialism: Egypt, Great Britain, and the Mastery of the Sudan*. Berkeley: University of California Press, 2003.

Qattan, Najwa. "*Dhimmīs* in the Muslim Court: Legal Autonomy and Religious Discrimination." *International Journal of Middle East Studies* 31 (1999): 429–444.

Quataert, Donald, ed. *Consumption Studies and the History of the Ottoman Empire, 1550–1922: An Introduction*. Albany: State University of New York Press, 2000.

———. *Ottoman Manufacturing in the Age of the Industrial Revolution*. Cambridge: Cambridge University Press, 1993.

Quzma-Khuri, Yusuf. *Rajul Sabiq li-'Asrihi: Al-Mu'allim Butrus al-Bustani, 1819–1883*. Beirut: Bisan; Amman: Al-Ma'had al-Malaki lil-Dirasat al-Diniyya, 1995.

Racy, Ali Jihad. "Record Industry and Egyptian Traditional Music: 1904–1932." *Ethnomusicology* 20 (1976): 23–48.

Radhakrishnan, R. "Nationalism, Gender, and the Narrative of Identity." In *Nationalisms and Sexualities,* edited by Andrew Parker, Mary Russo, Doris Sommer, and Patricia Yaeger, 77–95. New York: Routledge, 1992.

Rafeq, Abdul-Karim, "Ownership of Real Property by Foreigners in Syria, 1869 to 1873." In *New Perspectives on Property and Land in the Middle East,* edited by Roger Own, 175–239. Cambridge, MA: Harvard University Press, 2000.

Ragette, Friedrich. *Architecture in Lebanon: The Lebanese House during the 18th and 19th Centuries.* Beirut: American University of Beirut, 1974.

Rieder, William. "Bentwood Furniture." *Architectural Digest* 53 (1996): 106–111.

Robson, Laura. *Colonialism and Christianity in Mandate Palestine.* Austin: University of Texas Press, 2011.

Roche, Daniel. *A History of Everyday Things: The Birth of Consumption in France, 1600–1800.* Cambridge: Cambridge University Press, 2000.

Rosenthal, Steven. "Urban Elites and the Foundation of Municipalities in Alexandria and Istanbul." *Middle Eastern Studies* 16 (1980): 125–133.

Rubin, Avi. "Legal Borrowing and its Impact on Ottoman Legal Culture in the Late Nineteenth Century." *Continuity and Change* 22 (2007): 279–303.

Russell, Mona L. *Creating the New Egyptian Woman: Consumerism, Education, and National Identity, 1863–1922.* New York: Palgrave Macmillan, 2004.

Rybczynski, Witold. *Home: A Short History of an Idea.* New York: Viking, 1986.

Ryzova, Lucie. *The Age of the Efendiyya: Passages to Modernity in National-Colonial Egypt.* Oxford: Oxford University Press, 2014.

Saalman, Howard. *Haussmann: Paris Transformed.* New York: G. Braziller, 1971.

Said, Edward W. *Orientalism.* New York: Vintage Books, 1994.

Saisselin, Rémy G. *The Bourgeois and the Bibelot.* New Brunswick, NJ: Rutgers University Press, 1984.

Saliba, Robert. *Beirut 1920–1940: Domestic Architecture between Tradition and Modernity.* Beirut: Order of Engineers and Architects, 1998.

Salim, Ahmad Muhammad, ed. *Al-Rasa'il al-Zaynabiyya.* Cairo: Al-Hay'a al-Misriyya al-'Amma lil-Kitab, 2007.

Sami, 'Abd al-Rahman. *Qawl al-Haqq fi Bayrut wa-Dimashq.* Beirut: Dar al-Ra'id al-'Arabi, 1981.

Sand, Jordan. *House and Home in Modern Japan: Architecture, Domestic Space, and Bourgeois Culture, 1880–1930.* Cambridge, MA: Harvard University Asia Center, 2003.

Sarkis, Khalil. *Al-'Adat fi al-Ziyarat wa-l-A'ras wa-l-Ma'atim wa-Adab al-Mahafil wa-Ghayriha Mimma Huwa Jarin wa-Mustalah 'Alayhi 'inda al-Shu'ub al-Mutamaddina.* Beirut: Al-Matba'a al-Adabiyya, 1911.

Sayyah, Huda. "Sahifat *Thamarat al-Funun.*" Master's thesis, Lebanese University, 1974.

Sedghi, Hamideh. *Women and Politics in Iran: Veiling, Unveiling, and Reveiling.* Cambridge: Cambridge University Press, 2007.

Sehnaoui, Nada. *L'occidentalisation de la vie quotidienne à Beyrouth, 1860–1914*. [Beirut]: Dar An-Nahar, 2002.

Shakry, Omnia. "Schooled Mothers and Structured Play: Child Rearing in Turn-of-the-Century Egypt." In *Remaking Women: Feminism and Modernity in the Middle East*, edited by Lila Abu-Lughod, 126–170. Princeton, NJ: Princeton University Press, 1998.

Sharif, Malek. *Imperial Norms and Local Realities: The Ottoman Municipal Laws and the Municipality of Beirut (1860–1908)*. Beirut: Orient Institute, 2014.

Shaw, Stanford J. "The Ottoman Census System and Population, 1831–1914." *International Journal of Middle East Studies* 9 (1978): 325–338.

Shaw, Stanford J. and Ezel Kural Shaw. *History of the Ottoman Empire and Modern Turkey*, 2 vols. Cambridge: Cambridge University Press, 1976–1977.

Shbaru, 'Isam Muhammad. *Jam'iyyat al-Maqasid al-Khayriyya al-Islamiyya fi Bayrut, 1878–2000*. Beirut: Dar Misbah lil-Fikr, 2000.

Shechter, Relli. *Smoking, Culture and Economy in the Middle East: The Egyptan Tobacco Market, 1850–2000*. London: I. B. Tauris, 2006.

———, ed. *Transitions in Domestic Consumption and Family Life in the Modern Middle East: Houses in Motion*. New York: Palgrave Macmillan, 2003.

Sheehi, Stephen. *Foundations of Modern Arab Identity*. Gainesville: University Press of Florida, 2004.

———. "A Social History of Early Arab Photography or a Prolegomenon to an Archaeology of the Lebanese Imago." *International Journal of Middle East Studies* 39 (2007): 177–208.

Sorensen, André. *The Making of Urban Japan: Cities and Planning from Edo to the Twenty-First Century*. London: Routledge, 2002.

Tahtawi, Rifa'a Rafi' al-. *Manahij al-Albab al-Misriyya fi Mabahij al-Adab al-'Asriyya*. 2nd ed. Cairo: Matba'at al-Ragha'ib, 1912.

Tamari, Salim. "Jerusalem's Ottoman Modernity: The Times and Lives of Wasif Jawhariyyeh." *Jerusalem Quarterly File* 9 (2000): 5–27.

Tarrazi, Filib di. *Tarikh al-Sahafa al-'Arabiyya*, 4 vols. Beirut: Al-Matba'a al-Adabiyya, 1913–1933.

Thabit, Jad. *Al-I'mar wa-l-Maslaha al-'Amma: Fi al-Turath wa-l-Hadatha*. Beirut: Dar al-Jadid, 1996.

Thompson, Elizabeth. *Colonial Citizens: Republican Rights, Paternal Privilege, and Gender in French Syria and Lebanon*. New York: Columbia University Press, 2000.

———. "Public and Private in Middle Eastern Women's History." *Journal of Women's History* 15 (2003): 52–69.

———. "Sex and Cinema in Damascus: The Gendered Politics of Public Space in a Colonial City." In *Middle Eastern Cities, 1900–1950: Public Places and Public Spheres in Transformation*, edited by Hans Chr. Korsholm Nielsen and Jakob Skovgaard-Petersen, 89–111. Aarhus: Aarhus University Press, 2001.

Thomson, William M. *The Land and the Book; or, Biblical Illustrations from the Manners and Customs, the Scenes and Scenery, of the Holy Land.* Vol. 1. New York: Harper & Brothers, 1859.

Thoumin, Richard Lodoïs. *Géographie humaine de la Syria centrale.* Paris: Librairie Ernest Leroux, 1936.

Toprak, Zafer. "The Financial Structure of the Stock Exchange in the Late Ottoman Empire." In *East Meets West: Banking, Commerce and Investment in the Ottoman Empire*, edited by Philip L. Cottrell, Monika Pohle Fraser, and Iain L. Fraser, 143–159. Aldershot, UK: Ashgate, 2008.

Traboulsi, Fawwaz. *A History of Modern Lebanon.* London: Pluto Press, 2007.

Troelenberg, Eva-Maria. *Eine Ausstellung wird besichtigt: Die Münchner "Ausstellung von Meisterwerken muhammedanishcer Kunst" 1910 in kultur- und wissenschaftsgeschichtlicher Perspektive.* Frankfurt am Main: Peter Lang, 2011.

Tucker, Judith E. *In the House of the Law: Gender and Islamic Law in Ottoman Syria and Palestine.* Berkeley: University of California Press, 1998.

Twain, Mark. *The Innocents Abroad.* Project Gutenberg, 1869. http://www.gutenberg.org/files/3176/3176-h/3176-h.htm.

Unat, Faik Reşit. *Hicrî Tarihleri Milâdî Tarihe Çevirme Kılavuzu.* 6th ed. Ankara: Türk Tarih Kurumu Basımevi, 1988.

Unsi, 'Abd al-Basit al-. *Dalil Bayrut.* Beirut: Matba'at Jaridat al-Iqbal, 1909–1910.

Veblen, Thorstein. *The Theory of the Leisure Class.* Oxford: Oxford University Press, 2007.

Warner, Charles Dudley. *In the Levant.* 19th ed. Boston: Houghton, Mifflin, 1894.

Watenpaugh, Keith David. *Being Modern in the Middle East: Revolution, Nationalism, Colonialism, and the Arab Middle Class.* Princeton, NJ: Princeton University Press, 2006.

———. "Middle-Class Modernity and the Persistence of the Politics of Notables in Inter-War Syria." *International Journal of Middle East Studies* 35 (2003): 257–286.

Weber, Stefan. "Images of Imagined Worlds: Self-image and Worldview in Late Ottoman Wall Paintings of Damascus." In *The Empire in the City: Arab Provincial Capitals in the Late Ottoman Empire*, edited by Jens Hanssen, Thomas Philipp, and Stefan Weber, 145–171. Beirut: Orient Institute, 2002.

———. "Reshaping Damascus: Social Change and Patterns of Architecture in Late Ottoman Times." In *From the Syrian Land to the States of Syria and Lebanon*, edited by Thomas Philipp and Christoph Schumann, 41–58. Würzburg: Ergon Verlag, 2004.

Wedeen, Lisa. *Peripheral Visions: Publics, Power, and Performance in Yemen.* Chicago: University of Chicago Press, 2008.

Weiss, Max. *In the Shadow of Sectarianism: Law, Shi'ism, and the Making of Modern Lebanon.* Cambridge, MA: Harvard University Press, 2010.

West, Michael O. *The Rise of an African Middle Class: Colonial Zimbabwe, 1898–1965.* Bloomington: Indiana University Press, 2002.

Williams, Raymond. "Advertising: The Magic System." In *Culture and Materialism: Selected Essays,* 170–195. London: Verso, 2005.

Wolfe, Joel. *Autos and Progress: The Brazilian Search for Modernity.* Oxford: Oxford University Press, 2010.

Wollstonecraft, Mary. *A Vindication of the Rights of Woman.* New York: W. W. Norton, 1975.

Woodward, Michelle L. "Between Orientalist Clichés and Images of Modernization: Photographic Practice in the Late Ottoman Era." *History of Photography* 27 (2003): 363–374.

Worringer, Renée. *Ottomans Imagining Japan: East, Middle East, and Non-Western Modernity at the Turn of the Twentieth Century.* New York: Palgrave Macmillan, 2014.

Yahusha', Ya'qub. *Tarikh al-Sahafa al-'Arabiyya fi Filastin fi al-'Ahd al-'Uthmani, 1908–1918.* Jerusalem: Matba'at al-Ma'arif, 1974.

Yarid, Nazik Saba. *Al-Katibat al-Lubnaniyyat: Bibliyughrafiya, 1850–1950.* Beirut: Dar al-Saqi, 2000.

Young, George. *Corps de droit ottoman,* 7 vols. Oxford: Clarendon Press, 1905–1906.

Young, Iris Marion. *Justice and the Politics of Difference.* Princeton, NJ: Princeton University Press, 1990.

Zachs, Fruma. *The Making of a Syrian Identity: Intellectuals and Merchants in Nineteenth Century Beirut.* Boston: Brill, 2005.

Zachs, Fruma and Sharon Halevi. "From *Difā' al-Nisā'* to *Mas'alat al-Nisā'* in Greater Syria: Readers and Writers Debate Women and Their Rights, 1858–1900." *International Journal of Middle East Studies* 41 (2009): 615–633.

———. *Gendering Culture in Greater Syria: Intellectuals and Ideology in the Late Ottoman Period.* London: I. B. Tauris, 2015.

Zaman, Muhammad Qasim. "The 'Ulama of Contemporary Islam and their Conceptions of the Common Good." In *Public Islam and the Common Good,* edited by Armando Salvatore and Dale F. Eickelman, 129–155. Leiden: Brill, 2004.

Zandi-Sayek, Sibel. *Ottoman Izmir: The Rise of a Cosmopolitan Port, 1840–1880.* Minneapolis: University of Minnesota Press, 2012.

Zaydan, Jurji. *Tarikh Adab al-Lugha al-'Arabiyya,* 4 vols. 2nd ed. [Cairo]: Matba'at al-Hilal, 1937.

Ze'evi, Dror. "The Use of Ottoman Shari'a Court Records as a Source for Middle Eastern Social History: A Reappraisal." *Islamic Law and Society* 5 (1998): 35–56.

Zeidan, Joseph. *Arab Women Novelists: The Formative Years and Beyond.* Albany: State University of New York Press, 1995.

INDEX

Page numbers in italics refer to illustrative material.